Ethnicity, Identity and Music

BERG
Ethnic Identities
SERIES

General Editors:
Shirley Ardener, *Director, Centre for Cross-Cultural Research on Women, University of Oxford*

Tamara Dragadze, *School of Slavonic and East European Studies, University of London*

Jonathan Webber, *Institute of Social and Cultural Anthropology, University of Oxford*

Book previously published in the Series

Sharon Macdonald (ed.), *Inside European Identities: Ethnography in Western Europe*

Forthcoming title:

Joanne Eicher (ed.), **Dress and Ethnicity**

Ethnicity, Identity and Music

The Musical Construction of Place

EDITED BY
Martin Stokes

BERG
Oxford/New York

First published in 1994 by
Berg Publishers
Editorial offices:
150 Cowley Road, Oxford, OX4 1JJ, UK
70 Washington Square South, New York, NY 10012 USA

Paperback reprinted in 1997.

© Martin Stokes 1994, 1997

All rights reserved.
No part of this publication may be reproduced in any form
or by any means without the written permission of
Berg Publishers Limited.

Library of Congress Cataloging-in-Publication Data

A catalogue record for this book is available from the British Library.

British Library Cataloguing in Publication Data

A catalogue record for this book is available from the British Library.

ISBN 0 85496 877 6 (Cloth)
1 85973 041 8 (Paper)

Printed in the United Kingdom by WBC Bookbinders, Bridgend,
Mid-Glamorgan.

Contents

Acknowledgements vii
Notes on Contributors ix

1 Introduction: Ethnicity, Identity and Music
　Martin Stokes 1

2 Thoughts on Celtic Music
　Malcolm Chapman 29

3 The Role of Music in the Creation of an Afghan National Identity, 1923–73
　John Baily 45

4 National Anthems: The Case of Chopin as a National Composer
　Zdzislaw Mach 61

5 Macunaíma's Music: National Identity and Ethnomusicological Research in Brazil
　Suzel Ana Reily 71

6 Place, Exchange and Meaning: Black Sea Musicians in the West of Ireland
　Martin Stokes 97

7 Identity, Place and the 'Liverpool Sound'
　Sara Cohen 117

8 'The Land is Our Märr (Essence), It Stays Forever': The Yothu–Yindi Relationship in Australian Aboriginal Traditional and Popular Musics
　Fiona Magowan 135

9 Personal and Collective Identity in Kalasha Song Performance: The Significance of Music-making in a Minority Enclave
　Peter Parkes 157

10 Music, Literature and Etiquette: Musical Instruments and Social Identity from Castiglione to Austen
　Hélène La Rue 189

Index 207

Acknowledgements

This book discusses the significance of music in relation to ethnicity. There are a number of interrelated reasons for this. Firstly, theories of ethnicity have made a distinct mark on recent ethnomusicological and musicological scholarship, and this book is intended as a contribution to a growing area of interest. Secondly, it provides an obvious potential area of overlap for the anthropologist interested in music. Thirdly, it arose from a series of seminars initiated by Edwin Ardener dedicated to the study of identity and ethnicity. The contributors to the music seminar were either ethnomusicologists with social anthropological experience of some kind or another, or social anthropologists with a keen interest in music. The intention of the seminar was to provide a forum in which anthropologists could discuss 'the significance of music'.

Thanks are due in the first instance to the convenors of the seminar, who brought this group of people together, and turned each meeting into a lively exchange: Shirley Ardener, Tamara Dragadze and Jonathan Webber. Thanks are also due to colleagues and students at the department of Social Anthropology and the department of Music at The Queen's University of Belfast. The relationships between a sense of place, identity and music are powerfully marked in this noisy city. Ideas which took shape in the Oxford seminar took on a new and sometimes curious lease of life in seminars and classes in Belfast, and the process of editing these essays, as well as my own contributions to this volume have been heavily influenced by this environment. For contributing to this environment, and for their comments on drafts of the introduction, I am indebted to Richard English, Mike Kenny, Suzel Reily, Elizabeth Tonkin, David Wilson, Desi Wilkinson, Fintan Vallely, Helen Brennan-Corcoran, Aideen Morrisey, Bronagh Coyle, Hae-Kyung Um, Kevin Dawe, Tony Langlois, Ian Woodfield, Colin Irwin, and Bob Gilmore. Outside Queen's, I would like to thank Philip Bohlman, Jocelyn Guilbeault, John Davis, Michael Gilsenan, Nelson Graburn and Ruth Davis.

Valerie Miller and Hazel Bland kindly provided their time and help in the preparation of the manuscript. Lucy Baxandall read through many sections of this text. I continue to be indebted to her unfaltering sense of literary style and great patience. The mistakes that remain are my own.

Notes on Contributors

John Baily is Lecturer in Ethnomusicology at Goldsmith's College, The University of London. His publications and films include *Music of Afghanistan: Professional Musicians in the City of Herat*, and the film, *Amir*.

Malcolm Chapman currently teaches at the Bradford University Management Centre. He is author of *The Gaelic Vision in Scottish Culture* and *The Celts: The Construction of a Myth*.

Sara Cohen is a lecturer at the Institute of Popular Music Studies, Liverpool University, and is the author of *Rock Culture in Liverpool: Popular Music in the Making*. She is currently researching the role of kinship in popular culture in Liverpool.

Hélène La Rue is the curator of musical instruments at the Pitt Rivers Museum and Institute of Social and Cultural Anthropology, Oxford University.

Zdzislaw Mach teaches Anthropology at the Department of Sociology, the Jagellonian University in Warsaw.

Fiona Magowan teaches Anthropology at the Department of Social Anthropology, Manchester University. She is currently completing her D. Phil dissertation on music in North East Arnhem Land, Australia at the Institute of Social and Cultural Anthropology, Oxford University.

Peter Parkes is lecturer in Social Anthropology at Goldsmith's College, London. His work includes *Kalasha Society: Practice and Ceremony in the Hindu-Kush* and the Granada Disappearing World film, *The Kalasha Rites of Spring*.

Suzel Ana Reily is lecturer in Ethnomusicology and Social Anthropology at The Queen's University of Belfast. She received an MA from Indiana University and her PhD from the University of São Paulo. She is currently working on a book based on research which she has been conducting since the early 1980s on Brazilian music and popular catholicism.

ix

Martin Stokes teaches Ethnomusicology and Social Anthropology at The Queen's University of Belfast. He is the author of *The Arabesk Debate: Music and Musicians in Modern Turkey*.

Introduction: Ethnicity, Identity and Music

Martin Stokes

The musicologist Joseph Kerman once sympathised with the plight of ethnomusicologists 'as they struggle to make themselves heard in the seemingly tone-deaf conclaves and enclaves of anthropology' (1985: 181). After at least two decades of well published discussion of music in university departments of sociology, politics, cultural studies and even art history, anthropologists have less reason than ever to maintain the 'tone-deafness' that Kerman was undoubtedly correct in identifying. In accordance with the highly pervasive fiction of an earlier musicology,[1] music is still however considered a domain of a special, almost extra-social, autonomous experience. What ethnomusicologists deal with in the societies they study, is – anthropologists are residually inclined to assume – either the diversionary or the arcane. By definition they cannot be dealing with the kinds of events and processes that make up the predominantly verbal and visual 'real life' of which social reality is assumed to consist. Ethnomusicologists disagree, but they often have little choice but to put up with, and enjoy as best they can, the limited benefits of a precarious periphery.

This is a crude characterisation, but there is a struggle, and it has its problems. It might be argued that the response has been to overstate, to overargue the significance of music, to present a social world in which nothing exists outside of an overarching definition of music. This response was endorsed, if in a somewhat whimsical fashion, by Lévi-Strauss, for whom, in *The Raw and the Cooked* (1986), the

---

1. For an influential statement of this argument, see Wolff 1987. For recent contributions to this deconstruction of musicology's 'objects', see Nettl 1992 and Randel 1992.

essence of mythic thinking could be seen in music. Principles of symmetry, inversion, equivalence and homology which constitute the structures of mythic thought are illustrated by comparison with the repertoire of baroque and classical compositional technique. Music for Lévi-Strauss, in line with post-war serial thinking (especially that of Pierre Boulez), deals with pure, abstract structures of potentially infinite expansion (Lévi-Strauss 1986: 23).

Lévi-Strauss's only excursion into Amerindian conceptions of music and musical instruments is a relatively brief passage (for a book dedicated 'to music') in *From Honey to Ashes* (1973: 360–470). Ethnomusicologists have however subsequently argued (see for example Turino 1989, Seeger 1987), that music is of central significance in South American Indian societies. Seeger, working amongst the Suyá of the Upper Xingu in Brazil, described his monograph as a 'musical anthropology'. This formulation reversed Merriam's seminal description of ethnomusicology as 'the study of music in culture'. But music is not just a thing which happens 'in' society. A society, Seeger argues, might also be usefully conceived as something which happens 'in music'; it is through music and dance performance that fundamental aspects of Suyá social organisation (in particular moiety affiliations) are recognised, social time is ritually articulated, and an entire cosmological system is grasped. Suyá society as a totality might be understood in terms of their music; as Seeger points out, 'Suyá society was an orchestra, its village was a concert hall, and its year a song' (1987: 140)

Seeger's monograph is a powerful argument which, amongst other things, overcomes the theoretical divide between the study of music and the study of society. It is one of a small number of recent ethnomusicological monographs of 'remote' tribal peoples, in which our own distinctions between the ritual and the technical, the cultural and the natural, music, dance, speech and other forms of communication have to be rethought from scratch (see also Feld 1982). But how is the anthropologist to make use of these kinds of insights in societies more like our own? In our own technologised and industrialised existence, the ritual forms of music have become peripheralised, and the rest, social dances, bar sessions, concert attendance, listening to a new CD at home in the evening or the radio during the day fit into gaps created by work, or at least, the working day. Music often seems to do little more than fill a silence left by something else.

Introduction

And yet the social and cultural worlds that have been shaped by modernity (that is to say, the industrial–capitalist order, the nation-state, and secular rationalism) would be hard to imagine without music. My own awareness of 'the modern' itself, in a remote Anglican choir school in Herefordshire, was decisively formed through music. I had heard a recording of Honegger's *Pacific 231* before I had travelled on a large train. The sound of Messaien's *Les Corps Glorieux*, thundering from the organ whilst we processed out of chapel one Whitsun day, intimated a world of radical, violent and bitterly contested change. Music is clearly very much a part of modern life and our understanding of it, articulating our knowledge of other peoples, places, times and things, and ourselves in relation to them.

Performance and Place

This becomes particularly clear when we think about the ways in which music informs our sense of place. Place, or 'locale', following Giddens (1990: 18) 'refers to the physical setting of social activity as situated geographically'. Giddens points out that one distinct consequence of modernity is the 'phantasmagoric' separation of space from place, as places become 'thoroughly penetrated by and shaped in terms of social influences quite distant from them' (ibid). This dislocation requires an anxiety ridden process of relocation or, to use Giddens' term, 'reembedding' (ibid.: 88). Amongst the countless ways in which we 'relocate' ourselves, music undoubtedly has a vital role to play. The musical event, from collective dances to the act of putting a cassette or CD into a machine, evokes and organises collective memories and present experiences of place with an intensity, power and simplicity unmatched by any other social activity. The 'places' constructed through music involve notions of difference and social boundary. They also organise hierarchies of a moral and political order. The insistent evocation of place in Irish balladry or the 'Country and Irish' heard on juke-boxes in bars in Ireland and amongst migrant communities in England and the United States is a striking example, defining a moral and political community in relation to the world in which they find themselves. In this particular process of relocation, the places, boundaries and identities involved are of a large and collective order. People can equally use music to locate themselves in quite idiosyncratic and plural ways. A private collection of records, tapes or CDs, for example, articulates a number of highly idiosyncratic sets of places and boundaries. A moment's reflection on our own musical practices brings home to us the sheer profusion of identities and selves that we possess.

The idea that music symbolises social boundaries might seem an obvious enough starting point for an anthropological approach to music. Ethnomusicologists, with anthropologists, have however become less interested in the structuralist proposition that performance simply reflects 'underlying' cultural patterns and social structures. Firstly, as A. Cohen pointed out, 'the view that any event or process or structure somehow replicates the essence of a society's culture has now ... been properly discredited' (1982: 8). Social performance, following writers such as Bourdieu (1977) and De Certeau (1984), is instead seen as a practice in which meanings are generated, manipulated, even ironised, within certain limitations. Music and dance, as all of the contributors to this volume stress, do not simply 'reflect'. Rather, they provide the means by which the hierarchies of place are negotiated and transformed. The case of the private collection of records, tapes and CDs illustrates the ways in which music can be used as a means of transcending the limitations of our own place in the world, of constructing trajectories rather than boundaries across space. To take a different example, identification with urban genres provides the means by which rural–urban migrants can transform themselves from peripheralised proletarians to urbanites, 'become' members of the 'clean' middle class (Peña 1985), become members of groups which represent in some way or another specific migrant interests (see Reily 1992).

Music does not then simply provide a marker in a prestructured social space, but the means by which this space can be transformed. To take another example, documentary and advertising clichés denoting place do more than reflect a knowledge already 'there'. They preform a knowledge of other places that is borne out by subsequent experience, and this knowledge has a distinct role in the definition and control of problematic 'others'. The augmented second denoting 'the orient' in the old Turkish Delight advertisement has little to do with Turkish musics, but it informs us in the context of our own musical language of an imagined world of violence and repressed sexuality. These deeply rooted images simultaneously justify the Western use of the Orient as the basis of collective sexual fantasies, and allow its governments to mobilise their armies against Middle Eastern populations the moment their supply of oil is threatened. The popular images and sounds (currently much in vogue with advertising copywriters) of overweight Italian operatic singers denote to North Western Europeans a decaying and sensuous Mediterranean which we can simultaneously fantasise about in our collective historical myths as the root and source of 'European culture', and at the same time exploit for tourism and cheap labour. Clearly, these musical images do not just reflect knowledge of 'other places' but preform them in significant ways.

Secondly, as ethnomusicologists have recently come to insist, it is important that music and dance in these kind of rituals are not just seen as static symbolic objects which have to be understood in a context, but are themselves a patterned context within which other things happen (Waterman 1990: 213). What is important is not just musical performance, but *good* performance, if music and dance are to make a social event 'happen'. Complex aesthetic vocabularies, or single terms covering a complex semantic terrain point to minute and shifting subtleties of rhythm and texture which make or break the event. The Yoruba *ariya*, neotraditional celebrations described by Waterman marking namings, weddings, funerals, and business ventures are crucially dependent upon the *idùnnún* ('sweet stomachedness'), *itúraká* ('unfolded body') and *igbádùn* ('sweetness reception') provided by *Jújù* musicians. In Ireland terms such as *craic* ('crack'), and 'nyah' (Wilkinson 1991), and in Greece, the Balkans and the Middle East, terms derived from the Arabic words *keyf* or *zevk* (see for example Cowan 1991, Sugarman 1989) point to the crucial relationship between the music and ritual. Without these qualities, however they are conceived in a particular society, the ritual event is powerless to make the expected and desired connections and transformations.

I would argue therefore that music is socially meaningful not entirely but largely because it provides means by which people recognise identities and places, and the boundaries which separate them. The contributions to this volume illustrate some of the ways in which musical performance, as well as the acts of listening, dancing, arguing, discussing, thinking and writing about music, provide the means by which ethnicities and identities are constructed and mobilised. The fact that 'music' is left as a vague category is not a problem; it will be clear from the contributions to this volume that music 'is' what any social group consider it to be, contrary to the essentialist definitions and quests for musical 'universals' of 1960s ethnomusicology, or text-orientated techniques of musicological analysis.

Ethnicity

Ethnicity is perhaps the more problematic word. Ethnicity is 'an arguable and murky intellectual term' (Chapman, McDonald and Tonkin 1989: 11), but one which nonetheless continues to be useful for a variety of reasons. Barth's seminal essay (1969) introduced the term in his analysis of boundary construction and maintenance. Ethnicities are to be understood in terms of the construction, maintenance and negotiation of boundaries, and not on the putative social 'essences' which fill the gaps within them. Ethnic boundaries define and maintain social identities, which can only exist in 'a context of opposition and relativities' (Chapman, McDonald and Tonkin 1989: 17). The term ethnicity thus points to the central anthropological concern with classification. It allows us to turn from questions directed towards defining the essential and 'authentic' traces of identity 'in' music (a question with which much nationalist and essentially racist folklore and ethnography is explicitly concerned) to the questions of how music is used by social actors in specific local situations to erect boundaries, to maintain distinctions between us and them, and how terms such as 'authenticity' are used to justify these boundaries.

Chapman's contribution to this volume illustrates the point that it is always the categories and not the content that remain important. The immense significance of 'Celtic' music lies in the fact that whilst it is a strictly defined category (as a romantic 'other' in binary oppositions such as European periphery vs. centre, Celt vs. Anglo-Saxon or French) its content is capable of a great deal of variety and left relatively undefined. 'Celtic' music is thus always potentially easy, participatory, and crosses national borders. Consequently it allows people access to – in their own terms – a domain of 'Celtdom' denied to them by the complexities of, for example, a Celtic language, or the theoretical and practical difficulties of maintaining a coherent political identity. 'Celtic music' is then something which has been created by certain ways of classifying musical experience, and is certainly not a residue of authentic 'Celtness' waiting to be discovered in the many and various musical styles and genres played in the Celtic world.

'Authenticity' is a term that was frequently raised in questions during the seminar. Clearly, notions of authenticity and identity are closely interlinked. What one is (or wants to be) cannot be 'inauthentic', whatever else it is. Authenticity is definitely not a property of music, musicians and their relations to an audience. It is not even a Benjaminesque 'aura' of uniqueness that surrounds a live situation as opposed to mechanically reproduced music, even though one frequently hears the term used in this way. We are inclined to make the mistake of hearing a word and assuming that the various things it points to are similar, if not the same.[2] Instead, we should see 'authenticity' is a discursive trope of great persuasive power. It focuses a way of talking about music, a way of saying to outsiders and insiders alike 'this is what is really significant about this music', 'this is the music that makes us different from other people'. The ways in which authenticity is structured, defined and employed in discursive contexts are discussed in a number of contributions to this volume, particularly those by Chapman, Cohen and Stokes. This kind of perspective enables the interested anthropologist to see music less as a fixed essence with certain definable properties than as a wide field of practices and meanings with few significant or socially relevant points of intersection. Without understanding local conditions, languages and contexts, it is impossible to know what these practices and meanings are. Ethnicities, as Ardener pointed out, positively 'demand to be seen from the inside' (1989: 111); the same is true of their musical strategies.

The 'emic' perspective is not however the end of the story. Ethnicities can never be understood outside the wider power relations in which they are embedded, as a number of well-established critiques of the term as used by anthropologists point out (see the contributors to Asad 1973). This is more clear now than ever. The notion of the 'ethnic' today (particularly in journalistic language) points to an area of experience around which some of the most violent conflicts in Europe are being played out, particularly in the context of 'ethnic conflict' in the former Soviet Union, 'ethnic cleansing' in Bosnia, and 'ethnic violence' in British cities. Perhaps this will mark a final break with the romantic notion of 'the ethnic' as the harmless and colourful 'folklore' on the remote peripheries of our own societies.

Groups are self-defining in terms of their ability to articulate differences between self and other, but issues of colonialism,

---

2. Wittgenstein repeatedly pointed to the ways in which we are mislead by this kind of language in the *Philosophical Investigations*: 'What this language primarily describes is a picture. What is to be done with the picture, how it is to be used, is still obscure. Quite clearly, however, it must be explored if we want to understand the sense of what we are saying. But the picture seems to spare us this work: it already points to a particular use. This is how it takes us in.' (1958: 184)

domination and violence have to be taken into account. Recognition of difference is seldom reciprocal. Dominant groups oppose, with a violence which is either explicit or 'douce' (Bourdieu 1977), the construction of difference when it confronts their interest. Ethnicities are violently suppressed and excluded them from the classification systems of the dominant group. There is hardly an area of social difference which is not contested in these kinds of terms. When we are looking at the way in which ethnicities and identities are put into play in musical performance, we should not forget that music is one of the less innocent ways in which dominant categories are enforced and resisted. In Magowan and Parkes's contributions to this volume, which discuss music as a marker of identity in, respectively, colonised and enclave groups, the relationships of domination and subordination are particularly marked. As Parkes's discussion of music amongst the Kalasha of the Hindu Kush shows, these external relations have profound implications for internal relations. Ceremonial musical performance provides the principal means by which the resulting contradictions between an egalitarian ethos and intense competition between factional leaders are socially managed.

The violence which enforces dominant categorisations is seldom far away from musical performances in many situations. Two examples from my own immediate experience will make this point. A problematic boundary patrolled, as it were, and enforced by musicians is that between 'Irish' and 'British' identities in Northern Ireland. The 12 July parades by Protestant Orangemen are militaristic extravaganzas of uniformed flute and drum bands, consisting almost entirely of young men, which commemorate the Protestant victory over Irish Catholics at the Battle of the Boyne in 1690. They also define central city space in Belfast as the domain of Ulster Protestants and British rule. The Protestant communities of Ulster continue to dominate political life at every level, but an increasing Catholic population (now securing sizeable majorities in many town councils and electoral wards), and a paralysed embarrassment on the part of the British government has begun to erode this domination. The embattled attempts by 'Orange' hardliners to assert their 'Britishness' would appear to many as an attempt to swim against the tide. The symbolic control of urban space through graffiti, flags, the language of signs and colour coding[3] is a daily fact of life for

---

3. The colours of British and Irish flags painted on kerbstones indicate respectively Loyalist and Republican areas. Red letter-boxes are painted green in republican West

the people of Northern Ireland. Public symbols stressing the relationship between Ulster and the Republic of Ireland, for example the Dublin–Belfast maracycle which disrupts traffic in the city for a couple of days every June, increasingly challenge the political/symbolic means by which Unionists have hitherto asserted their 'Britishness' and justified their power in Ulster, and Belfast in particular.

The marches are aggressive occasions. It is impossible to disentangle the musical aspect of the parades from the militarism of the banners, and scarcely concealed displays of machismo and supremacism on the part of the marching musicians. Chants of 'UVF'[4] accompany drums and flutes, particularly when marchers are marching past or through republican areas. The lambeg drums are as objects vital symbols of the pride and integrity of Protestant communities, but at the same time, as extremely loud musical instruments, they constitute an assault on the ears. No alternative thought is possible. The drums demand that people either march in time to them, or go away. The space patrolled in these marches consists of more than a route which could be traced on a map, but the wide area in the city from which the sounds of the lambeg drums can be heard.

Another example concerns what is widely (but not entirely correctly) considered to be 'Catholic' music. The expression 'diddle-de-dee' music, by its detractors, suggests a world of harmlessly folkish and essentially 'Irish' concerns. 'Irish Traditional' music is however one of the many ways in which public recreational space is intensely politicised. Where political issues are at stake, questions of definition assume great importance. Whilst the bozouki and a number of other 'foreign' instruments, as Chapman points out in this volume in the 'Celtic' context, do not dilute the 'Irishness' of the music, the guitar, according to many, does. A guitar player turned up for a session in a GAA[5] club determined to chip in, in spite of being frozen out by the other musicians. He was asked to leave and, when he didn't, told to clear off; the guitar 'wasn't an Irish instrument' and this was an 'Irish session'. Eventually he

---

Belfast. The Post Office repaints them, and the process starts again. In these kinds of ways there is a constant battle between Loyalists, Republicans and the apparatus of the British state for symbolic control of the city's public space.

4. Ulster Volunteer Force, an outlawed loyalist paramilitary organisation.
5. Gaelic Athletics Association. 'Irish' sports have played a vital role in organising and socialising resistance to British rule in Northern Ireland.

did, but the damage had been done; he was apparently attacked the next day by masked men, and his left hand was mutilated with an axe. Perhaps the most significant details were omitted when this event was related to me. If anything it was a friendly warning, perhaps exaggerated to make the point, that Irish music was something that people would be prepared to fight about to maintain a desired purity and authenticity, and that I should tread lightly. What it did convey however was a recognition by a local musician that the boundaries constructed in musical contexts defining 'Irish' and 'British' are as much a part of the violence of the political situation as shooting and bombs.

This point runs against the grain of a Platonic strand in our thinking about music, in which music, understood as an extraterrestrial 'essence', controls, regulates, and harmonises social relations. Our informants too often tell us the same story, presenting to us in normative statements a world in which music and dance unite and bring together. Music and violence are thus doubly difficult to think about in the same breath. In the Black Sea region of Turkey my informants constantly told me that the *horon* dance 'brings us all together'; global peace was imagined as a *horon* line stretching across the whole world. What I remember however was a series of dramatic events; a man being shot in the stomach whilst dancing by a rival in a feud, and some weeks later a lad dancing next to me being clubbed almost senseless by an old woman with a piece of wood the size of a log for apparently eyeing her granddaughter. These dance events in fact seemed not to allow for the temporary suspension of the everyday boundaries between competing kin groups, men and women. On the contrary it brought people separated by these boundaries into an intense and potentially explosive proximity. Dance sometimes did allow for a temporary suspension of disbelief, but this could never be taken for granted.

Identity and the Nation-State

Music is intensely involved in the propagation of dominant classifications, and has been a tool in the hands of new states in the developing world, or rather, of those classes which have the highest stake in these new social formations. This control is principally enacted through state control or influence over universities, conservatories and archives, and is disseminated through its media systems. These processes might be dismissed as part of the coercive apparatus of the state (see for example Harker 1985), or vociferously defended by ideologues whose jobs, presumably, are at stake (see for example Bashir 1978). More usefully perhaps they may be considered as a terrain of meanings somewhere between those invented and those provided by other 'traditions' which professional musicians, instrument makers, media planners and their audiences have to negotiate.

However they are seen, the definition and construction of national styles is seldom unproblematic. Who does the defining? Who can be paid (and trusted) to do the spade work of modifying instruments, training musicians, creating archives and repertories? What entrenched interests in the existing music world will this affect? Will it be accepted or rejected? These problems are discussed by Baily, in this volume, in a situation where radio was practically the only means by which a coherent sense of national identity could be imparted to the complex mix of ethnic groups (*qaum*) that constituted modern Afghanistan. Music was a vital arm, and not just a reflection of state cultural policy. The creation of what is now perceived as a distinct 'Radio Afghanistan' style was, as he points out, the largely unexpected end result of quite diverse plans. The intentions of Afghan ideologues were different from those of the specialists available to put them into operation. Whilst the resulting bricolage of Hindustani *rag* and *tal*, Persian *ghazal*, Pashtun and Tadjik *kiliwali* now thought of as 'Afghan music' enjoys substantial popularity, this was not always the case. As Baily notes, the radio was so intensely associated with modernist reformism that the radio station was destroyed following the deposition of Amanullah in 1929.

Why should music be worth this trouble to the modernising state? There are a number of answers to this question, which do not add up to a total explanation of all the phenomena mentioned, but may apply in varying weights in different cases. Where communications are generally inadequate the radio is an important means of propagating the notion of national unity. Radio listening outside the developed world is often conducted in public space (see also Baily in this volume). According to Güngör (1990: 55) there were 4,834 registered radio sets in rural Turkey in 1935, at the height of nationalist reformism. These village radio sets were kept in village 'guest rooms'. Educational programmes (disseminating 'new' Turkish language, history, folklore), news bulletins and newly approved musical genres representing Turkey's 'European' identity thus became a property of public space in rural areas at a critical phase of Turkey's nation building. The control of media systems by states, through ownership of the technology and its ability to exclude through censorship rival systems, is a tool of social control that few authoritarian states have overlooked. It is worth pointing out, however, that media systems are not a watertight means of enacting social control. They are often 'leaky', to use Enzenburger's expression (1976): meanings cannot be totally controlled, and the technologies are seldom foolproof. For example, Western classical music had little appeal to Turkish villagers in the period discussed above. Villagers would either simply turn off (Szyliowicz 1966: 100), or, far worse, use their radio sets to tune into Egyptian radio, broadcasting more powerfully at a readily available frequency (Stokes 1992: 93). The argument through music that Turks were Europeans rather than Arabs fell flat on its face. The rapid changes in recording and sound reproduction technology in recent years have arguably (see Cutler 1984) democratised recording and listening, and consequently weakened the grip of state and music industry monopolies.

But why have modernising, and often extremely poor states, lavished so much funding on the establishment of musical archives, the development of folklore as an academic field, the training of orchestras and academics, the establishment of schools and conservatories? We might perhaps first look at what musics often *do* rather than what they are held to *represent* (the two not always being the same thing). Musics are invariably communal activities, that brings people together in specific alignments, whether as musicians, dancers or listening audiences. The 'tuning in' (Schutz 1977) through music of these social alignments can provide a powerful affective experience in which social identity is literally 'embodied'. The relationships which are activated through music might involve the community as a whole – indeed one of the only occasions on which the community does come together, as in the case of the Venda *Tschikona* described by Blacking (1976: 50), or the Miri *Tendung*, by Baumann (1987: 173). Thus, in certain societies, music and dance are the only means by which the wider community appears as such to itself.

For regions and communities within the context of the modernising nation-state that do not identify with the state project, music and dance are often convenient and morally appropriate ways of asserting defiant difference. As in the case of Black South African Zionist church music, they can literally embody a different social order based on the moral values of their own community (Blacking 1981). The parallel association of music and dance with social licence, sexual adventure, drink and drugs establishes these communal musical events as a vital and pleasurable part of life. The fact that pleasure is involved is immensely important. As Foucault repeatedly pointed out, pleasure becomes a significant arena of political experience and a focus of control, through the definition of what pleasures 'are' and whether or not they are permitted, and, conversely, through resistance to that control.⁶ The association of pleasure, licence and a festival atmosphere with music and dance makes them experiences which are distinctly 'out of the ordinary'. It is perhaps this that distinguishes the kinds of ethnicity discussed in this volume from the 'everyday' practices of boundary construction and maintenance with which much social anthropological writing on ethnicity is concerned (Cohen 1982: 3). Even though they are out of the ordinary experiences, music and dance (and talk about music and dance) do encourage people to feel that they are in touch with an essential part of themselves, their emotions and their 'community'. It is perhaps for this reason that the 'resistance through rituals' discussed by Hall involved the rituals of subcultural groups enacted principally through music and behaviour in relation to music (Hall and Jefferson 1976). Just as musical performance enacts and embodies dominant communal values, it can also enact in a powerful, affective way, rival principles of social organisation. Control of media systems provides the state with the means by which this might be countered.

Musical styles can be made emblematic of national identities in complex and often contradictory ways. The significance of 'national' composers is a case in point. Mach's contribution to this volume is an account of the ways in which Chopin has been successively redefined by the Polish intelligentsia in terms of the changing contexts of Polish nationalism. Chopin was an international composer with very little experience of Polish peasant music. By the turn of the century in newly independent Poland, he had come to stand for a distinctly Polish contribution to a universal (i.e. European) culture. What was celebrated in this cult was the ability of the composer to

6. Hall discusses the extent to which resistance is itself construed and held within the bounds of disciplinary power in an illuminating interview with Lawrence Grossberg (1986). Hall argues against Foucault's 'proto-anarchism' (ibid.: 48). Resistance is not, he points out, simply summoned up from nowhere, but organised in terms of alternative 'regimes of truth'. These may be subordinated within an overall power field, but they nonetheless have distinct places within them. If this is the case, one could claim, following Hall, that musics, like languages, have to be seen in relation to one another in a field of power which is structured but not entirely determined by the dominant ideologies.

sublimate his Polish musical identity and attain the rank of genius in terms of an international musical culture. Chopin thus embodied a fantasy of Poland's political role in early twentieth century Europe. His late romantic style itself denoted revolution, and the struggle of the individual against the world; a highly appropriate image for the ideologues of a new nation-state. This formulation was however entirely reversed in socialist Poland. Chopin was celebrated for his adherence to his roots and his refusal to conform to the bourgeois aesthetics of romanticism.

Ideologues appear to have a free hand in deciding what criteria are in play in the definition of national style, even in the most unlikely circumstances. Reily's paper points out that music could provide the symbolic means by which a modernising intellectual, Mário de Andrade, could argue for the national integration of Brazil's seemingly irreconcilable ethnic diversities.[7] De Andrade envisaged a Brazil united by a music which brought together European, African and Amerindian identities. His work provided the bedrock of his, and a subsequent generation of social and folkloric research, which sought to effect the means by which this non-racial utopia could be brought into being. The power of figures such as De Andrade to control what they create is more problematic. Reily's paper examines the significance of this imagined ethnicity in Brazilian anthropological and folkloric research in later decades, and the ways in which it was deflected and redefined in changing political circumstances. The significance of a style, a composer or a projected multi-ethnic national musical identity emerges under specific ideological circumstances. The papers of Baily, Mach and Reily point to the diversity of these contexts, and the sheer variety of strategies employed within them, which the blanket notion of 'reinvented traditions' does not really address.

The nature of this kind of appropriation as a form of internal cultural colonialism can be seen when we look at 'traditional' music in overtly colonial contexts. The ways in which the British in West Africa promoted 'tribal' identities and their musics at the expense of syncretic creole forms, since creole mercantile élites formed a

---

7. The cult of Chopin spread far and wide. Mach points out the popularity of Chopin in Japan. In Brazil, Reily notes that 'Mário de Andrade saw Chopin as an ideal of the nationalist composer, because he was unselfconsciously national. His roots were so ingrained in his subconscious that he did not have to produce them "artificially", as Brazilians would have to do. Chopin was presented as the model Brazilian composers were meant to strive towards.' (personal communication)

substantial threat to British economic interests, has been discussed by Collins and Richards (1989). To take a slightly different example, the role of Western ideas about 'the Orient', as is well-known from Said's influential critique (1978), has had immense implications for Middle Eastern musicians today. The French orientalist D'Erlanger maintained his own mock court orchestra in Tunisia, and used it to militate against 'new' instruments (such as the harmonium), and resurrect old instruments and genres (Davis 1993). The 1932 Congress of Arab music in Cairo featured one of his ensembles, actually after D'Erlanger had died, playing music even then obsolete. The fact that instruments such as the Maghrebin *ud* and the *ghazal* are performed in Tunisia today testify to the extent to which this form of cultural colonialism, with its ideas of order, rationality and authenticity, continue to operate in the Middle East.

Hybridity and Difference

Clearly music has to be seen as a field of symbolic activity which is highly important to nation-states. The promotion of supra-national entities by nation-states is not an exception, allowing them to argue the right to participate in a sphere of cultural and political involvement (Turkey's commitment to the Eurovision Song Contest being a case in point), or the right to control this sphere (as in the case of Egypt's hosting the Arab Music Congress in 1932). Celtic, Arab, African, Mediterranean, European musics, to name but a few, are defined and constructed in competitions, festivals, conferences and tourist promotions. This highly widespread domain of musical experience is not one with which ethnomusicologists have been happy. Chauvinist agendas are all too obvious, staged 'folklore' has little in common with what it purports to represent, music and dances become alienated from their real settings, their currency worthless out of context (Blacking 1987: 133–4). These events are hardly 'popular', and seldom make any claims to high artistic value, but they are however events which account for a great deal of musical experience. Contexts are constructed by musicians, audiences and media in these events, in which meanings are generated, controlled and negotiated.

My own contribution to this volume looks at one such event, a trip to Ireland by a group of Black Sea Turkish musicians. The event was seen by the organisers as one of musical exchange; the Turkish musicians would give something and get something – an experience of

Irish music – in return. The ways in which the parameters of meaning were defined, stage managed and, in the end, quietly contested by organisers and musicians in the micropolitics of the bar sessions were certainly unusual, in both Irish and Turkish terms. However, they do perhaps illustrate a more general process of a highly flexible, creative construction of ethnicity which is increasingly common as tourism, 'world music' events and media bring together unlikely groups of musicians and listeners. Even now, when musicians are overwhelmed by a consciousness of other musics, they struggle to make sense of them, incorporate them, relegate them to lower rungs on ladders of complexity, difficulty, interest and so on, in terms dictated by their own musics and views of the world. In spite of the language of global participation, these events are power struggles. The idea of the pleasure of unexpected juxtapositions and 'proximities' of genres and styles (Chambers 1985), the semiotic free-for-all celebrated by some post-modernist theory, does little justice to the complexities of increasingly common 'multi-cultural' musical events. In the final analysis, whatever else goes on at these kind of events, music is a form of public display which the state and other social groups have an interest in controlling for obvious purposes of self-promotion.

A final reason why music is so important to 'top down' ethnicities is that musicians often appear to celebrate ethnic plurality in problematic ways. Musicians in many parts of the world have a magpie attitude towards genres, picked up, transformed and reinterpreted in their own terms. The proliferation of instruments and styles in the context of the Irish music session (I have heard Appalachian, Breton, Rumanian, Bulgarian, French *chanson*, Kletzmer, even *conjunto*) is a problem for extreme nationalists in Northern Ireland, as my earlier anecdote makes abundantly clear. The significance of 'Black' music styles in British rock has been the subject of a number of studies (Chambers 1985, Hebdige 1979). Chilean *Nueva Cancion* (Fairley 1985) plays on the exoticism of Andean musics. The Mediterranean, historically divided between Christians, Jews and Muslims, provides a number of striking examples. Greek *Rebetika* (see Holst 1975, Herzfeld 1987), Turkish *Arabesk* (Stokes 1992) and Israeli *Rock Mizrahi* (Shiloah and Cohen 1983), even Andalucian *Flamenco* (Manuel 1989) celebrate an oriental 'other' which is highly subversive in the contexts of official nationalist discourses which explicitly reject their internal 'orients' as aspects of a backward past. Where official ethnicities are defined through opposition to a pernicious otherness embodied by neighbouring states, this celebration of ethnic profusion in what we might loosely call the popular musics it seeks to control is always a potential threat. The questions that have previously concerned ethnomusicologists, shaping a number of now classic studies on which the chapters of this volume build, have been how and why different styles are embraced. Ethnomusicologists have noted with great frequency the fact that musics are seldom stable in contexts of social change. Merriam pointed out the value of musical data in understanding processes of 'culture contact', providing a laboratory domain of retentions and changes susceptible observation at a musical level (1959). Two aspects of 'culture contact' have proved to be of enduring interest to ethnomusicologists. Firstly, the gradual musical changes that come about in small-scale, isolated communities as they are absorbed into wider political entities. Since ethnomusicology as a discipline was developed in the United States, the changing experience of the North American Indians provided the most relevant point of reference (see for example Herzog 1935). The response of musicians in 'small' communities to the encroachments of the outside world have been a common theme. More recently, and in Europe, Baumann has used the term 'reintegration' in his discussion of how the Miri of Northern Sudan have sought to recreate their community in their own terms using song and dance in the face of the expansion of the Sudanese state, the Arabic language and Islam in the Miri hills. Whilst Miri 'grindstone songs' have been pervaded by Northern Sudanese musical tropes and expressions in Arabic, Sudanese popular songs (*daluka*, celebrating urban love) are only permitted to be sung by unmarried girls; on their marriage they must cease (1987: 94). A changing and essentially unequal relationship with the world outside their community is thereby controlled and symbolically dealt with in their own terms. The outside world is 'domesticated' through music.

The incorporation and 'domestication' of musical difference is an essential process of musical ethnicity. To take a quite different case, in Suyá cosmology and in Suyá musical practice, all of their songs come from outside their own society – taught to them by the animal world, or learned from captives from neighbouring tribes. Each incorporates and controls a power emanating from beyond Suyá society. All were however made their own by the context and style of Suyá vocal performance, and, what is more, came to act as 'assertions of identity in a multi-ethnic social situation' (Seeger 1987: 105) in the Upper Xingu area in which Gê, Tupi, Arawak and Karib groups travel widely and attend one another's ceremonies.

Discussion of the use of music and dance in the construction of urban, especially migrant identity has also been a common theme. In 1956, Mitchell pointed out the importance of the Kalela dance as a focus for the recreation and reformulation of migrant identity in the copper belt of former Northern Rhodesia. The abundance of immigrant communities (and the residual power of the 'melting-pot' ideology) in most cities in the United States again has again provided American ethnomusicologists with fieldwork sites on their own doorstep (Kerman 1985: 160). Subsequent 'urban ethnomusicological' research has discussed degrees of assimilation, counter-acculturation and inter-generational differences in the perception of identity on the part of migrant communities, or urban environments transformed by rural–urban migration (see for example the contributions to Nettl 1978). Migrants and refugees might identify with the popular genres produced by the dominant group, especially if these have sentimental points of connection with an imagined rural world and uncorrupted moral order (for example Country and Western in Ireland), or if it embodies aspirations of participation in an urban high life (for example West African 'High Life', Texas Mexican *Orquesta*), or, more simply, if it is the only way to be able to carry on being a professional musician (as in the case of the Afghan refugee musicians in Baily's film *Amir*). They might also best be served by maintaining a defiant difference, as is frequently the case with political refugees whose politics are either encouraged or merely tolerated by the host society.

Ethnicity, Class and Media

The recreation of rural identities and their performance in music and dance by urban migrant communities points to the complex relationship of ethnicities and class identities. Ethnicity and class identity in the case of migrant communities can be hard to distinguish, especially in societies in which one group provides nearly all of the cheap labour for another. The situation is rarely of course this simple. Rapid but highly selective mobility in capitalist economies, and their hegemonic ideologies make class relationships difficult to see. Looking at the relationship between 'American' and 'Mexican' identities in Texas, Peña (1985) argues that the distinction between *orquesta* and *conjunto* amongst Mexican migrants marked the difference between Mexicans who had adopted the dominant ideology of assimilation in the American melting-pot, and those who did not. It not only marked this distinction, but provided the means by which Mexicans could move themselves and their families upmarket, and publicly associate themselves with the 'clean' middle class by identifying with *orquesta* rather than *conjunto*. The semiotics of *orquesta* precisely mirrored the 'contradictory class locations' (ibid.: 177) of the Texas–Mexican middle classes. Significantly Peña concedes that it is ultimately difficult to draw a fixed line between the two genres, their musicians and clienteles. *Conjunto* musicians and *orquesta* musicians maintain a certain fluidity; aspects of style pass from one to the other. In the end, *orquesta* and *conjunto* merged as Chicanos began to see themselves in opposition to non-Chicano Americans. One should not conclude that an analysis which discusses class if misdirected, but that the relationships between classes, ethnicities and their musics are more complicated than a simplistic model equating class with musical style would allow.

Classes rarely cohere in terms of – to paraphrase Volosinov – musical 'sign communities' (Hebdige 1979: 17). Adorno also warned against the simplistic notion that a class could be simply matched with musical style of cultural expression; genres carry the marks of the contradictory tendencies of the society as a whole (Adorno 1976: 69). Subsequent Marxian theorists have sought a more flexible and sophisticated way of conceptualising the relation of classes and music. Subcultural theory dealt with this complex situation in more explicitly Gramscian terms (Hall and Jefferson 1976). Subcultures borrow from the dominant culture, inflecting and inverting its signs to create a bricolage in which the signs of the dominant culture are 'there' and just recognisable as such, but constituting a quite different, subversive whole. In sartorial terms, as Hebdige points out, this can be seen in the use of bin liners as items of dress, and safety pins as ornaments (1979). In musical terms, the material of post-war popular cultures has essentially been the harmonic-melodic vocabulary of the dominant culture (that of eighteenth- and nineteenth-century Viennese tradition), but one which is subverted through repetition (Middleton 1992), speed and volume, texture and timbre (Shepherd 1991: 153). The dominant culture, through the music industry and media, attempts to reappropriate the space for its own purposes. The moment it does this, new stylistic criteria for articulating an inflected 'difference' *vis-à-vis* the dominant culture are found by the subcultural group. The art was to stay a step ahead; Mod style, as Hebdige points out, 'concealed as much as it stated' (1979: 52). The point was that it confounded attempts by the dominant culture to identify what it really consisted of.

Ethnicities are rather like classes in this respect; frequently they are defined or excluded in terms of the classificatory systems of the dominant group whose guiding motive is the control and cooption of potentially problematic 'others'. Neither ethnicities nor class subcultures can operate outside this control. Frequently they have to define themselves within dominant classifications. This, as Ardener pointed out in a seminal essay, is a characteristic of all 'muted groups', by which he meant all groups (specifically, but not just, those constituted by gender) whose expressions of identity are either silenced or not acknowledged by the dominant group (1972). The criteria by which the boundaries are erected and maintained are not always easy to see, and are capable of shifting quickly, enabling a core of insiders to redefine themselves as ethnicities or class subcultures in the face of encroachment on the part of predatory outsiders. The complicated ways in which ethnicities are manifested in music make some sense in these terms. The 'Irish' music session with its profusion of musics makes sense partly in terms of the 'session' situation, and partly in terms of instruments and playing styles that make everything potentially 'Irish'. The Scandinavian Irish music enthusiast and the American ethnomusicologist/folklorist (both stock comic figures in Irish music circles), with their intent concentration on authentic repertories miss precisely the integrated profusion of styles which lies at the heart of many 'Irish music' sessions.[8]

I have been arguing that the means by which ethnicities (as well as class subcultures) define themselves in music have to take into account the power relations which pertain between the groups defining and being defined. An important and powerful agent in the process of definition has been the recording industry. The media technologisation of popular musics does little in itself to affect perceptions of authenticity on the part of musicians and audiences, especially since new recording technologies no longer imply quite the same kind of dependence upon large companies, and indeed,

---

8. In relation to Basque ethnicity and music, Urla points out that 'new Basque musical production, with its inspired irreverence toward tradition and authenticity, calls into question the notion of a bounded Basque culture and identity that underlies both nationalist discourse and the language movement. It is in this sense that we can view these forms of popular culture as involving a very different notion of difference and modernity' (1993: 115). The Irish practices described here also constitute, through kind of supervised eclecticism, a claim to a 'real Irishness' which simultaneously subverts the categories of official folklore, and those of visiting academics.

themselves form an integral part of the production of popular music through dubbing, scratching and sampling in rap, hip hop, rave. Cohen's chapter in this volume looks at the ways in which an authentic 'Liverpool Sound' is constructed in Liverpool in terms of a series of oppositions (technological/acoustic, synthesised/raw, contrived/ authentic) in which Liverpool is principally opposed to Manchester. This insistence on locality and authenticity contradicts a post-modernist argument in which history has disappeared in the pursuit of the instantaneous, and authenticity has been supplanted with a celebration of surfaces. This disintegration of history and authenticity has been promoted by, and is in turn a product of, the media industries who, after all, have to sell their product to as many people as possible. The disintegration is frequently held to effect a significant 'delocalisation' of the experience of listening. Cohen argues that on the contrary we should see a dialectical opposition of the global to the local, in which the local languages of authenticity retain their significance. The production of the 'Liverpool Sound', she concludes, is ultimately a resource through which demeaning stereotypes and a dependence upon South-East England can be reinterpreted and redefined.

Magowan's chapter in this volume looks at the recasting of Aboriginal concepts of place in the Australian popular music industry. In North-East Arnhem Land song performance at funerals constitutes the most important ritual occasion in which relationships between kin, tribal moieties and their territory are both asserted and challenged. The aesthetic and ideological force of the performance can be understood in relation to the concept of *yothu–yindi* relationships, which are considered to embody a certain harmony between certain groups and their claims to territory. Recent aboriginal popular bands, notably *Soft Sands* and *Yothu–Yindi* have recast elements of this aesthetic to express pan-tribal solidarities. This reformulation articulates a vision of just and equitable relations between aboriginals and white Australians, and respect for their claims to political and geographic space.

Gender and Identity

A final area in which boundaries are 'performed' in music is that of gender, which connects the issues addressed in this volume to the already well established study of gender in historical musicology, popular music studies, and ethnomusicology. As La Rue points out in this volume, musical instruments and ways of playing them not only define ranks and hierarchies but gender. Castiglione's *Book of the Courtier* (translated into English in 1561) provides a wealth of detail on not just the appropriate instruments, but the ways in which behaviour in relation to performance itself correctly conveyed politely gendered behaviour. A man should above all hide the effort involved, which might confuse his status with that of a professional musician – then merely a servant. His skills should appear 'natural' and not learned. A woman should never initiate a performance, but always be asked, and feign reluctance. Even then, she must make sure she doesn't do it too well; her performance should be 'sweet' rather than 'cunning'. It is not difficult to see in these formulations ideals which underpin an entire domestic and sexual ideology in Europe from the sixteenth to the late nineteenth century. Music thus provides the means by which men learn to be gentlemen and women to be gentlewomen.

Since gender is a symbol of social and political order, and the control of gender behaviour is a means of controlling that order, gender boundaries cannot be separated from other social and political boundaries. Gender boundaries articulate the most deeply entrenched forms of domination which provide basic metaphors for others, and thus constitute the most intensely 'naturalised' of all our boundary making activities (Ortner 1974). The boundaries which separate male and female and assign to each proper social practices are as 'natural' as the boundaries which separate one community from another. Musical practices are no exception – it is as 'natural' that men will make better trumpeters as it is 'natural' that women will make better harpists. Musical performance is often the principal means by which appropriate gender behaviour is taught and socialised (see Sugarman 1989).

But this is not all. Music, as mentioned above, does more than underscore, or express differences already there. Music and more particularly dance provides an arena for pushing back boundaries, exploring the border zones that separate male from female. Cowan's recent study of Greek dance (1990) provides a case study. Following Williams's definition of culture, Cowan sees dance less as a domain of shared and agreed meanings than one of conflict and control. Whilst dance is a vital means of gender socialisation, and an enactment of masculinity and femininity at ritual occasions such as weddings, it is also an arena in which gender categories can be contested. But dance is not 'normal' behaviour: the rules which apply outside dance do not necessarily apply inside. The fact that dance can ultimately be understood as a Simmelian 'play form' of culture means that these danced semiotic deconstructions cannot legitimately be confronted with the overt violence with which rural Greek society traditionally deals with its deviants.

Musicians are deeply implicated in these processes of gender 'play', even when this is not recognised by the dominant (male) social model. Social dance bringing together unmarried men and women in public space is a problem in any society in which social and moral order is imaged in terms of marriage and the confinement of sexuality within the domestic unit (see Leppert 1988). The fact that musicians preside over these occasions in the very real sense of controlling the 'flow' of the socio-musical space (as Waterman describes in the context of Yoruba *ariya* ceremonies), makes them powerful and problematic figures for the society at large. The extent of this problem can be seen in terms of the efforts to which a society goes to 'degender' musicians. Male musicians are with great frequency portrayed in societies in which gender hierarchies simultaneously constitute the basic symbol and fact of domination as men without social power, passive homosexuals and transsexuals, or at the very least, inappropriate choices for a husband. Conversely they are held to possess an extra-social, diabolic power (as in Mann's *Dr. Faustus*, and myths in European folklore of the devil's violin), or a kind of inspired madness (Baily 1988). Whilst this kind of otherness is often interpreted as an empowering liminal quality (Turner 1974) it should not be forgotten that the image of the musicians flouting the gender specific laws of society also has the basic ideological function of control. As anthropologists of the Mediterranean world have constantly argued, the moral order of many societies is entirely predicated upon the separation of gender and the control of sexuality; behaviour which threatens this, such as music and dance, is a complicated and conflict ridden terrain. Culturally desexing the musicians is one way of effecting this control.[9]

This volume aims to show how anthropologists might use musical material in their discussions of the social construction, exploration and control of identity categories and their boundaries. Perhaps it will not succeed in answering the telling question; with

---

9. The significance of the *castrati*, male musicians castrated to preserve aa boy's voice in eighteenth and nineteenth century Italy, illustrates this argument in a drastic way.

all this exploration, does music provide any means by which the boundaries might be challenged in any lasting way? Answers range from the specific to the general. Many East German scholars considered the role of East German popular musicians in bringing down the Berlin wall to have been critical.[10] At the other end of the continuum, Attali has argued that music prefigures social history; the forms of one era herald the social processes of the next. Twentieth century political forms are rooted in the political philosophy of the nineteenth century, which were present 'in embryonic form' in the musical forms of the eighteenth (1985: 4). His sweeping and slightly ecstatic generalisations have often been criticised, but they have the virtue of suggesting that we might at least get the idea of how things could be from music.

It is unlikely, to say the least, that what music 'does' is always traceable in simple cause and effect terms. As Frith points out: 'What music (pop) can do is put into play a sense of identity that may or may not fit the way we are placed by other social facts' (1987: 149). A sense of identity can be put into play through music by performing it, dancing to it, listening to it or even thinking about it. Depending upon how we are placed by other social facts it can confine and entrap us in a narrowly chauvinist or sexist sense. Depending upon how we are placed by other social facts, it can also leap across boundaries and put into play unexpected and expanding possibilities. Social Anthropologists have much to learn from the study of music, and much to contribute to its future development. The collapse of, or at least disillusion with, the grand explanatory schemata and renewed attention being given by anthropologists to the resourceful and prolix creativities of everyday life provides anthropologists with an opportunity to observe and engage with music as a vital form of social creativity. It is an opportunity which musicologists, ethnomusicologists and social anthropologists should seize together.

References

Adorno, T.W., *Introduction to the Sociology of Music*, New York, continuum, 1976.

Ardener, E.W., 'Belief and the Problem of Women' in J.La Fontaine (ed.) *The Interpretation of Ritual*, London, Tavistock, 1972.

---

10. Peter Wicke put this point in his opening address at the Sixth International Conference on Popular Music Studies in Berlin, 15 July 1991.

———, 'Social Anthropology and Population', in M. Chapman (ed.), *The Voice of Prophecy and Other Essays*, Oxford, Basil Blackwell, 1989.
Asad, T., (ed.) *Anthropology and the Colonial Encounter*, New York, Humanities Press, 1973.
Attali, J., *Noise: The Political Economy of Music*, Manchester, Manchester University Press, 1985.
Baily, J., 'Amin-e Diwaneh: The Musician as Madman', *Popular Music*, vol. 7, no. 2, 1988, pp. 133–46.
———, *Amir* (film) Royal Anthropological Institute, London, 1986.
Barth, F., *Ethnic Groups and Boundaries: The Social Organisation of Culture Difference*, London, George Allen and Unwin, 1969.
Bashir, M., 'Musical Planning in a Developing Country: Iraq and the Preservation of Musical Identity', *The World of Music*, vol. 20, no. 1, 1978, pp. 74–8.
Baumann, G., *National Integration and Local Integrity: The Miri of the Nuba Mountains in the Sudan*, Oxford, Clarendon Press, 1987.
Blacking, J., *A Common Sense View of All Music: Reflections on Percy Grainger's Contribution to Ethnomusicology and Music Education*, Cambridge, Cambridge University Press, 1987.
———, *How Musical is Man?*, London, Faber, 1976.
———, 'Political and Musical Freedom in the Music of some Black South African Churches' in L. Holy and M. Stuchlik (eds), *The Structure of Folk Models* [ASA monographs no. 20], London, Academic Press, 1981.
Bourdieu, P., *Outline of a Theory of Practice*, Cambridge, Cambridge University Press, 1977.
Certeau, M. de, *The Practice of Everyday Life*, Berkeley, University of California Press, 1984.
Chambers, I., *Urban Rhythms: Pop Music and Popular Culture*, London, Macmillan, 1985.
Chapman, M., E. Tonkin and M. McDonald, 'Introduction' to E. Tonkin, M. McDonald and M. Chapman (eds), *History and Ethnicity*, London, Routledge, 1989.
Cohen, A., *Belonging: Identity and Social Organization in British Rural Cultures*, Manchester, Manchester University Press, 1982.
Collins, J. and P. Richards, Popular Music in West Africa', in S. Frith (ed.), *World Music and Social Change*, Manchester, Manchester University Press, 1989.
Cowan, J., *Dance and the Body Politic in Northern Greece*, Princeton, Princeton University Press, 1990.
Cutler, C., 'Technology, Politics and Contemporary Music: Neccesity and Choice in Musical Forms', *Popular Music,* vol. 4, 1984, pp. 279–300.
Davis, R., 'Tunisia and the Cairo Congress of Arab Music, 1932', *The Maghreb Review*, vol. 18, nos. 1–2, 1993, pp. 83–102.
Enzenburger, H., 'Constituents of a Theory of the Media' in *Raids and Reconstructions*, London, 1976.

Fairley, J., 'Karaxú and Incantation: When does 'Folk' Become Popular?', *Popular Music Perspectives*, vol. 2, Göterborg, IASPM, 1985, pp. 278-86.
Feld, S., *Sound and Sentiment; Birds, Weeping, Poetics and Song in Kaluli Expression*, Philadelphia, University of Pennsylvania Press, 1982.
Finnegan, R., *The Hidden Musicians: Music Making in an English Town*, Cambridge, Cambridge University Press, 1990.
Frith, S., 'Towards an Aesthetic of Popular Music' in R. Leppert and S. McClarey (eds), *Music and Society: The Politics of Composition, Performance and Reception*, Cambridge, Cambridge Univerity Press, 1987.
Giddens, A., *The Consequences of Modernity*, Cambridge, Polity, 1990.
Güngör, N., *Arabesk: Sosyokültürel Açıdan Arabesk Müzik*, Ankara, Bilgi, 1990.
Hall, S., 'On Postmodernism and Articulation (Interview with Lawrence Grossberg)', *Journal of Communication Enquiry*, 1986, pp. 45-60.
Hall, S. and T. Jefferson (eds), *Resistance Through Rituals: Youth Subcultures in Postwar Britain*, London, Hutchinson, 1976.
Harker, D., *Fakesong: The Manufacture of British 'Folksong', 1700 to the Present Day*, Milton Keynes, Open University Press, 1985.
Hebdige, D., *Subculture: The Meaning of Style*, London, Methuen, 1979.
Herzfeld, M., *Anthropology through the Looking-Glass: Critical Ethnography in the Margins of Europe*, Cambridge, Cambridge University Press, 1987.
Herzog, G., 'Plains Ghost Dance and Great Basin Music', *American Anthropologist*, vol. 37, 1935, pp. 403-19.
Holst, G., *Road To Rembetika: Music of A Greek Subculture. Songs of Love, Sorrow and Hashish*, Athens, Denise Harvey, 1975.
Kerman, J., *Musicology*, London, Fontana, 1985.
Leppert, R., *Music and Image*, Cambridge, Cambridge University Press, 1988.
Lévi-Strauss, C., *An Introduction to the Science of Mythology, Vol. 2: From Honey to Ashes*, New York, Harper and Row, 1973.
——, *The Raw and the Cooked*, Harmondsworth, Penguin, 1986.
Manuel, P., 'Andalusian, Gypsy and Class Identity in the Contemporary Flamenco Complex', *Ethnomusicology*, vol. 33, no. 2, 1989, pp. 47-65.
Merriam, A., 'African Music' in W. Bascom and M. Herskovits (eds), *Continuity and Change in African Cultures*, Chicago, University of Chicago Press, 1959.
Middleton, R., '"Play It Again Sam": Some Notes on the Productivity of Repetition in Popular Music', *Popular Music*, vol. 3, 1983, pp. 235-67.
Mitchell, J.C., *The Kalela Dance*, The Rhodes Livingstone Institute, Manchester, Manchester University Press, 1956.
Nettl, B., (ed) *Eight Urban Musical Cultures: Tradition and Change*, Urbana, University of Illinois Press, 1978.

———, 'Mozart and the Ethnomusicological Study of Western Culture' in K. Bergeron and P.V. Bohlman (eds), *Disciplining Music: Musicology and its Canons*, Chicago, University of Chicago Press, 1992.

Ortner, S., 'Is Male to Female as Nature is to Culture?' in M. Rosaldo and L. Lamphere (eds), *Woman, Culture and Society*, Stanford, Stanford University Press, 1974.

Peña, M., *The Texas-Mexican Conjunto: History of a Working-Class Music*, Austin, University of Texas Press, 1985.

Reily, S.R., 'Musica Sertaneja and Migrant Identity: The Stylistic Development of a Brazilian Genre', *Popular Music*, vol. 11, no. 3, 1992, pp. 337–58.

Said, E., *Orientalism*, Harmondsworth, Penguin, 1978.

Schutz, A., 'Making Music Together: A Study in Social Relationship' in J. Dolgin, D. Kemnitzer and D. Schneider (eds), *Symbolic Anthropology*, New York, Columbia University Press, 1977.

Seeger, A., *Why Suyá Sing: A Musical Anthropology of an Amazonian People*, Cambridge, Cambridge University Press, 1987.

Shepherd, J., *Music as Social Text*, Cambridge, Polity Press, 1991.

Shiloah, A., and E. Cohen, 'The Dynamics of Change in Jewish Oriental Music in Israel', *Ethnomusicology*, vol. 27, no. 2, pp. 227–37.

Stokes, M., *The Arabesk Debate: Music and Musicians in Modern Turkey*, Oxford, Oxford University Press, 1992.

Sugarman, J., 'The Nightingale and the Partridge: Singing and Gender among Prespa Albanians', *Ethnomusicology*, vol. 33, no. 2, pp. 191–215.

Szyliowicz, J., *Political Change in Rural Turkey*, The Hague, Mouton, 1966.

Turino, T., 'The Coherence of Social Style and Musical Creation among the Aymara in Southern Peru', *Ethnomusicology*, vol. 33, no. 1, pp. 1–30.

Turner, V., *Dramas, Fields and Metaphors*, Ithica, Cornell University Press, 1974.

Urla, J. 'Contesting Modernities: Language Standardisation and the Production of an Ancient/Modern Basque Culture', *Critique of Anthropology*, vol. 3, no. 2, 1993, pp. 101–18.

Waterman, C.A., *Jújù: A Social History and Ethnography of an African Popular Music*, Chicago, University of Chicago Press, 1990.

Wilkinson, D., 'Give Me A Lonesome Reel: The Flute Playing of Sligo and North Leitrim', unpublished MA dissertation, The Queens University of Belfast, 1991.

Wittgenstein, L., *Philosophical Investigations*, Oxford, Basil Blackwell, 1958.

Wolff, J. 'Foreward: The Ideology of Autonomous Art' in R. Leppert and S. McClarey (eds), *Music and Society: The Politics of Composition, Performance and Reception*, Cambridge, Cambridge University Press, 1987.

Thoughts on Celtic Music

Malcolm Chapman

The author of this piece makes no claim to be a specialist in Celtic music, or any kind of musicologist. It is probably true, however, that study of any self-conscious ethnicity will throw up musical examples, as part of the more general phenomenon; this is certainly true in the Celtic case(s). Since 1975, I have been involved, as a social anthropologist, with those peoples conventionally called 'Celtic'; I have made a particular study of the Scottish Highlands and islands, and Brittany, and of their associated 'Celtic' languages: Scottish Gaelic and Breton. This has involved considerable periods of fieldwork.

During this time, I have almost always carried music with me, in the form of a guitar of some kind. On this, I have been able to make a more or less proficient attempt to play most varieties of music – classical, jazz, blues, ragtime, 'folk', popular song, and so on. In the Hebrides and in Edinburgh, in Finistère, and in Rennes, I played for myself, played for others, and played with others. I have played set pieces on party occasions; I have played at musical evenings, before seated audiences willing to be pleased; I have played under the moon on the far western beaches of Eurasia, Celtic faery in the minds of those about, and the waves breaking on the shore. So, the Celts and music have come together in my own thoughts and experience, because I have been, on the one hand, an anthropologist that has studied the Celts, and, on the other, a reasonably competent amateur musician. The question of music, and musicality, has inevitably risen many times during my fieldwork, and the following comments are based on this. The background is prosaic, but real.

There are doubtless many other ways of approaching the issues raised by Celtic music. One, perhaps the most obvious, the most commonly pursued, would be to go to those sources that are self-styled in their concern with 'Celtic' music. There are books and articles, and, more importantly, records and tapes of many popular and gifted musicians. The efforts of modern musicians in this area are typically based upon a sense of 'tradition', and the traditions and associated music are also well-documented. Once within this sphere of enthusiasm, many possibilities open up: detailed musicological analyses of the 'traditional' Celtic instruments and musical styles, enthusiasm for the capture of dying traditions, assertions of the idiosyncratic splendour of the Celtic inheritance, the forging of musical embellishment for political separatism, and so on.

I have not indulged in any of these; indeed, I regard them as part of my object of study. We might at this stage note that we are dealing with two rather distinct spheres: one, the area of self-conscious 'Celtic' activity (in the sphere, say, of language, music or politics); and two, genuinely popular activity in the 'Celtic' areas of Scotland, Ireland, Wales, Brittany, Cornwall (and so on). The innocent observer might expect there to be a large degree of overlap between these, even a simple congruity. There is not. We will come at this problem from a variety of directions, but it can be bluntly illustrated: in, say, a small Breton village, it is entirely typical that 'traditional Breton music', as played on 'traditional Breton instruments', should be totally absent; if it is indeed present, then it is in all probability the province either of intellectual incomers with folkloric tastes, or of some small part of the university-educated local youth who might listen to such music on record-player or tape recorder (or whatever newer technology comes to offer itself). Locally born, full-time residents, and (crucially, perhaps) speakers of the local Celtic language, that is, the great majority of local people, often know little or nothing about this music, and have no interest in it. It is not *their* music. *They* have derived their musical tastes in much the same way as the greater British or French populations, within much the same rhythms of taste and demography. Within this genuinely vernacular local sphere, the popular instruments are not, say, the harp or the bagpipe, but rather the piano accordion, the electric organ, the electric guitar, the radio and the television; the popular heroes are Maurice Chevalier and Perry Como, Edith Piaf and Tina Turner, John Lennon and Freddy Mercury.

The problem is well illustrated by the following quotation, from an interview in the 'folk-music' magazine *Folk Roots*. The interviewee is talking about the *Cercles folkloriques* in France, organisations which make it their business to dance the 'local' dances, sing and play the 'local' music, wear the 'local' costume, and so on. A good deal of harmless fun is had thereby; local children are often participants in these *cercles folkloriques*; and the more skilled exponents of dance, music and costume often turn out for tourist festivals of various kinds. The *cercles* might be regarded as a sort of cross between a rather esoteric youth organisation, and a local history society. The interviewee says:

> All over France you find the Cercles folkloriques (in Brittany – Cercles Celtiques) . . . Some of them are dire, making up picturesque costumes and even dances if the originals aren't pretty enough for the tourists, but many of them do a good deal of vital research. Even the worst of them at least have kept some sort of local identity alive. . . . It means for example that all Bretons, all Berrichons, all Auvergnats have a rough idea of what their local music sounds like and what the dances look like, even if they can't stand the stuff' (*Folk Roots* 1988: 23).

It is all there. I do not mean to take sides in the question of what is or is not 'dire'. On the one hand we have those involved in the *Cercles folkloriques*, who are for the most part aware that theirs is a minority interest; I do not mean 'minority', in the sense of ethnic minority (Breton, Auvergnat, and the like), but wish rather to imply specialist enthusiasm, that is, limited to a small like-minded group, as it might be train spotters, or tennis players. Within such a *cercle* there is commonly nostalgia for, as it were, the traditional past, and perhaps a good deal of naïvety about the nature of that past; there is also, however, a necessarily realistic assessment of the relationship of the activity of the *cercle* to the ambitions and habits of the majority of people living round about. A *cercle* does not see itself as seeking to embody 'local identity'. They are also, for the most part, very little politicised and do not see their folkloric activities as part of a separatist politics. This depoliticisation is much deplored by the more serious-minded would-be Celts, and regarded, with portentous disapproval, as the most significant politicisation of all.

What is more interesting about the above quotation is that the interviewee, candid enough in his admission, is prepared to speak of a 'local identity' which is kept alive by the make believe of a minority, and of 'local music' which the local people either know nothing about, or dislike. He is not, however, prepared to revise his notion of 'local' in order to re-accommodate what most would regard as the legitimate and common meaning of the term, something to do, perhaps, with what the majority of local people thought and did. 'Celtic music', like many other aspects of Celtic ethnicity, is borne out of definitional conundrums of this kind.

I will go back to my own early ethnographic interest in the Celts, to seek another approach to this. When I began fieldwork, in 1976, it was still easy to imagine that an anthropologist's task was to go to a far and exotic corner of the world, and document it for the benefit of those back home. There were discernible problems in this approach, even then. I was troubled, at the time, by what might be called 'exoticism'. I had read many ethnographies of 'exotic' peoples in Africa India, South-East Asia, South America. These were various mixtures of theory and description, and I had begun to wonder whether their appeal, charm, and apparent theoretical and observational subtlety, were due not to any merit, but simply to their exotic provenance. I do not claim that this was a sophisticated insight, but it moved me to consider doing fieldwork 'close to home'. The logical thing, perhaps, would have been to have the courage of one's convictions, and study an English town, perhaps one of its middle-class suburbs. Instead, I opted for the half-way solution, and went to the Scottish Highlands and islands. What I found there was so different from what I expected, that my first thoughts about it became largely irrelevant. It is not without interest, however, that I turned out to be riding a fashion, unknowingly, which led anthropologists to the conceptual and geographical fringes of European life. I was not the only person deciding, at the time, that the Celts might be an appropriate object of study. Indeed, Edward Condry (my immediate contemporary at Oxford) and myself were, in October 1975, both sent away for a few days by our shared supervisor, Edwin Ardener, to think about where we might concentrate our anthropological interests. We both returned, within a few hours of one another, and without any collusion, with the same answer: Gaelic Scotland. Since then, ethnic minorities have become the most fashionable anthropological topic of all.

It was not only anthropologists that found the Celtic fringe of consuming interest at the time. There was a general interest, in the 1960s, in 'alternatives', and the Celts were, from within the British Isles, apparently the alternative most readily available. So, for every anthropologist treading a path to Brittany or the Hebrides, there was also a small cohort of smallholders, porters, painters, weavers, craft-shop keepers, and social security *rentiers*. The anthropological taste for 'otherness' was more or less congruent, at this time, with a more general intellectual enthusiasm.

I have referred to the old-style anthropological ambition, that of documentation of a previously inaccessible 'exotic', because it bears upon the Celts and their peculiarities. The Celts, however defined, have been closely involved with mainstream European events for as long as we have records. There has been no dividing line, no impenetrable forest, no mountain range, no sundering sea, which has systematically prevented their close involvement with other peoples and polities. At the same time, however, the Celts have always had, and retain, an aura of mystery and inaccessibility; out of the world, behind the world, exempt from the world, and so on.

Much of my work over the past fifteen years has been an exploration of the structure of this apparent paradox. The immediate evidence of the paradox, when I went to begin my studies of Scottish Gaelic in the Outer Hebrides, was that I became one of a large army of people all assiduously studying Scottish Gaelic culture, its language, music and habits, and attempting to emulate them. We had, *en masse*, travelled to this distant and inaccessible location, and as a group we cultivated its ancient traditions. The paradoxes of 'remoteness', since delineated by Edwin Ardener (see Ardener 1987), first began to present themselves. I earlier expressed the problem thus:

> As part of my attempts to learn the Gaelic language I went, in the summer of 1976, to Sabhal Mor Ostaig, to attend a course intended to teach the spoken language. There were people from all over the world there, and we were well looked after and well entertained. Almost every evening had its *ceilidh*, its dancing, its singing or its drinking. One of the teachers there, a girl from one of the smaller islands of the Outer Hebrides, expressed some concern that we were in danger of getting a totally false idea of what Gaelic life was like. 'It isn't like this', she said, 'normally nothing happens for weeks on end'. Yet there we all were, Gael and Gall alike, drawn into a common conspiracy to celebrate the Gaelic world that we all felt should exist (Chapman 1978: 232).

Many of the 'Gaelic' skills that we cultivated were musical. Indeed, musical events were a predominant part of the pedagogy, and we spent a good deal of time learning and singing Gaelic songs. There was a good linguistic point to this, no doubt, since the tunes were catchy, and the words were remembered along with the tunes. There was also, however, a real reflection of the structure of interest in Scottish Gaelic in Scotland. Much the largest group of the would-be Gaels learning Gaelic were those who, throughout Scotland, sing in what are known as 'Gaelic choirs'. These choirs were originally intended to be a forum within which the Gaels could celebrate their own culture, and they were particularly intended for those who had migrated from the Highlands and islands to the industrial towns of the Lowlands. The choirs are, however, open to anybody interested, and most of the people involved today have only a tenuous claim to being 'Gaelic'. There are few native Gaelic speakers among them. The choirs might be regarded as an assertion, throughout Scotland, of a sort of residual Gaelic-ness of the entire country. The choirs sing in Gaelic, and ability at least to pronounce the language, if not to understand it, is therefore necessary. Those involved in the choirs, therefore, commonly learn a smattering of Gaelic for the purpose.

These choirs vie with one another in regional competitions called 'mods'; there is a prestigious annual 'national Mod', in which the best of the local choirs compete for the highest prizes of all (the 'national Mod' in Scotland bears many resemblances to the Welsh 'Eisteddfod', upon which it was initially modelled). There are other categories of competition besides those for choirs, notably individual singing events, and instrumental sections (particularly for bagpipe and for violin). It is the Gaelic choirs, however, that bring the largest number of contestants, and that give the events their characteristic flavour. The Mod is sometimes irreverently called 'the whisky Olympics'. The most prestigious prizes are the gold medals for individual singing. These demand, as a formal condition of participation, a reasonable competence in spoken Gaelic, of about '0-level' standard. In Gaelic language classes, therefore, there was always a sprinkling of aspirants to these prizes, people with voices like angels, struggling with nouns and verbs among lesser mortals. The gold medal prize was no trivial one, since a mod winner can reasonably expect recording contracts and the like.

The 'Celtic' ethnicities are defined by, among other things, their languages. The number of people speaking the different Celtic languages has fallen continuously for most of the last hundred years or so.[1] Most ordinary speakers of the Celtic languages are not greatly concerned about the gradual decline of their mother tongue, an indifference that is routinely deplored by enthusiasts. There is, in each case, a small and vociferous minority who are such language enthu-

---

1. The rhythms vary slightly, with Brittany something of an exception, in that the maximum number of speakers of Breton was probably attained rather late, in about 1914.

siasts, and who bring together aims of linguistic revival and aims of political and cultural autonomy. It is generally true (with significant exceptions) that those involved in such linguistic enthusiasm are not ordinary native speakers of the Celtic languages, but rather have learnt them as teenagers or adults. These language enthusiasts are, both in their own eyes and often in the eyes of less linguistically privileged enthusiasts, the élite of Celtic ethnic consciousness.

The Celtic languages are, however, very difficult to learn. This is not (as is commonly said) because they are in themselves 'difficult' languages. It is, rather, for intractable sociolinguistic reasons. Learning any language is difficult; where, however, there is only a small and largely unwilling population of bilingual native speakers to practise on, the problems are great indeed.[2] Learning such a language to complete fluency requires a nearly full-time investment over many years; it also often requires a restriction of social horizon to those involved in the same linguistic attempt. Few people are prepared to make such a commitment, or to hold their social horizons within this kind of monomaniacal enthusiasm

Music, by contrast, offers a pleasant and easy participation for the dilettante. It is generally true, in consequence, that the musical manifestations of the various Celtic ethnicities tend to overwhelm the linguistic. One might point in example to a typical 'Celtic' bookshop. There is at least one such bookshop in most medium sized Breton towns. While there may be many books on display about the Celts and the Celtic nations, and many books in the Celtic languages, there is always 'Celtic' music playing. Indeed, such a shop relies for its profitability on sales of music, of records, tapes, sheet music and so on.

The most striking and publicity-worthy 'ethnic' festivals in the two areas where I have worked are also essentially musical – the Mod in Scotland, and the Fête Interceltique in Brittany. There are literary and linguistic aspects to these, but their main substance is musical. Music is the attraction for the majority of contestants, performers and attenders. Politics, if it is present at all, is often given musical clothes. People routinely sing songs in languages that they do not speak.

I will pause here to reiterate two important general points. Firstly, there is often a great gulf between the real representatives of an 'ethnicity' (the man and woman in the street, so to speak), and the

---

2. For a full exposition of the problems, see Chapman 1986.

self-conscious and enthusiastic exponents of the same 'ethnicity'. This is manifest as much in musical as it is in other matters. Secondly, music provides an entry into the practices and sentiments of ethnic belonging, for those whose commitment is small, and who require entertainment rather than effort.

In a general treatment of the Celts, within which musical examples form only a very small part, I have tried to sort out the various processes which have led to the creation of the Celts as we know them today (see Chapman 1992, for the full argument). In summary, there are four relevant processes:

1. The elaboration of an opposition 'self/other', with the 'Celts' (under various related titles) figuring as the 'other' of a more dominant European tradition. Oppositions like Greek/Keltoi, Roman/Galli, Anglo-Saxon/*walxas, English/Celtic, succeed one another. Geographically and conceptually, the second of each of these pairs is peripheral (although the objective location of the relevant geography moves about over the millennia). The content of the second (or, say, what is noticeable about the second) is primarily determined by the content of the first, and the requirements of dramatic symbolic opposition of one to the other.
2. The steady progression of fashions from a centre to a periphery, with new fashions appealing at the centre, and steadily moving to the periphery, replaced in their turn by the same continuing process. This process is in many respects indifferent to boundaries constructed under the first process. The *content* of categories constructed under the first process can change continuously, while the categories themselves appear stand.
3. A systematic function of the meeting of incongruent category systems, causing the perceiving culture to construct the perceived as inconstant, unreliable, irrational, colourful, dramatic, given to excess and inadequacy, and so on.

Processes 2 and 3 provide constantly renewed material for process 1. It is often difficult to sort out the effects of these different processes, for they overlie one another; the observations resulting from them are in many respects incompatible, and so are the object of a good deal of creative forgetfulness and fudging (in order, for example, that process 2 should always seem to provide support for process 1). The picture is further complicated by Romanticism, which I call the fourth process:

4. Romanticism: this glamorises the 'other' that is constructed in processes land 3, and introduces a complicated refraction, an apparent counter-current, into the observation of process 2.

We can illustrate all these processes through musical examples.

Process 1

This might be exemplified in the modern period by a general assertion such as 'Celts play the pipes; we (the English, the French) do not.' The example is particularly telling, in that the three-drone bagpipe, a relatively modern Scottish invention, has now been adopted, within the principles of the above opposition, throughout the world of 'Celtic' music making; it is played, for example, in Ireland and Brittany. It is also played throughout the world of the Scottish diaspora, where the native discrimination between Highland and Lowland Scotland has been subsumed by the internationally more visible opposition between England and Scotland.

The early musical examples are little documented[3] but I am in no doubt that the relevant ethnic opposition could always have taken musical form, for any interested commentator. The exact form would, of course, have varied over time, which takes us to process 2.

Process 2

Within process 2, there is a constant shift of musical fashion from centre to periphery. We can use the bagpipe again as an example. In the ancient world, a version of the bagpipe was the mainstream instrument of popular and sophisticated entertainment (see Collinson 1975). By the seventeenth century, it had been replaced in European mainstream music by lutes, viols, violins (and all their related instruments), and keyboard instruments. Versions of the bagpipe survived, however, as instruments of popular entertainment. In Brittany, for example, the single-drone *biniou* survived into the twentieth century in genuinely popular (unselfconscious, unfolklorised) use. In northern Britain, the bagpipe, in its Highland, lowland Scottish and Northumbrian forms, was essentially moribund by the end of the eighteenth century. It would probably have died out altogether, as it

---

3. For some interesting comments from the late twelfth century, see Gerald of Wales, 1905: 495–7.

had from most of the rest of Europe, had it not been for Romanticism (see below).

The history of the harp is rather similar, except that the process was more advanced before the re-evaluations of Romanticism appeared. The harp had disappeared from both Wales and Scotland by the eighteenth century, before any adequate written transcriptions had been made. The tradition was effectively lost. Ireland, that much further behind on the road to fashionability, has retained some fairly authentic semi-classical harp music from a related tradition, best associated with the name of the harpist Carolan (1670–1783).

Any instrumental or musical fashion is apt to follow processes of innovation and abandonment of this kind. I do not mean to say that the Celtic fringe has not produced innovations and abandonment leads from centre to periphery, over the centuries and decades. There are plenty of modern evidences of this. The piano accordion, for example, has become a *Scottish* instrument in the minds of many, like the bagpipe and the harp before it. An unlikely combination of banjo, penny whistle, violin and acoustic guitar has come to seem, for many, to characterise Irish 'traditional' music. Instruments that were popular throughout western France in the nineteenth century have now come to seem like Breton specialities. It may be that universally available media of television, radio and pre-recorded music will put a stop to these processes, or so muddle them that they are no longer discernible. It may he that process 1 will completely take over. Or things may carry on as they have for centuries, with process 2 providing constantly renewed material for process 1.

Process 3

Process 3 can be readily exemplified by music, although the examples may seem rather esoteric.

A first example concerns musical scales. An *a cappella* pentatonlc song tradition (such as that of much 'traditional' Celtic music), when viewed from within the more tightly structured cage of classical harmony and seven-note scales, gives an impression of a rather capricious freedom. Within a seven-note scale system, a note can vary only a little before it starts to sound like another note. It is like a vowel phoneme in a twelve-vowel system (and the analogy is fairly exact): it cannot move very far before it starts to sound like another vowel. Within a pentatonic scale, there are only five notes to accommodate, not seven. As a result, notes have a larger range of possible variation open to them, before they stop 'being themselves'. The phenomenon is most commonly noticeable in the 'bent' notes that characterise 'blues' music. Skilled *a cappella* singers can make considerable technical and emotional use of this freedom, within a pentatonic framework.

The effect, however, on an ear trained within twelve-note harmony, is of a kind of wild freedom, an emotional excess, or a lack of order and control. Words like 'wailing' commonly occur in attempts to describe this perception. I have, in conversation with 'Celtic musicians', been told that the freedom of Celtic singing was a manifestation of the more general freedom from rules that characterises the Celts, as compared to the rule-bound French and English. This is true, as well; not perhaps in the simple sense that these musicians meant, but in the sense that all perceptions of one system by another, in all the areas of human representation, are prone to throw up conclusions and perceptions of disorder, excessive freedom, and absence of rule. The Celts are, in my view, constructed through an accumulation of perceptions of this kind; all of them *perceptions by others*. The confrontation of older pentatonic styles, with newer melodic and harmonic conventions, has been a gradual move across the social and geographical map of the kind described under process 2. It has, however, often been concretised by observers, under process 1, as a Celtic/non-Celtic-Celtic feature (see, for example, Brekilien 1973: 33).

It is worth noting that those arranging Gaelic songs for performance by the Gaelic choirs referred to above, have regularly used classical harmonic structures. Arranging tunes for several voices, as is the common pattern, effectively closes any other option This has the unfortunate effect, however, that pentatonic tunes of great beauty are de-natured by their passage through a system based on a twelve-note tempered scale and functional harmony; the two systems are fundamentally incompatible, and much is lost in the translation from one to another.[4]

Another example which we might take to exemplify process 3, concerns the very category of 'music' itself. This, in common with other abstract categories like religion, art, work and so on, is a product of a particular form of social understanding. We might say, to be

4. Marjory Kennedy Frazer is responsible for many early popular arrangements of this kind, much sung in school choirs throughout the English-speaking world; see Kennedy Frazer 1810.

brief and crude, that for most urban people in Britain in the nineteenth century, religion was something you did on Sundays, art was something in galleries, work was what you did every day except Sunday, and music was what happened in music halls, concert halls, and hymn-time at church. Nineteenth century observers, however, found, in the Celtic areas, that stories were chanted in 'musical' form, that minor invocations to God, Mary and the Saints were constantly made in rather similar vein, and that tedious manual labour was often enlivened by working songs. These features were widespread in pre-Reformation and pre-industrial Europe, and they survived in many areas, slowly retreating before the Protestant ethic, generalised agnosticism, mechanised industry, and alternative forms of entertainment. They were, once again, features subject to process 2, viewed at a particular historical moment through process 1. Those who regarded art, music and religion as particularly high-minded specialised activities, found on looking at Celtic rural life in the nineteenth century that things that looked like art, music and religion seemed to penetrate the most banal and prosaic aspects of daily life. The conclusion readily drawn was that all of life, for the Celts, was a kind of artistic performance, imbued with religiosity. The picture was an appealing one.

It was, however, based upon a series of category errors. From a Saussurean point of view, the categories of music, art and religion, as they took their form in the semantic structures of (say) English urban life, were specific to that life. They encouraged inappropriate conclusions, gave forth inappropriate resonances, when they were applied to 'Celtic' life. There, they gave the impression of 'excess' of music, or art, and of religion. These are, again, enduring features of perception of the Celts. So in this case we have process 3 phenomena, generated across the rolling fashions of process 2, and providing material for process 1.

Process 4

Process 4 is Romanticism (my definition is somewhat idiosyncratic; I will try below to explain the shorthand). Romanticism glamorises the 'other' that is constructed in processes 2 and 3, and introduces a complicated refraction into the observation of process 2. Process 4 is a relatively modern phenomenon, dating, say, to the middle eighteenth century in Britain, and to almost a century later in France (the datings are arguable in every respect; I mean these to apply to the romantic discovery of internal 'ethnic' minorities, of which the Celtic examples, in both France and Britain, were primary).[5] The timing of the intervention of process 4 into process 2 is critical for the construction of 'Celtic tradition', including its musical features. Because of the timing difference between Britain and France, 'Celtic tradition' in Britain has a strong tendency to display late eighteenth and early nineteenth century features; 'Celtic tradition' in France, by contrast, is characteristically late nineteenth or early twentieth century. This is not a hard and fast rule, and retrospective effort can bring together all manner of anachronisms; nevertheless, the musical examples in general conform to this: the most visible and immediately convincing manifestations, however, are the forms of 'traditional dress' (see Logan 1820, Creston 1978, Chapman 1986, ch. 5).

Romanticism is not primarily a creative process, but a re-evaluative process. In the sense that I use the term here, Romanticism is a re-evaluation, in the centre, of peripheral features. The motivation to the re-evaluation is that those in the centre who carry it out, benefit from it. They benefit from it because they acquire some feature, abstract or tangible (instrument, language, dance, attitude, costume, furniture), which is dying out on the periphery (and so apt to being 'cornered' by the fast movers of fashion), and very little known in the centre; if moral and political conditions in the centre are appropriate, this transported peripheral feature can be turned, at the centre, into a fashionable and glamorous rarity. The process requires a distance between centre and periphery, in terms of process 2, and it also requires that the feature in question be coming, even on the periphery, to the end of its process 2 life (as the Highland pipes and Highland dress were doing in the middle eighteenth century, Disclothing Act notwithstanding; the harp had already completely disappeared by this time). The reason for this can be readily demonstrated. If you are an aesthetically minded nineteenth century Edinburgh lady, you can play the Celtic harp in your Georgian drawing room, and expect to elicit admiration and nostalgia for the misty and fugitive beauties of this forgotten tradition, and for your own sensitivity in recapturing it. The trick does not work, however, if outside on the street every peddler and roughneck has a 'Celtic' harp, which he habitually uses to accompany the latest bawdy songs. Con-

---

5. I have, in several seminar papers since 1979, discussed reasons for the difference in timing as between Britain and France; a version of the argument given in these can be found in Chapman 1986 and 1992.

ditions in Edinburgh in the late nineteenth century were kind, in this sense, to the revivers of the harp.

I have argued that features apt to the Romantic re-evaluation need to be coming to the end of the process 2 life. As such, they will be peripheral, unfashionable, and little documented. Their transmutation makes them famous, but cannot alter the facts of their previous decay and obscurity. There is, in consequence, a constant problem of authenticity about 'Celtic traditions', and irresolvable ambiguity about the true pre-Romantic state of affairs. This is conspicuously true, for example, of the Scottish Highland piping tradition (see Lorimer 1983, Collinson 1975, Trevor-Roper 1983, Campsie 1980). Argument over authenticity, and accusations of forgery, invention and retrospective embellishment, flourish in such an environment. One example might be regarded as fortuitous, but the phenomenon is so general that it demands a general explanation, such as I have tried to provide (for detail, see Chapman 1978 and 1992). We might even say that problems over authenticity were a *necessary feature* of 'Celtic tradition', as it is interpreted in the modern world (this general statement can be applied, of course, to other 'ethnic' traditions as well).

Conclusion

The scarcity of real people, other than enthusiastic outsiders, inside the shell called 'Celtic music', is generated by the interaction of processes 1,2 and 4. We need not, however, be surprised by the lack of people. The 'Celts', in the British context, simply form the largest regiment in the phantom army of 'folk' who are the notional makers of 'folk-music'. The 'folk', as a musical ethnicity, englobe the 'Celts'; there is, however, a strong tendency for the tail to wag the dog, and for the 'folk' category in British music to be usurped by Celtic material, or to assume a Celtic accent of some kind. There are good symbolic and geographical reasons for this, given flesh through the processes already described (the easy congruence of 'the folk' and 'the Celts' can be seen, for example, in the activities of the major British folklorists, as described by Dorson 1968).

'Folk' music now exists, as a genre, recorded, performed, published, sung and listened to, in the nearly complete absence of any 'folk' to provide the fall social context that once (in whatever arguable and murky sense) might have existed; the social context of 'folk' music today is one of vinyl and magnetic tape, recording studios, published works, media performance and specialist gatherings. 'Celtic' music is going the same way, and has always been closely related to 'folk' music in these respects. There are many ways in which these features are common to the entirety of music in the modern Western world. The tendency to removal of all forms of music into electronic media and specialist performance is well-known, and, whatever its social merits or demerits, needs no further adumbration here.

I have written as if 'Celtic music' exists. It is a point of view, and one which many practitioners and listeners, folklorists and enthusiasts, accept without comment. Nevertheless, if process 2 is regarded with a sufficiently detached eye, and processes 1 and 4 are not allowed to interfere, it is often much harder to defend the existence, on strictly musical grounds, of any such category.[6] The ethnomusicologist Bruno Nettl, in a chapter entitled 'The Germanic peoples', and under the sub-heading 'The style of English folk music', deals with the Celts in the following summary manner:

> At this point we must mention also the Celtic-speaking inhabitants of the British Isles, particularly the Irish and the Welsh, peoples whose musical culture has played so important a part in their history that the Irish national emblem is the harp. Irish folk song today is almost entirely in the English language, and, indeed, the songs of Irish origin have contributed greatly to the English-language heritage of the United States, Canada and Australia. On the whole, their musical style does not differ greatly from that of the English folk tunes of eighteenth- and nineteenth-century origin (1973: 669).

Finally, I wish to put in a disclaimer. My attempt to sort out the structures and processes underlying the category 'Celtic music', is not intended as any form of judgement upon the excellence or otherwise of the music that it contains. I stress this, since I know from experience that an approach such as I have adopted often seems, to those wedded to a certain kind of faith in authenticity, and to a (by

---

6. The Basque example has many features in common with the Celtic, including a general and permanently renewable aura of antiquity. The interaction of processes 1,2 and 4 generates this readily enough. Again, however, if process 2 is considered on its own, the phenomena under observation can seem rather prosaic. Nettl writes of the Basques: 'Legend has it that the Basques are the oldest people in Europe, but they seem to have retained little of their ancient heritage of folklore. On the contrary, they seem to have partaken of the traditions of Northern Spain and South-western France, and their culture is a repository of archaic forms of that region, both French and Spanish' (Nettl 1973: 116).

no means discreditable) sentimental atavism, to be cheapening or critical. It is not intended to be, nor should it be. The music flourishes, acoustically, in a space entirely untouched by my comments.

References

Ardener, E., 'Remote areas – some theoretical considerations', in A. Jackson (ed.), *Anthropology at Home*, London, Tavistock, 1987.
Brekilien, Y., *Alan Stivell ou le Folk-Celtique*, Quimper, Nature et Bretagne, 1973.
Campsie, A., *The MacCrimmon Legend*, Edinburgh, Canongate, 1980.
Chapman, M., *The Celts: The Construction of a Myth*, London, Macmillan, 1992.
——, *The Gaelic Vision in Scottish Culture*, London, Croom Helm, 1976.
——, 'Plouhinec in Cap-Sizun: A Social Anthropological Study of a Breton Fishing and Farming village, with Celtic Comparisons', unpublished D. Phil thesis, Oxford University, 1986.
Collinson, F., *The Bagpipe*, London, Routledge and Kegan Paul, 1975.
Creston, R., *Le Costume Breton*, Paris, Tchou, 1978.
Dorson, R., *The British Folklorists*, London, Routledge and Kegan Paul, 1968.
Folk Roots '"French Fashion", Paul Wright describes the local music to Paul James', no. 61, 1988.
Gerald of Wales (circa 1146–1223) *The topography of Ireland and the history of the conquest of Ireland* (trans. T. Forester), and *The itinerary through Wales, and the description of Wales* (trans. R. Colt Hoare), all revised and edited by T. Wright, London, George Bell, 1905.
Hobsbawm, J. and Ranger, T. (eds), *The Invention of Tradition*, Cambridge, Cambridge University Press, 1983.
Kennedy Frazer, M., *The Song of the Hebrides*, vol. 1, London, 1810.
Logan, J., *The Costumes of the Highland Clans*, London, 1820.
Lorimer, R., 'Traditional phrase patterns employed in *ceol-mor*', paper read to the Seventh International Congress of Celtic Studies, Oxford, 1983.
Nettl, B., *Folk and Traditional Music of the Western Continents*, Englewood Cliffs, Prentice-Hall, 1973.
Trevor-Roper, H. (Lord Dacre), 'The Invention of Tradition: the Highland Tradition of Scotland', in E. Hobsbawm and T. Ranger (eds), *The Invention of Tradition*, Cambridge, Cambridge University Press, 1983.

The Role of Music in the Creation of an Afghan National Identity, 1923–73

John Baily

Issues of cultural identity seem likely to constitute some of the major problems confronting humanity in the twenty-first century. In various places around the world we see heterogeneous political entities of various sizes – from large empires to relatively small countries – disintegrating into their constituent parts, a process often accompanied by a frightening degree of conflict. We become increasingly aware of the extraordinary tenacity of this phenomenon we call 'culture', and of the way its meaning and importance persist for the culture bearers.

Afghanistan may be taken as a paradigm of this process. Confronted with the cultural and political fragmentation that has occurred since the Marxist *putsch* of 1978 one wonders what kind of unity ever prevailed in the past. What was it that held this country of 15 million people together? Was it a unity that was imposed and maintained by force, or was there a real degree of social consensus? And if one can identify the processes that gave political cohesion in the past, how can they be revived, assuming that would be the best outcome for the people of Afghanistan and their neighbours?[1]

---

1. The fieldwork on which this paper is based was conducted between 1973 and 1977, in Herat, a provincial city near the Iranian border, and Kabul, the capital of Afghanistan. The research was supported by grants from the Social Science Research Council. Some of the data and ideas discussed here have been published in Baily (1988). I did not specifically focus on issues of 'identity' in my research, and there are many areas where the inadequacies of my data are only too apparent. However, some of these deficiencies are compensated for by the subsequent help given to me by the Afghan historian Professor S.Q. Reshtia, who had the unique experience of being the Director of Radio Kabul during a crucial period between 1940 and 1945,

Does the study of *music* in Afghanistan tell us anything specific about these issues? Arguably it does. Following a line of inquiry initiated long ago by Mark Slobin – who conducted extensive fieldwork in northern Afghanistan in the late 1960s – I shall attempt to demonstrate that music certainly 'illuminates patterns of inter-ethnic contact' (Slobin 1976: 1), reveals a good deal about the dynamic processes involved in the emergence of a national identity in modern Afghanistan, and served as an agent for creating that identity.[2]

Music and Identity

In ethnomusicology certain kinds of explanation are couched in terms of analytical concepts and arguments about music and social/cultural identity. Ideas about the special link between music and identity are frequently offered to explain why a particular social group – a community, a population, a nation – cultivates outmoded and seemingly irrelevant musical practices. Blacking noted that:

> The most interesting and characteristically human features of music are not stylistic change and individual variations in performance, but non-change and the repetition of carefully rehearsed passages of music. It is truly remarkable that anyone in 1977 should want to perform or listen to Mozart, or *Khyal*, or *Wayang*, long after the circumstances that gave rise to these genres have passed (Blacking 1977: 7)

Although Blacking was addressing here problems of musical change, the 'ethnic identity' hypothesis can readily be invoked to

---

after which he was in charge of the Cultural Department of the Ministry of Information and Culture until 1951. In 1985 and 1987 he was kind enough to read and offer copious comments on drafts of several sections of my book, confirming the account I had given as substantially correct, and offered much new information, some of which is included here for the first time. I wish to thank Professor Reshtia for his help, kindness, and enthusiasm for what I have written. My thanks are due also to Veronica Doubleday, Nabi Misdaq and Anthony Pryer for reading and commenting upon early drafts of this paper, and to Martin Stokes for his encouragement and perceptive editorial comments.

2. The role of music in the creation of an Afghan national identity is but one part of a wider pattern of musical change related to processes of modernism and modernisation in Afghanistan, as discussed at length in Baily (1988). The dates 1923–73 have been selected because they span the modern era of Afghan history. Amanullah came to the throne in 1919, and by 1923 his programme of reform and modernisation was well in place. Fifty years later, in 1973, King Zaher Shah was deposed and the Republic of Afghanistan set up. This was also the year when I began my fieldwork in western Afghanistan.

explain the 'repetition of carefully rehearsed passages of music'. This argument is sometimes put forward to explain why immigrant groups in large multi-cultural cities such as New York often cling tenaciously to their traditional musics – they are 'maintaining group identity in a multiethnic society', as Allen and Groce (1988: 4) put it in their forward to a collection of papers rich in such statements. For example, discussing why gospel quartets thrive in New York City: 'they raise money for financially strapped churches and charitable causes, and attract new members for small, struggling churches. But perhaps most importantly, these groups provide their listeners with aesthetic pleasure, spiritual uplift, and a sense of shared ethnic and historical identity as southern black Christians' (Allen 1988: 20).

A similar explanation has been offered for the continued patronage of European art music.

> It is my belief that a symphony concert is a celebration of the 'sacred history' of the western middle classes, and an affirmation of faith in their values as the abiding stuff of life. As these values, and those of industrial society in general, come more and more under attack from both critics and the pressure of events, so the concert becomes more vital as a ritual of stability in an unstable world (Small 1987: 19).

The implication is that the symphony concert is a ritual re-enactment of middle-class values which serves to maintain a bourgeois identity.

We are dealing here with a species of functionalist theory; the function of music in this situation is to give people a sense of identity, and so to promote the successful continuation of the social groups concerned. Curiously, Merriam does not talk about cultural, social or ethnic identity in his exhaustive discussion of the functions of music in society, but it clearly fits into his functionalist framework, especially in his treatment of music and the integration of society (Merriam 1964: 226–7). Rather similar ideas have also been advanced by Lomax with respect to music and *individual* identity, and a specific mechanism described:

> The child begins to learn the musical style of his culture as he acquires the language and the emotional patterns of his people. This style is thus an important link between an individual and his culture, and later in life brings back to the adult unconscious the emotional texture of the world which formed his personality... Thus from the point of view of its social function, the primary effect of music is to give the listener a feeling

of security, for it symbolises the place where he was born, his earliest childhood satisfactions, his religious experience, his pleasure in community doings, his courtship and his work – any or all of these personality-shaping experiences (Lomax 1959: 929).

A second and rather different approach to ethnicity regards ethnic identity as something that is invoked by individuals in particular circumstances when it suits their purposes and helps them attain their goals. This is the view of ethnicity that Slobin adopted in his book, and it is appropriate to the arguments put forward here. Slobin cites the work of Barth:

> Ethnic categories provide an organizational vessel that may be given varying amounts and forms of content in different socio-cultural systems. They may be of great relevance to behaviour, but they need not be; they may pervade all social life, or they may be relevant only in limited sectors of activity. There is thus an odious scope for ethnographic and comparative descriptions of different forms of ethnic organisation (Barth 1969: 14)

Barth argued that 'Ethnic boundaries are maintained in each case by a limited set of cultural features' (ibid.: 38), and Slobin (1976: 1) suggests 'music may be one of those features of social interrelationship that reflect underlying patterns of ethnic boundary maintenance'. Of course, one has to agree with Slobin that music may in this 'reflective' sense be indicative of wider socio-cultural processes, but Barth's approach suggests it may also be used in a more active manner. The point is surely that music is itself a *potent* symbol of identity; like language (and attributes of language such as accent and dialect), it is one of those aspects of culture which can, when the need to assert 'ethnic identity' arises, most readily serve this purpose. Its effectiveness may be twofold; not only does it act as a ready means for the identification of different ethnic or social groups, but it has potent emotional connotations and can be used to assert and negotiate identity in a particularly powerful manner.

Cultural Diversity in Afghanstan

Afghanistan would seem to be typical of many modern countries with linguistic and cultural diversity whose boundaries were drawn up by colonial powers. Afghanistan was established in 1747 by Afghan tribesmen from Kandahar who had for several generations been élite mercenaries in the Iranian army. Although invaded by British troops in 1839 and 1879 and again attacked in 1919, Afghanistan was never the colony of a European power, but was rather the buffer between the Russian and British empires. Its borders were finally specified to the north and south-east by treaties with its imperial neighbours, leaving local populations cut in two by artificial frontiers, sowing the seeds of future problems.

The term *qaum* is of some consequence for the present discussion. *Qaum* refers to consanguinial social groups of varying size; for example, to an ethnic group, such as Pashtuns, Tajiks or Hazaras, or to a tribe, lineage, or clan, or simply to families with whom inter-marriage can reasonably be contemplated due to putative common ancestry. The two principal *qaums* (in the sense of 'ethnic' groups) inhabiting Afghanistan are Pashtuns (the 'true Afghans'), who speak the Pashto language, and Tajiks, who are Persian speaking agriculturalists and townspeople.[3] The country has been dominated politically since its creation by the Pashtuns, who make up about half of the total population of 15 million people, while the Tajiks amount to 3 or 4 million (these are pre-war figures). Both groups were extended over much of the territory of Afghanistan, with the Pashtun heartland in the south and south-west, and Pashtuns having migrated to thinly populated regions in other parts of the country. Provinces near Kabul, such as Parwan, Wardak, and Logar are notable for having large mixed Pashtun–Tajik populations. In addition, there are a number of other smaller groups in Afghanistan: Hazaras, Uzbeks, Turkmen, Pashai, Baluch, Kazakhs, Kirghiz, Aimaq, Nuristanis, and others, usually restricted to specific regions of the country. The Afghan royal family (deposed in 1973) were Persianised Pashtuns, who by the twentieth century hardly spoke Pashto. Dari (Afghan Persian) was the language of the court and administration.

'A principal theme in the political history of Afghanistan has been the effort to create a unified nation-state' (Poullada 1973). The 'nation-state' is a eurocentric concept but may still be usefully applied in this case, for that was the model Afghan rulers sought to emulate.

---

3. The label for this language is problematic, politically as well as academically. We are dealing with variants of Persian, which in Iran is known as Farsi. The version of this language spoken in Afghanistan, and which is sometimes referred to as Afghan Persian, is officially designated Dari, though widely termed Farsi within Afghanistan. In Tajikistan the local version of Persian is called Tajiki, and it would perhaps be appropriate to call the Persian spoken in northern Afghanistan Tajiki rather than Farsi or Dari.

Two factors hindered this development in the nineteenth century. Firstly, conflicts within and between the dominant Pashtun tribes prevented the emergence of Afghanistan as a state. For example, rivalry between the Sadozai and Mohammadzai sections of the ruling Durrani tribe meant that western Afghanistan was a more or less autonomous region for more than sixty years. Secondly, the number of different ethnic groups inhabiting the territory, with different languages, and to some extent different cultures, has hindered the development of the people into a single nation.

Afghanistan began to emerge as a nation-state in the 1880s, under Amir Abdur Rahman. By building a powerful regular army which could confront the tribes he was able to bring the whole of the country under the control of Kabul. It is clear that at this stage the political integrity of Afghanistan was created and maintained by force. In the 1920s, under the enlightened and modernising rule of Abdur Rahman's grandson Amanullah, Ataturk's Turkey served as a sociopolitical model. Amanullah's close relative and father-in-law, Sardar Mahmud Tarzi, had lived much of his life in exile in Syria and Turkey. With the assumption of Amanullah to power, Tarzi's ideas of how to bring about social change and modernisation were implemented by the new ruler in the style of Ataturk, by decree. It is at about this point in Afghanistan's recent history that one can discern the beginnings of an Afghan national music. But before discussing that process it is first necessary to examine some of Slobin's ideas about music and culture contact in Afghanistan.

Slobin's Notion of the 'Shared Music Culture'

Slobin's research in Afghan Turkestan, a culturally diverse area shared principally by Tajiks and Uzbeks, has already been mentioned. Slobin's stated aim was to focus on music as it illuminates patterns of inter-ethnic contact. He is perhaps most convincing when discussing the interaction of Tajik and Uzbek culture and language in various regions of what was then Soviet Central Asia, drawing on extensive researches by Soviet scholars. Here he certainly demonstrates that musical interactions conform to patterns established in other cultural domains. But the extension of his argument to northern Afghanistan leaves many questions unanswered.

He shows that northern teahouse music was a genre shared by Uzbeks and Tajiks. Teahouse music consisted essentially of the singing of quatrains, accompanied by the *dambura* (long-necked lute), *zirbaghali* (goblet drum) and *tāl* (small cymbals). The song texts were in either Uzbek or Tajiki, and it was common to alternate quatrains in the two languages.[4] The mixed Uzbek and Tajik audience, predominantly bilingual, was able to participate in the cultural inter-play at work here, in a social arena where male members of the two communities interacted. Slobin did not analyse these issues in any detail. He did not elicit actors' views and elucidate individual interpretations and manipulations of performance events, nor show how the song/music style might be a combination of Uzbek and Tajik elements. He did not consider how the shared music culture might symbolise or otherwise express different aspects of the shared culture. What does it mean when two culturally distinct communities come to share the same music?

The answers to some of these broader questions are suggested in another publication, in which Slobin discusses the role of radio in Afghan musical life.

> Radio Afghanistan is one of the few unifying factors in a country unusually marked by ethnic and linguistic fragmentation . . . For the Afghan villager or nomad . . . the radio has drastically reduced the restrictions on the scope of his imagination . . . he shares in the music of the Kabul studio, one of the few manifestations of an emerging pattern of national values and expression that may eventually comprise a pan-ethnic, distinctively Afghan society (Slobin 1974: 248)

The formation of a shared music culture in northern teahouses was indicative of a wider process involving the emergence of an Afghan national music, first in the context of the royal court, and later in the context of the radio station in Kabul. Let us now examine some of the characteristics of this national music.

The Character of Afghan National Music

Afghanistan is surrounded by countries – such as Iran, Uzbekistan, Tajikistan and Pakistan – whose inhabitants claim considerable antiquity for their art musics. To a large extent their beliefs about their music histories are supported by contemporary documents and sci-

---

4. Excellent examples of northern teahouse music can be found on Slobin's 1969 LP record *The Music of Afghanistan. Vol. 1: Music of the Uzbeks*. Anthology AST 4001.

entific treatises. In contrast, for Afghanistan there is very little in the way of such documentation, and the musical past is open to speculation and assertion.

Afghan experts, including some musicians, make nationalistic claims to Hindustani music. They maintain that what we know today as 'North Indian classical music' originated in Balkh, 'the mother of cities', whose ruins lie in northern Afghanistan. This music was carried to India in the thirteenth century by Amir Khosrow Balkhi, an important Sufi and literary figure at the Delhi court of the Khilji and Tughlak sultans, who is also credited with a number of innovations in Indian music, such as the invention of the *sitār*, the *tabla*, and the musical genre of *qawwāli*. In the Afghan view, music progressed and developed in the more tolerant culture of India, where the mullahs had little control over people's lives. Recently, according to these ideas, Hindustani music had been brought back and re-established in Afghanistan. The Moghuls, great patrons of music, also enter into this popular history, having conquered much of North India from their base in Kabul, where Babur, the first Moghul emperor, is buried. This version of Afghan music history accommodates the fact that there are indubitably strong links between the two regions. The Afghan ruler Amir Sher Ali Khan is acknowledged to have brought a number of Indian court musicians to Kabul in the 1860s (see Baily 1988: 25), and since then the court music of the Afghan rulers has been strongly orientated towards Hindustani music.

By the early twentieth century an Afghan national music came into being, sometimes termed by Afghans *musiqi-ye melli*, 'national music'. This term embraces genres of both art and popular music. Afghan art music consists of *ghazal* singing, while popular music, termed *kiliwāli*, comprises a variety of vocal and instrumental types, many originally identified with specific regions of Afghanistan. What is the relationship between the creation of these genres of national music and the emergence of an Afghan national identity? Once we start looking in terms of constituent elements we begin to discover some interesting relationships, especially in terms of regional, or ethnic, origins. Specifically, we seem to be dealing with three constituent elements, which we can label: Pashtun, Tajik and Hindustani. National music synthesised elements of the music cultures of the two main ethnic groups in Afghanistan, 'systematised' and 'improved' in the light of Hindustani theory and practice.

The following discussion of how these elements have been combined is for the purposes of illustration and is not intended to recapitulate an actual historical sequence of events.

Pashtun Regional Music

The basis of Afghan national music is Pashtun regional music, a solo vocal music with *rubāb* (plucked lute), *sarinda* (bowed lute), and *doholak* (double-headed barrel drum) accompaniment. The *rubāb* is regarded by Afghans as their national instrument. It is a short-necked plucked lute with a complex morphology, having two sound chambers and sets of drone and sympathetic strings. The *rubāb* is the Pashtun regional instrument *par excellence*, used both to accompany singing and to play instrumental music.

There are various vocal genres in Pashtun music, such as *tappā*, *chahārbeita, loba, rubāi* and *dastān*, distinguished by types of text and standard melody types for their performance. In this Pashtun music sung verses alternate with instrumental sections played at a fast tempo, employing heavily emphasised rhythmic cadences (terminating patterns) followed by short breaks. It is rhythmic structure and the dynamic use of rhythm that characterise Pashtun music most clearly. The tonal system is essentially diatonic, with little use of microtones. A division of the octave into twelve approximately equal semitones is implicit in the fretting of the *rubāb*. Pashtun music uses a simple system of melodic modes, corresponding to the Ionian, Dorian and Phrygian modes.

The Afghan *Ghazal* at the Court of Amanullah

The principal vocal art music genre of Afghan national music is the *ghazal*. The word is derived from Arabic, and refers to one of the principal forms used in Persian and Pashto poetry, constructed of a series of couplets following a particular rhyme scheme. The term *ghazal* also indicates a musical form for the singing of this kind of poetry, a form which is also well-established as a 'light-classical' genre of Hindustani music. The Kabuli *ghazal* generally uses Persian texts, often from the great poets of the Persian language such as Hafez, Sadi, and Bedil. The music is based on the *rāg*s (melodic modes) and *tāl*s (metrical cycles) of Hindustani music, but has certain distinct features, notably a cyclical rhythmic organisation with fast instrumental sections interpolated between units of text. The fast, even frenetic, tempos of these instrumental sections and the use of emphatic rhythmic cadences are features of the *ghazal* which can be linked to Pashtun music.[5] The art of *ghazal* singing depends in part on skill in the interpolation of apposite couplets from other poems. Such an interpolation is called a *fard*, and is usually sung in free rhythm, with no regular pulse. This sort of metrically free singing is characteristic of various types of Tajik music, such as the ubiquitous *chahārbeiti*, the rural style of singing quatrains, and unaccompanied *na't* (religious *ghazal*s) sung in the context of Sufi ritual. It finds an equivalent in *āvāz* singing in Iran (Tsuge 1970). The interpolated *fard* signifies the incorporation of this aspect of Tajik music into the *ghazal* form.

The *ghazal* style of Kabul that is found today seems to have been developed and perfected at the court of Amanullah in the 1920s, during this progressive, modernistic, and liberal era of Afghan history. The principal singer at the Kabuli court in the 1920s was Ustad Kassem, a master of *ghazal* singing, combining a deep knowledge of Persian poetry with a broad training in Hindustani music. There were many other less famous *ghazal* singers in Kabul in his time. The style was not confined to Kabul, but spread through personal contact to other cities, such as Herat, Kandahar, and Mazar-e Sharif, where Kabuli musicians would perform and acquire local pupils. For example, Kabuli art music was introduced in Herat in the 1930s (Baily 1988: 28).

Since at least the 1920s it has been usual for the *ghazal* singer to accompany himself with the hand-pumped Indian harmonium, backed by a small group including *rubāb, tabla* (drum pair), and often bowed lutes such as *sārangi* and *delrubā*, and the *tānpurā* drone. Apart from the *rubāb* all these instruments have been adopted from India. In Herat the fourteen-stringed Herati *dutār* was often added to the basic ensemble after the invention of this instrument in the 1960s (Baily 1976).

Regional Musics of the Kabul Area

The provinces around Kabul, notably Parwan, Logar and Wardak, are relatively densely populated with a mixture of Pashtuns and Tajiks.

---

5. An example of *ghazal* singing by the Herati singer Amir Jan Khushnawaz is discussed by Baily (1988: 62–6) and can be heard on the audio cassette which accompanies the book (Example 1).

It is highly significant that in these areas a shared Pashtun–Tajik music culture developed, in which the song texts were mainly in Dari and the music Pashtun in style. The Pashtun basis of this music is most clearly manifest in the choice of melodic modes and in rhythmic features like the use of accelerating instrumental sections and pronounced rhythmic cadences. The genre known as *chahārbeiti shomāli*, which originates from Parwan region, shows the mixture of Pashtun and Tajik elements very clearly. The vocal sections are sung in Persian, in a very slow tempo that approaches the free rhythm of unaccompanied *chahārbeiti* singing, and the instrumental sections are Pashtun dance pieces of the kind known as *logari*.[6] An important addition to the instrumentarium of national music from this region was the *tanbur*, which has special associations with Parwan. The *tanbur* is a large long-necked lute with sets of drone and sympathetic strings (see Slobin 1976: 235–40).

Afghan Popular Music (*Kiliwāli*)

The Pashto term *kiliwāli*, meaning 'local', has come to refer to a variety of types of Afghan popular music which have been disseminated by the radio station in Kabul. The song texts of this repertoire are usually in Pashto or Dari, and the musical style is clearly based on Pashtun prototypes. Many new songs in the *kiliwāli* style were created by composers and musicians working at the radio station. Others were originally local folk songs (either brought by provincial singers to the radio station, or actually collected by station staff making trips to different parts of the country) and performed in the *kiliwāli* style. In this way many of the folk songs of Afghanistan were given a new lease of life by radio broadcasting (see Baily 1981). There was also an input from the Indian and Pakistani films regularly shown in the cinemas of Afghanistan, and from the popular musics of other neighbouring countries such as Iran and Tajikistan. The musical style that developed for this national popular music can be readily understood as an extension of the regional Pashtun–Tajik music of the areas around Kabul, which already embodied this cultural synthesis.

The radio station used a variety of instruments – Afghan, Indian,

---

6. An example of *chahārbeiti shomāli* by the Kabuli singer Amir Mohammad is discussed by Baily (1988: 85–6) and can be heard on the audio cassette which accompanies the book (Example 7).

and European – to accompany popular music. For example, the *Orkestra Bozorg*, the 'big orchestra', I saw in rehearsal with a singer in 1976 consisted of: two *rubābs*, two *tanburs*, mandoline, Spanish guitar, *tulak* (cross-blown wooden Afghan flute), Boehm flute, piccolo, two tenor saxophones, clarinet, piano, string bass (plucked), *tabla*, *sitār*, and *delrubā* (Baily 1981: 110).

What this brief discussion of the elements in Afghan national music shows is that the contemporary musical 'style' is a synthesis of distinct cultural items from different sources. Is there any way in which we can understand how these elements were put together which relates to other political, economic and social trends in Afghanistan during this period? To answer this question we have to examine briefly the issue of an Afghan national identity.

The Creation of an Afghan National Identity

After the fall of Amanullah in 1929 and the brief Bacha Saqao interregnum, a new nationalist trend became clearly discernible in Afghanistan. According to Reshtia (p.c.), 'The nationalist movement was a deliberate initiative which originated in 1935-6.' Gregorian (1969) gives an account of the arguments put forward by nationalist writers of the time. They recognised that one of the country's problems was its ethnic diversity, and the nationalists were preoccupied with establishing a common history, religious background, and ethnic origin for all the peoples of Afghanistan, claiming that they were descended from the same Aryan stock. The Pashto language was given great importance in this nationalist ideology. In the 1933 constitution Pashto and Dari were specified for the first time as the official languages of the country. It was argued that Afghanistan needed the development of a modern national culture.

> Many urged that Afghanistan's folklore and traditional music be collected, and called for the development of a new literature reflecting both the nation's historical legacy and its present social realities, needs and aspirations. Poets and writers were exhorted to see themselves as vehicles of social change and their role as the awakening of the Afghan people (Gregorian 1969: 349).

Pashtun poets also wrote to promote Afghan nationalism, as this couplet by Malang Jan illustrates:

Chay ay mor'i -a de khawra zaqawalay
Ka po har zhaban goyaa day khow Afghan day

That person who was given birth by his mother on this soil, Whatever language he speaks, he is still an Afghan.

Radio Broadcasting and Afghan Popular Music

A brief consideration of the history of radio broadcasting from Kabul sheds some light on the way music served to foster nationalism. Radio broadcasting from Kabul has been of crucial importance in the creation and dissemination of the popular forms of Afghan national music. Broadcasting in Afghanistan was initiated in 1925 during the reign of Amanullah. For a few years radio achieved a small breakthrough, with an estimated 1,000 receiving sets in Kabul by 1928. The radio station was destroyed in 1929 in the uprising against Amanullah, and there was no serious attempt to resume transmissions until Radio Kabul was officially opened in 1940. From this time the radio station started to take over from the royal court as the main patron of musicians and institutional sponsor of new developments in music, employing most of the important musicians in the country. The stated aims of the radio station were to spread the message of the Holy Koran, to reflect the national spirit, to perpetuate the treasures of Afghan folklore, and to contribute to public education. According to Reshtia (p.c.), the government saw radio as the best and quickest way to communicate to and inform the population of its policies and development programmes.

During the Second World War broadcasting was seriously hampered by difficulties in obtaining new equipment or spares. An effective broadcasting service that could be received in most parts of the country was not established until the mid-1940s. Ownership of radio receivers was very limited and to ensure the dissemination of broadcasts, receiver appliances in a number of cities were linked to loudspeaker systems in their main streets. They broadcast the news, music, and other programmes, to a predominantly male audience in public places. This project was launched in 1940 and completed by 1945 in the main provincial towns (Reshtia, p.c.). The buildings of Kabul Radio were located on the edge of the old city, not far from Kucheh Kharabat, the musicians' quarter. In the 1960s a new radio station for what was now Radio Afghanistan was built in the outskirts of Kabul.

Afghan popular music originated in response to the need to create a music suitable for radio broadcasting. The regional music of Parwan and other mixed Pashtun–Tajik areas provided the models on which the new national popular music broadcast by the radio station was built. The new music brought together Dari texts, Pashtun musical style, and Hindustani theoretical concepts and terminology. The development of Afghan popular music (*kiliwāli*) took place with the assistance of the *ustāds* (master musicians), descendants of Indian court musicians, whose knowledge of Hindustani music theory and terminology and high standards of performance were important for organising small ensembles and large orchestras at the radio station. They played a key role in training musicians, both professionals and amateurs, and can be likened to foreign experts who had the technical expertise necessary to help the Afghans upgrade and improve their music. In this way their role anticipated that of American, Russian, and other music advisers brought to the station in the 1960s. The contribution of the Afghan *ustāds* seems to have been much more acceptable to the Afghans and altogether more successful than the efforts of Western experts, whose frustrations are described by Slobin (1974: 244–5).

Conclusions

It is clear from the data discussed above that music played a significant role in expressing and creating an Afghan national identity. The obvious question to arise at this point concerns the intentionality behind the process. To what extent can one talk about the 'architects' of this national music? Was it planned or was it the unforeseen result of actions taken to achieve some other set of goals? According to Reshtia (p.c.) one must incline to the latter interpretation: it would be wrong to imagine a committee in the Ministry of Information and Culture sitting down to discuss how to institute a national music which could then be used to create and promote an Afghan national identity. The controllers of radio broadcasting had their own agenda, and could not predict in detail the results of their actions. The broad goal of fostering national identity was defined by the government with no clear idea of how to achieve it. It would be interesting to discover what musicians involved in the process might have to say about the national style bringing together elements of Pashtun and Tajik music, but this has not yet been possible.

Music and the Afghan National Identity

Finally, we return to our original questions about the cultural and political fragmentation that has occurred in Afghanistan since 1978. If one can identify the processes that gave political cohesion in the past, how can they be revived? It is at this stage not possible to reach any reliable conclusions as to what has happened to Afghan music since 1978, both inside and outside the country. There is obviously a need for research. Much of the oral history of the war will be found in the context of epic songs (*dastān*) recounting the exploits of various commanders and their *mujāhideen* groups. In terms of stylistic parameters, music seems to have remained relatively static through the conflict, with little in the way of innovation, just changes in song texts. Musicians who remained in Kabul sang songs praising the communist government, while those who were in exile extolled the bravery and fighting skills of the *mujāhideen*. The only *musical* innovation I can report is the imitation on the *tabla* of various firearms and artillery by Afghan refugee musicians in Peshawar, in whose hands the rhythmic cadences of the Pashtun style became even more dramatic and pyrotechnic, adorned with these iconic representations of the sounds of war.

Compared with periods of musical innovation in the 1920s and 1940s–50s, when genres of national music were emerging, Afghan musical culture seems to have remained static since the start of the war. Neither side in the conflict laid claim to a distinct style, what differed was the overall attitude towards music. The communist government in Kabul, with its secular educated middle-class Marxist ideology, supported music, and party members and their cohorts were enthusiastic patrons of live performance for small gatherings. Musicians in Kabul seem to have prospered at this time. In contrast, Afghan refugees in Pakistan and Iran were strongly discouraged from even listening to music, and the musicians amongst them had to live and operate outside the refugee camps, which were run by the mullahs in a state of perpetual mourning. After the fall of the communist regime in 1992 music was more or less proscribed by the new Islamic government. The Kabul mullahs, as in 1929, have cited the 'soul corrupting' aspect of music to justify this ban.

As a result of this stagnation in the arts during the years of armed conflict, Afghan national music retains the mixture of Pashtun and Tajik elements that it had before, and is available again to play its role in promoting a pan-Afghan identity. But for music to fulfil its potential for reconciliation there must be a revival of musical patronage, and if the past is anything to go by, that will have to be inspired by a new government initiative.

References

Allen, R., 'African-American Sacred Quartet Singing in New York City', *New York Folklore*, vol. 14, nos. 3–4, 1988, pp. 7–22.

——, and N. Groce, 'Introduction: Folk and Traditional Music in New York State', *New York Folklore*, vol. 14, nos. 3–4, 1988, pp. 1–6.

Baily, J., 'Cross-cultural Perspectives in Popular Music: The Case of Afghanistan', *Popular Music*, vol. 1, 1981, pp. 105–122.

——, *Music of Afghanistan: Professional Musicians in the City of Herat*, Cambridge: Cambridge University Press (with accompanying audio cassette), 1988.

——, 'Recent Changes in the *Dutār* of Herat', *Asian Music*, vol. 8, no. 1, 1976, pp. 29–64.

Barth, F. *Ethnic Groups and Boundaries*, Boston, Little, Brown and Co., 1969.

Blacking, J., 'Some Problems of Theory and Method in the Study of Musical Change', paper read at ICTM Conference, Honolulu, 1977 and later published in modified form in *Yearbook for Traditional Music*, vol. 9, 1977, pp. 1–26.

Gregorian, V., *The Emergence of Modern Afghanistan*, Stanford, Stanford University Press, 1969.

Lomax, A., 'Musical Style and Social Context', *American Anthropologist*, vol. 61, 1959, pp. 927–54.

Merriam, A.P., *The Anthropology of Music*, Evanston, Northwestern University Press, 1964.

Poullada, L.B., *Reform and Rebellion in Afghanistan 1919–1929: King Amanullah's Failure to Modernise a Tribal Society*, Ithica, Cornell University Press, 1973.

Slobin, M., 'Music in Contemporary Afghan Society', in L. Dupree and L. Albert (eds), *Afghanistan in the 1970s*, New York, Praeger, 1974.

——, *Music in the Culture of Northern Afghanistan*, Viking Fund Publications in Anthropology No. 54, Tucson, University of Arizona Press, 1976.

Small, C., 'Performance as Ritual: Sketch for an Enquiry into the true Nature of a Symphony Concert', in A.L. White (ed.) *Lost in Music: Culture, Style and the Musical Event*, Sociological Review Monograph 34, London, Routledge & Kegan Paul, 1987.

Tsuge, G., 'Rhythmic Aspects of the *Āvāz* in Persian Music', *Ethnomusicology*, vol. 14, no. 2, 1970, pp. 205–27.

4
National Anthems: The Case of Chopin as a National Composer

Zdzislaw Mach

Contemporary nation-states are identified by a triad of official symbols, which are legally defined and protected by law. These elements are: a flag, an emblem and an anthem. They serve as an identification of states and state representatives at political meetings, sports competitions and other international gatherings. Abuse of them is punished by law, and they are supposed, according to the official state ideology, to represent the ideas and values of the nation and the state, with which citizens are expected to identify. Often the symbols are rooted in the nation's tradition, in its history, in the heroic periods of its mythical creation or its fight for sovereignty. They frequently illustrate Hobsbawm and Ranger's well known concept of the invention of tradition, since history which is represented in the condensed form of national symbols is constructed and interpreted in order to create a coherent ideological image (Hobsbawm and Ranger 1983). Sometimes national symbols are openly invented and their ideological content, their meaning, is clearly stated in documents. An example would be the flag of the state of Tibet, designed by the Dalai Lama's government in exile.

National flags, emblems and anthems symbolically represent both the nation and the state, and especially the link between the two. From the point of view of the state authorities it is essential that the symbols have proper respect and are sacred for citizens, since they represent the ideological and political unity of the nation and its political organisation. For this reason, radical changes of power, especially revolutions, usually end with changes of national symbols, and with the invention of new elements compatible with the new state ideology. Official national symbols are also contested by those groups of citizens who do not identify with the state ideology.

Revolutionaries often deliberately desecrate symbols which for them represent the state but have nothing to do with the nation, as they define it, or with a particular social class. A good example may be the case of the US flag displayed in the Institute of Art in Chicago in 1989 by a young artist. The flag was a central element of an object of art, and was placed on the floor in such a way that visitors had to step on it. The artist openly admitted that his intention was to provoke desacralisation of the flag as a black communist, and as such, wanted to show contempt to the state and to the political system he hated. There also exist other symbols of strong patriotic value which are not legally defined or protected, but are recognised as part of national symbolism. National mythology, heroes, music and literature often belong to one system of state and national symbols, and function in the same way as the classic three-element official set venerated by some and opposed by others.

In Poland, national symbols are closely related to the concepts of statehood and political sovereignty. The flag and the emblem have their origin in medieval times, but assumed a new significance in the nineteenth century when they symbolised the independence the country had lost. The Polish national anthem, known as the *Dabrowski Mazurka*, was written by a poet, Josef Wybicki, in 1797 to a folk tune for the Polish military units fighting in Italy in alliance with Napoleon. The soldiers sang the song which became widely known as a patriotic song and part of the national symbolism developed in the romantic period in the first half of the nineteenth century. Polish national identity, with its concepts of heroism, its mythology, literature and art, was a product of Polish romanticism. Central ideas and values of Polishness were formed during this period. The great Polish poets: Adam Mickiewicz, Juliusz Slowacki, Zygmunt Krasinski and Cyprian K. Norwid, belong to this period, and they continue to be recognised as the most prominent creators of the Polish national culture. As heroes of Polish romanticism and leaders of national military uprisings, writers and artists have been venerated as founding fathers of the modern Polish nation. Frederick Chopin is one of those heroes, as important as the above mentioned poets, and the only composer and musician who achieved the status of a national hero and became the object of an almost religious cult.

Born in 1810 as a son of a Polish mother and French father, Chopin was brought up and educated in Warsaw, and as a young boy, gained recognition as a musician among aristocratic circles. The cosmopolitan culture of the Polish upper classes, which Chopin adopted, later made it easy for him to feel at home in Paris, where he spent the second half of his life. But he was also aware of other dimensions of Polish culture: the peasants whom he used to meet in the countryside every summer, where folk music inspired his own work, and the intelligentsia which was then in the process of formation as a new structure in Polish society. This consisted of the teachers, writers and other intellectuals who at that time were creating the foundations of Polish national mythology, patriotic values and ideas (Gella 1989). The national factor in Chopin's music has often been discussed (Jachimecki 1949, Callet 1966, Hamburger 1966, Searle 1966, Hedley 1947, Junien 1921, Brudnicki 1965). Many foreign authors claim that his works were really cosmopolitan and international, inspired by personal, romantic emotions rather than by something in the outside world. For Poles, to cite Norman Davies, 'Chopin's works were built on his experiences in the formative years in Warsaw, distilled from the Polish melodies, harmonies and rhythms that he heard in his youth, and inspired by a bitter sweet nostalgia for the land of his birth; they represent the quintessence of "Polishness"' (1981: 27). Chopin's musical genius is universal and is appreciated by listeners and artists who know nothing at all about Poland and its culture. Chopin is, for example, very popular in Japan. On the other hand, his Mazurkas, Polonaises and songs are undoubtedly inspired by Polish folk music. These inspirations, however, are not direct; whilst he articulated his desire to 'get to the heart of (Polish) national music' (Searle 1966: 215), he very rarely used a 'real' Polish folk song in his works, preferring to regard this repertory as a point of departure. There are few direct references to folklore in Chopin's compositions. Most of his dances, for example, cannot be traced to a single, definite folk model, but arise from a composite recollection of certain types of melodies and rhythms. In this respect, Chopin's 'Polishness' is rather like Dvorak's Czechness or Bloch's Jewishness (Hamburger 1966: 73).

    Chopin left Poland in 1830, a few weeks before a national uprising against the Russians began in November. His first Christmas abroad was spent in Vienna, where he composed the *Scherzo in B Minor* in which one can find the melody of a popular Polish Christmas carol (Jachimecki 1949: 57, Rawsthorne 1966: 65). The tragic news of the collapse of the uprising may have inspired Chopin to compose his so-called 'revolutionary study', the *Prelude in C Minor Op. 10, No. 12* (Hedley 1947: 42, Callet 1966: 133), although there is more doubt about the inspiration which lead to the creation of the *Preludes in A Minor* and *D Minor*.[1] There can be no doubt that for Chopin the news of the collapse of the national uprising was a shock. He suffered even more because he felt isolated from his family, and felt guilty for not taking part in the fighting. 'If it were not that I should be a burden on my father, I would come back. I curse the day I left', he wrote in one of his letters. Chopin was in Stuttgart when the news of the tragic end of the insurrection arrived. He then wrote in his notebook 'an incoherent jumble of lamentations and curses which show how worry, fear and regret had preyed on his overwrought nerves' (Hedley 1947: 4l). He speculated about the possible tragic fate of his family, and the inevitable tragedy of his country. It would have been strange if such strong emotions had found no effect on his works. Chopin's *Polonaise in A Major Op. 10, No. 1*, of which Robert Schumann remarked that it was a 'cannon buried in the flowers' (Davies 1981: 27), is for a Pole the proof and expression of his patriotic feelings, and one of the greatest masterpieces of Polish national culture.

When Chopin died in 1849, he became in official historiography a Polish 'national prophet', whose compositions were regarded as important for the national soul as the poems of Mickiewicz and Slowacki. The category of 'national prophets' plays an important function in the cultural construction of Polish national identity. It often refers to great artists and thinkers of nineteenth century romanticism, but also to those writers and painters in later years who made a special contribution to Polish national mythology, created heroes and legends and told stories of Poland's great past, tragic present and glorious future. They spoke about the role of the Polish nation in the history of mankind, and a Polish martyrology through which Poland will redeem the world. Polish nationalism is thus constructed on the basis of ideals and values of heroic struggles, glorious victories, and great personalities who fight, fall and, through tragic fate, become martyrs. The Polish past was constructed in the nineteenth century in such a way that it proved the metaphysical logic of history. National prophets give this logic its artistic expression.

The role of Chopin in Polish national culture reaches far beyond

---

1. The *Prelude in A Minor* belongs, according to Hedley (1947: 42), to the period of Chopin's visit to Majorca in 1838.

his artistic output. As part of Polish national identity his music is a component of the symbolic system, an element of Poland's 'Great Tradition' (Smith 1986: 14,42). Chopin has at least three functional aspects in Poland. Firstly, he was a composer of music; secondly, he was a national hero and prophet, and thirdly, he was a great man and Pole who contributed to the international recognition of Poland as a nation. The first aspect consists in understanding Chopin's music. His works are as popular among Polish pianists as they are among foreigners. Of course, most Poles do not have enough formal musical education to appreciate this kind of music, and prefer pop or jazz. Most cannot even recognise his major compositions. But for those who understand classical music, Chopin is among the first composers they listen to, and his works are very often broadcast and played. Musically educated Poles like Chopin and are proud of him. But his real role in Polish national identity lies in the second aspect mentioned above. For Poles, Chopin is a national hero and a national prophet. He is one of the greatest creators of the heroic, romantic period of struggle, tragedy and fame, the period that made the essential contribution to Polish nationalism. As Anthony Smith puts it, 'Chopin in Poland crystallised the ideal of an heroic age which could inspire fresh glories in a renewed nation' (Smith 1986: 193). As a result, pictures of him decorate classrooms in every Polish school, alongside those of Polish Nobel Prize winners, writers and scientists.

The cult of Chopin as a national hero grew throughout the second half of the nineteenth century and the first two decades of this century, until the Second World War, when Poland again became an independent nation-state. In 1910, the musician and politician Ignacy Paderewski, who later became a Prime Minister, spoke on the occasion of the hundredth anniversary of Chopin's birth:

> Everything is in Chopin: the sound of swords, the scream of the injured, the prayers of our hearts and the song of victory. He is now with us, in eternal glory and in gratitude of the nation, decorated with the flowers of our veneration and love. But he is not alone; with him there is Genius Patriae, the spirit of our country, of the nation. Our collective soul is reflected in him (Jachimecki 1949: 110).

Eleven years later, in newly independent Poland, a French–Polish author argued that

> Chopin was one of the greatest Poles, because he became the symbol of Polish music, and his music was the anthem of Poland, of the Polish

soul ... Chopin reached for the treasures of folk inspirations ... He also combined Polish and French elements in one harmony (Junien 1921: 5–6).

Such a harmony, the same author remarks, results from the fact that ideals of Polish and French nations merge in the same ultimate goals (ibid.). According to such a view, music is the essence of national soul, and Chopin added a Polish component to the great universal musical melting pot.

The third aspect of the role of Chopin in Poland is perhaps less openly admitted and less obvious, but undoubtedly present. Chopin satisfies the need for recognition; he is a remedy for the inferiority complex that the Polish intelligentsia often experiences and conceals in its mythology of greatness. The intelligentsia wants to be regarded as having made significant contributions to European high culture. The issue of the international recognition of Polish intellectuals, artists and writers is loaded with emotion. Poland is situated between Western and Eastern Europe, between Latin and Byzantine culture, and between Roman Catholic, Protestant and Orthodox Christianities. But the élite, high culture of the Polish intelligentsia belonged to the Western tradition. Poles often feel that the rest of Western Europe is not convinced of this fact, that for many British, German, French and Italian intellectuals, Europe ends at the eastern border of Germany. Therefore it is essential for Poles to show that their artists, writers and scientists have made important contributions to the high culture of Western European élites. Chopin is one of the very few Polish artists who are generally recognised as creators of 'European culture'. This is why the Polishness of Chopin and the Polish roots of his music are so important for Poles.

Despite the tremendous importance of Chopin in Poland, none of his music was chosen for the official national anthem. Perhaps, given the nature of Poland's relations with the outside world in the nineteenth century, its continuous struggle against foreign oppressors and the great symbolic significance of the national army, a simple military music was more appropriate than the subtle, more difficult romantic masterpieces of Chopin. The history of Polish national anthems shows that either military or religious music has been chosen. The first song to play this role, the medieval *Bogurodzica* ('Mother of God'), was sung by Polish knights before great battles. Another song, entitled *Rota*, a song composed to a poem by Maria Konopnicka in 1896, called upon Poles to resist the Germanisation of Prussia. Another religious song, *Boze Cos Polske* ('God Who Saves Poland'), is still sung in churches on patriotic anniversaries and on other occasions when patriotism can be expressed. *Boze Cos Polske* exists in two versions: one with a prayer to God for the blessing of a free Poland, and the other, which prays to God that He should make Poland free again. In the years between 1945 and 1989, the second version was sung by those who opposed the communist regime, whilst the first was sung by those loyal to it. The *Dabrowski Mazurka*, the present official national anthem, was written in 1797, and inspired by folk music. Its text expresses the idea of the nation alive, even if deprived of its own state. In 1927 it became the official anthem. The communists did not decide to replace it with another one, probably in order to gain legitimisation and to show their national character, and the continuity of the patriotic tradition (Russocki et al. 1963).

Chopin's music, even if it did not become the official anthem, played a central role in Polish national symbolism, as did Chopin himself. The ambiguity of musical symbols allows various contextual usages. For the communist authorities after the Second World War, it was essential to find legitimisation in national ideology, and so they tried to incorporate as many elements from the Polish national symbolic heritage as possible, as long as these elements did not openly contradict the communist world view. Religious music was out of the question, but Chopin, due to his universal value, unquestioned greatness, patriotic associations, and especially his folk inspirations, was very appropriate. Literature often provokes feelings and associations which may be unwelcome from a given ideological point of view, if, for example, a particular event is recalled, or a particular enemy named. Thus romantic Polish literature was dangerous because it aroused anti-Russian sentiments. But music was less explicit, and could be interpreted by state ideologues as generally patriotic, without particular associations.

In the case of Chopin's music, its roots in Polish folk culture were used as an argument that the healthy core of the national culture was of peasant origin, and not that of a decadent élite, since, the argument went, the greatest Polish music was inspired by peasant culture.[2]

2. This argument was generally put forward by Polish communist party ideologists and propagandists. According to the communist world view, the culture of peasants and workers was the most valuable, healthy, sound and dynamic component of the national culture. The best masterpieces of art and literature were supposed to be those which were folk-inspired, as opposed to the decadent, bourgeois culture of the West. Such views were often expressed at official celebrations organised by the state on the occasion of Chopin piano competitions.

The Polish nation could thus be identified with peasants and workers, and not with the nobility and aristocracy, and that was precisely the ideological aim of the communist rulers. For those Polish authors (for example Jachimecki 1949, Brudnicki 1965) who tried to strengthen the communist state's ideological position, there was no doubt as to the folk origin of Chopin's music: 'In the villages he encountered peasant music, which strongly influenced his entire artistic output . . . He found inspiration in the beauty of the Polish countryside and peasant song . . . coming from the folk and national music, he tried to transform it into masterpieces understandable for all nations' (Brudnicki 1965: 13–23).

Despite numerous attempts, the communist regime did not manage to inspire contemporary composers sufficiently to acquire a great 'socialist' music that could rival Chopin. Christel Lane mentions unsuccessful attempts of a similar kind in the Soviet Union (Lane 1981: 204). Conveniently, Chopin could be used instead, and so, in 1949, at the time when the communists in Poland consolidated their power, they celebrated the centennial anniversary of the death of Chopin.[3] The celebrations were a great event, with the participation of most of the high ranking politicians, including president Boleslaw Bierut. In his opening speech, Bierut spoke about a Chopin who made Poland famous, and whose music became part of everyday life for millions of Poles of all social strata and class, when the collapse of capitalism made it possible for workers and peasants to enjoy music. Chopin's nationalism came from simple people and their culture, he argued. He created simple and beautiful musical forms in the manner of folk song, and unlike the complicated, decadent music of the bourgeoisie. Chopin, according to Bierut, was a Slavic composer, whose music is particularly loved in the Soviet Union, and contributes towards 'the eternal friendship between Polish and Soviet people. Whoever read Chopin's letters discovered, Bierut continued, a man aware of contradictions and the dialectics of history – a true genius. Bierut quoted one of these letters in which Chopin commented on the Polish uprising in 1848: 'horrible things will happen, but in the end Poland will emerge: magnificent, great Poland'. Was it not, Bierut asked, a vision of genius (quoted in *Trybuna Ludu*

---

3. The celebrations consisted of a commemorative meeting with the participation of the political leaders of the communist party and the government, including the party's First Secretary, Bierut, members of the Politburo and the Prime Minister, Josef Crankiewicz. There were also articles in newspapers and extensive discussions in the media about Chopin, his life and work.

17/10, 1949)? Chopin competitions in Warsaw have been organised every five years, and have always been a source of pride for the state authorities. Chopin's music has always been present at state ceremonies, official concerts and artistic events wherever officials were to be present The year 1960 (the 150th anniversary of his birth) was officially declared 'The Year of Chopin'. His life was presented as the ideal life of a great man and patriot; his French father was portrayed in official biographies as a Polish patriot who took part in the Polish anti-Russian insurrection lead by Kosciuszko in 1794 (Brudnicki 1965: 9).

Chopin has been played on all occasions regarded by the state as important, whenever the authorities wished to appeal to patriotic sentiments. When General Jaruzelski declared martial law in December 1981, the radio broadcasted Chopin's music as a symbol of importance, solemnity and patriotic significance. This became such a regular feature of official events, that a prominent Polish intellectual once remarked, 'whenever I hear Chopin on the radio, I fear that something horrible has happened'.

Despite such frequent abuse of the symbolic meaning of Chopin, it seems that for most Poles, he and his music have never really been associated with the regime or with its ideology. The colour red of the worker's flag, by contrast, was so much associated with communism that the new Polish trade unions and workers' parties totally avoided using the colour. With Chopin, things have been different. Chopin's work could not be reduced to any political meaning; there always remained something else to be appreciated and understood, and read as a meaning alternative to what the ideologists interpreted as the true 'content' of the music. Perhaps this is always the case with music, that it leaves behind something beyond any interpretation, a basis for free, or at least, other associations and feelings. Whatever was said about Chopin, there always remained something to add and to start a new interpretation. Perhaps this is also an aspect of what constitutes Chopin's 'artistic greatness'.

References

Brudnicki, J., *Fryderyk Chopin*, Warszawa, Bibioteka Narodowa, 1965.
Callet, R., 'Studies, Preludes and Impromptus', in A. Walker (ed.), *Frederick Chopin*, London, Barrie and Rockliff, 1966.
Davies, N., *God's Playground: A History of Poland*, vol. 2, Oxford,

Clarendon Press, 1981.
Gella, A., *Development of Class Structure in Eastern Europe*, Albany, State University of New York Press, 1989.
Hamburger, P., 'Mazurkas, Waltzes, Polonaises', in A. Walker (ed.), *Frederick Chopin*, London, Barrie and Rockliff, 1966.
Hedley, A., *Chopin*, London, Dent, 1947.
Hobsbawm, E. and T. Ranger (eds), *The Invention of Tradition*, Cambridge, Cambridge University Press 1983.
Jachimecki, Z., *Chopin*, Warszawa, Instytut Wydawniczy 'Sztuka', 1949.
Junien, G., *O Chopinie Jako Muzycznym Wieszczu Polski*, Warszawa, Gebethner i Wolff, 1921.
Lane, C., *The Rites of Rulers*, Cambridge, Cambridge University Press, 1981.
Rawsthorne, A., 'Ballades, Fantasy and Scherzos' in A. Walker (ed.), *Frederick Chopin*, London, Barrie and Rockliff, 1966.
Russocki, S., S. Kuczynski and J. Willaume, *J. Godlo. Barwy I Hymn Rzeczypospolite*, Warszawa, Wiedza Powszechna, 1963.
Searle, H., 'Miscellaneous Works', in A. Walker (ed.), *Frederick Chopin*, London, Barrie and Rockliff, 1966.
Smith, A.D., *The Ethnic Origin of Nations*, Oxford, Basil Blackwell, 1986.

Macunaíma's Music: National Identity and Ethnomusicological Research in Brazil

Suzel Ana Reily

Macunaíma is the name of the main character in a novel published in 1928 by Mário de Andrade (1893–1945), a monument of Brazil's nationally oriented 'modernist movement'. The book itself is entitled *Macunaíma – the Hero with no Character*.[1] The contradiction implied by this title is not gratuitous. Macunaíma is something of an irreverent trickster figure, but in a literary sense he lacks character because he is not a definable 'psychological type': he is a mythic figure comprising a conglomeration of fragments of Brazilian cultures, past and contemporary. No attempt is made to transform this amalgam into a coherent whole. While there is literary logic to the book itself, there is no logic to Macunaíma as a character: the character he exhibits in one chapter is displaced by another in the next. He has been viewed by some critics as a turbulent figure representing the psychological chaos of the Brazilian people, in which the most diverse racial and cultural elements have been united, but have not as yet amalgamated (Proença 1974: 8).

Viewed in its entirety, the chapters of the book seem disconnected, but they are each internally coherent. Mário de Andrade himself called the book a rhapsody. Strictly speaking, a rhapsody is a

---

1. There are numerous editions of Mário de Andrade's book, *Macunaíma – O Herói sem Nenhum Caráter*, including an annotated edition organised by Telê Porto Ancona Lopez (1988). The book has also been translated into English by E.A. Goodland (Andrade 1984). Just as the author foresaw in a letter dated 12 December 1930 addressed to Manuel Bandeira, the translation is unable to capture the book's 'poetic-heroic-comical essence' (Andrade 1958: 318).

portion of an epic or a free medley of such portions sung in succession. As in a rhapsody, the parts – or chapters – of *Macunaíma* bring together a variety of popular motives based on some unifying principle. As Gilda de Mello e Souza (1979: 12–18) has demonstrated, it was precisely in these terms that Mário[2] described Brazilian traditional dramatic dance forms:

> What best characterises the contemporary aspect of all our dramatic dances is that . . . they do not form a coherent whole, in which a single idea – a single theme – is developed. . . . In general the thematic nucleus [of the drama] consists of a single, concise episode, which is then filled out with a series of themes built up around it. . . . Sometimes these incisions have no connection with the nucleus. . . . The episode that once formed the nucleus is now of no greater importance than the subsidiary episodes (Andrade 1982 (vol. 1): 54).[3]

While the nuclear plot of *Macunaíma* is the loss and retrieval of the *muiraquitã*, the hero's magic amulet, the book is constructed as a string of independent episodes depicting Macunaíma's adventures during his search. Each of these subsidiary narratives represents the fusion of a series of isolated fragments, which result in some phenomenon of Brazilian culture. The country's inter-racial mixture, for example, is embodied by the hero himself. Macunaíma is born pitch black of an Indian mother, but he becomes white after bathing in a magic puddle. Because he has dirtied the water, his brother, Jiguê, only manages to turn bronze-coloured (Indian) after his bath. Manaape, his other brother, is only able to lighten the palms of his hands and the soles of his feet, because Jiguê splashed most of the water out of the puddle. After the frenzy of each adventure, Macunaína – the tri-ethnic product of the tropics – lies back and exclaims: 'Oh, what laziness!'

It is significant that *Macunaíma* was published in the same year as one of Mário de Andrade's other major works: *Ensaio Sobre a Música Brasileira* (Essay on Brazilian Music). The *Ensaio* is not a novel, but a theoretical treatise, and it sets the agenda for much of his future musicological research. Mário de Andrade became the intellectual leader of an entire generation, and his influence extended

---

2. It is common practice in Brazilian academic writing for extremely well-known intellectuals such as Mário de Andrade to be referred to by their first names. I shall follow this personalised tradition in this chapter.
3. All translations are my own unless otherwise stated.

far beyond the musical sphere. He was in the forefront of the 'modernist movement' that brought together artists of various fields, including literature, painting, sculpture, architecture, and music. Mário de Andrade escapes any clear-cut professional categorisation: he was a novelist, a poet, a literary and music critic, a folklorist, a linguist, a music educationalist, a state cultural administrator, but above all a musicologist. Today we can legitimately consider him an ethnomusicologist as well, although the term had not been coined in Mário's time. Of the twenty volumes compiled to represent his *Complete Works*, seven relate to his musicological research.[4] Among these studies are several annotated collections of Brazilian folk songs and instrumental tunes, gathered on his extensive journeys throughout the country. His musical transcriptions are still among the most meticulous ever produced from such a wide-ranging corpus, and a comparison with Hungary's Bela Bartok is by no means misplaced.

With such an extraordinary range of activities, it may seem strange that Mário de Andrade did not compose. He only signed his name to one short piece, but he himself considered it an irreverent *jeu d'esprit*.[5] Despite this musical deficiency, his literary works – particularly *Macunaíma* – served to exemplify his project to the composers he was addressing. While *Macunaíma* is a literary 'composition',[6] the *Ensaio* calls on Brazilian composers to participate in the construction of a national serious music tradition through the use of Brazilian expressive elements. A musical transposition of the panoramic distortions used in *Macunaíma* feature prominently in the music of various Brazilian nationalist composers. José Miguel Wisnik's reading of Villa-Lobos's collection of *Choros*, for example, suggests a close affinity with Mário's project in *Macunaíma*.

[The *Choros*] absorb . . . a vast repertoire of diverse musical significance . . . . There is an (explicit) intention to capture the spectrum of the Brazilian musical psyche, through the recreation of orchestral landscapes

---

4. The volumes relating to Mário de Andrade's musicological research include single monographs, collections of essays, and collections of his shorter journalistic writings. His output, however, far exceeds the content of this collection. To my knowledge there is no comprehensive bibliography of his musicological studies at the moment.
5. His composition, *Viola Quebrada*, was based on the inversion of a piece by Catulo da Paixão Cearense, *Cabocla do Caxangá*. Because of this, he actually saw the piece as plagiarism (Mariz 1983: 27).
6. See G. de Mello e Souza (1979) on the various techniques of traditional music composition Mário de Andrade used in the construction of *Macunaíma*.

(jungles, backlands); occasional bird calls; citations and elaborations of Indian ritual songs; references to African dances, carnival parades, popular waltzes, children's songs, band tunes. ... These aggregations realise oneiric transformations of the musical material, ... resulting in an image of simultaneous forces, of an open-ended liberation of energy, and the infinite temporality of the clustered fragments. They are an aural transposition of an oneiric figuration that develops out of significants of a concept *brasil*: the 'country' (as unconscious) is the ungraspable whole of these forces, which the musical text tries to grasp in a sonic synthesis (Wisnik 1983: 166–7).

The idea of using national material was not a modernist invention. Since Carlos Gomes's (1836–96) opera, *Il Guarani*, there had already been a group of composers in the late nineteenth century, including such names as Alexandre Lévy, Alberto Nepomuceno, Ernesto Nazaré, among others, who had based their work on popular motives. Villa-Lobos had already been conducting his own field excursions in search of folk tunes to incorporate into his compositions at least twenty years before Mário de Andrade began his treks across the country to collect the national repertoire (Horta 1987: 18).

The novelty of the *Ensaio* resides in its ideological implications: here the nationalist proposition was presented to contemporary music circles in the form of an organised argument – almost as a manifesto. Mário believed that Brazilian cultural independence was viable, but it could only be realised through the *conscious agency* of the artistic world. It was up to them to break the habit of imitating European cultural models and search for their own *muiraquitã*. Like Macunaíma, the 'dis-interested' artist had to transcend the parochial 'interest' of local traditions, and thereby construct an autonomous culture reflecting the unique 'Brazilian' psyche. Self-recognition and self-esteem would only be possible once freedom from 'transplanted' cultures had been achieved. By integrating the particular to create the national, Brazilian culture would be able to participate as an equal in the 'concert of nations', with genuine and universally valid contributions. In effect, the composer was to serve as midwife to a truly *collective* national culture that would itself function within an *inter*-national arena. In Mário's own words:

> A national art cannot be created out of elements chosen arbitrarily and amateurishly: a national art already exists in the folk unconscious. All the artist has to do is give them an erudite transposition that will trans-

form popular [or folk] music into art music, music that is immediately disinterested (1962: 15-16).

Macunaíma is just such a transposition. The elements he chose were by no means arbitrary, and it took him years of research to collect them: hardly the work of a dilettante. Once collected though, the 'erudite transposition' must indeed have seemed simple to him: the actual book was written in six days, or so legend has it.[7] Whether or not others found the transposition to be as simple as Mário de Andrade did, his collections of folk music as well as his 'erudite transpositions' of folk material directly influenced at least fifty pieces by some of Brazil's major twentieth century composers.[8] Camargo Guarnieri, for example, composed *Quatro Poemas de Macunaíma* (Four Poems of Macunaíma) in 1931, and Batista Siqueira actually named one of his symphonic poems *Macunaíma*, composed in 1946.

Toward the end of Mário's life, however, his ideas acquired a more radical dimension, as he gained greater awareness of the social, cultural, and economic implications of Brazil's historic situation of dependency.[9] He turned progressively to Marxism, and his last literary works are more closely aligned with 'socialist realism' than with the 'modernist experimentalism' of *Macunaíma*. Ultimately, he found himself trapped by the contradictions of his own project: the desire for cultural autonomy, to be achieved through the construction of a national (individualistic) high art based on folk motives, and a determination to combat the structures sustaining the country's social inequalities, which would ultimately eliminate the popular (collective) base of his nationalist project. Mário de Andrade's solution was to fluctuate back and forth in his writings between these two self-exclusive propositions (Wisnik 1983: 137-8). This contradiction was to plague Brazilian intellectual circles throughout the twentieth century, setting the scene for the popularisation of the academic world, which deeply affected ethnomusicological enquiry in the country. Therefore, a closer look at Mário de Andrade's (ethno)musicological research, and the historical circumstances under which he was work-

7. Mário claims to have written *Macunaíma* in six days of uninterrupted work during the December holidays of 1926. He revised and extended the manuscript in January of 1927, and it was published in 1928 (G de Mello e Souza 1979: 9).
8. See Mariz (1983: 55-7), for a list of compositions inspired by or dedicated to Mário de Andrade.
9. An extensive analysis of Mário de Andrade's work in relation to dependency theory has been conducted in Schelling (1991).

ing, can help us understand the paths taken by Brazilian ethnomusicology in this century, and its relation to broader issues of national identity.

The Nationalist Project

Mário de Andrade's work was clearly influenced by European intellectual tides of the late nineteenth century. It has been claimed that his ideas developed out of his reading of Lévy-Bruhl, Taylor, Frazer, Freud, and later Marx (Schelling 1991: 195). But even if one can identify these immediate influences throughout his writings, his interpretations are unique, and must be viewed in relation to the debates going on within the Brazilian intellectual circles of his time. In this sense, the European eighteenth- and nineteenth-century romantic-nationalist movements seem a more likely point of departure. Much as in Herder's Germany, the Brazilian academic élites entered the twentieth century experiencing an 'identity crisis'; Brazilian culture – or the culture of the urban élites – was a 'transplanted' culture, coming to them from Europe, particularly from France. This feeling is expressed clearly by Júlio Mesquita in an editorial written in 1916:

> We are not yet a nation with an acquaintance of itself, with self-esteem; or we might more accurately say that we are a nation which as yet has not had the spirit to advance alone toward a vigorous and resplendent projection of its own personality. We have existed since our birth as a nation, whether as Empire or Republic, under the direct or indirect tutelage (if not political, at least moral) of Europe. We think with a foreign brain; we are dressed by foreign tailors; we eat a foreign diet; and to crown that act of collective servility, in our homeland we all too often stifle our mother tongue to speak a foreign language![10]

Brazil's colonisation process played an important role in the development of this 'inferiority complex' among the country's élites. The first Portuguese to come to Brazil did not intend their move to be permanent: they planned to exploit the riches of the new territory, and then return to a comfortable life in the motherland. But since the primary raw material of the Brazils was land (not gold), exploitation could only be achieved through prolonged settlement, and most colonisers were never to see their beloved Portugal again. Further-

---

10. Quoted in English in Martins (1970: 142–3).

more, Brazil was transformed into an 'earthly purgatory' for the dregs of Portuguese society. The mother country rid itself of its witches, Jews, rebels and criminals by shipping them off to the shores of Brazil (L. de Mello e Souza 1987: 80–83). The land was populated predominantly by 'savages' (Indians and Africans), whose racial inferiority was considered self-evident to any Christian. Images of Brazil as the 'devil's paradise' permeate the accounts of European travellers who visited the country between the sixteenth and early nineteenth centuries. All these factors contributed to the development and internalisation of a sense of inferiority among Brazilians, particularly among the upper classes, in relation to metropolitan Portugal.

The economic system set up in the colony reconciled the territory's natural resources – land and a favourable climate – with the demands of the international market. Vast isolated monocultural sugar cane plantations using slave labour were established along the coast, particularly in the north-east, which exported sugar to Portugal in exchange for manufactured goods. The Portuguese crown expressly prohibited the production of manufactured goods in the colony, so other than sugar cane, colonial production was limited to those goods necessary to immediate subsistence. In this way the mother country not only guaranteed a market for its manufactured goods, it also placed the colony in a position of economic and cultural dependency. Internally this 'latifundia' economy created a highly stratified society made up of a small minority of white landowners who dominated the political and economic arenas of the colony, a somewhat larger group of small landowners, merchant and craftsmen, and vast numbers of African slaves.

Independence in 1822 had little effect upon the colonial social structure, since the local landowners transferred their allegiance from Portugal to England, with an agreement to continue restricting local industrial development. The empire entered the 'free market' without restructuring its economic foundations: it remained a dependent agricultural export economy based on slave labour, and the élites continued to look to Europe for their cultural references.

Transformations of a more structural nature were achieved with the abolition of slavery in 1888 and the proclamation of the 'First Republic' just a year later. The emerging urban middle class was now in power, but their attempts to promote industrialisation and economic autonomy were obstructed by the strong alliances still prevailing between the local oligarchy and the British industrialists. Although the economic base remained firmly in the hands of the large landowners, the vast numbers of freed slaves could no longer be ignored. While the marginalised Indians could be romanticised, the African population was squarely integrated into the social fabric of the new republic. As free men, their place in Brazilian society would now have to be redefined.

Moreover, by the first decades of the twentieth century, the social configuration of the country's urban centres, especially São Paulo, had changed dramatically, and industrial development could now become a reality. The wealth generated by coffee in the southeast, along with the concentration of European immigrants in the region, provided a growing internal market, and São Paulo began to acquire the characteristics of a modern cosmopolitan city. Just as the power of the oligarchy within the country was finally beginning to recede, it was also necessary to free the country from the persistent importation of ready-made cultural models, and begin thinking about Brazil in new terms. The 'modernist movement' reflects this moment of transition, formalising an inversion in the value systems of the urban élites, whereby those qualities of the Brazilian previously considered negative could now be transformed into positive attributes (Schelling 1991: 90). Sectors of the intelligentsia set themselves the task of generating a more positive Brazilian identity by consciously creating a national art, and Mário de Andrade had a clear message for the artists of his time: 'Every Brazilian artist that now produces Brazilian art is an efficient being with human value. The one who produces international or foreign art – unless he is a genius – is useless, a non-entity. And a gigantic monument to idiocy'. (1962: 19)

If a national art tradition was to be established, one had to define the basis upon which to construct it. Previous European nationalist movements had already provided answers to this problem. For the German-speaking regions, Herder had proposed that a Germanic identity could only be recuperated through an investigation of the cultural representations of the German peasantry. They were the only true bearers of the 'national soul' still surviving in the land, and this could be verified by noting the 'emotional' (or irrational) element of their behaviour. While the aristocracy had been absorbed by the 'rationality' of the Enlightenment, the peasantry had remained at the margins of society, retaining their unique historical and ecological heritage. Thus the task facing the academic élites was that of recovering the lost Germanic culture among those that still bore its soul. This material could then be reworked by the élites in their elaboration of a true national culture. As in Herder's Germany – and then in other European countries – the Brazilian nationalist movement also saw folklore (or folk music) as the basis upon which to construct their own musical tradition. Given the peculiarities in the process of Brazil's colonisation, however, the country's situation was quite distinct from that of eighteenth century Germany. Brazil had no 'natural folk' comparable to the Germanic peasantry, to whom one could attribute the national soul. For the Brazilian context even a representative 'race' would have to be created artificially.

The ethnic synthesis embodied by Macunaíma reinterprets the racial ideologies of Mário's intellectual predecessors. By the late nineteenth century a clear discourse had been formulated by the Brazilian academic élites to explain the country's stunted development. Based on Spencer's social evolution and Buckle's climatic theories, Brazilian cultural inferiority was thought to be rooted in its racial make-up and the region's tropical climate. It had already been 'scientifically' proven that the intellectual capacities of Indians and Africans were significantly lower than those of European whites, while the vaporous conditions of the southern hemisphere were supposed to be conducive to indolence. The racial miscegenation of the population had further contributed to the development of a national character marked by sloth, a love of luxury, flexible moral standards, and uncontrolled sexual impulses. To move toward 'civilisation', a process of 'cultural Aryanisation' would be necessary, but the endeavour would have to be led by an enlightened élite.[11]

As the country entered the twentieth century this pessimistic characterisation of the Brazilian population was no longer acceptable to a nation anxious to see itself participating in the international arena. Now the 'myth of the three races' that meet and mix in the heat of the tropical jungles would have to begin to acquire more positive contours, and a powerful reinterpretation of this myth finds substance in the ambivalent figure of Macunaíma, the hero with no character. His multiplicity of personalities open an unlimited spectrum of alternatives, unhindered by the repressive forces of long-standing tradition. Even though Macunaíma is ultimately unable to control the onslaught of modern (foreign) civilisation, his irreverence and sensuality bring him back to life after successive deaths.

The full inversion of the racial ideology was to be mechanised in

11. On nineteenth-century racial ideologies in Brazil, see Ortiz (1986: 13–21).

the 1930s through the work of Gilberto Freyre (1966), whose *mestiço* is no longer inferior, but superior precisely because he is able to survive in the tropics. This image was further reinforced by Sérgio Buarque de Holanda's (1971) view of the Brazilian as a 'cordial' man. Both intellectuals argued that the informality of the colonial system (previously viewed as the inefficiency and laziness of an inferior race) and the lack of racial exclusivism of the Portuguese (formerly their degenerate tropical moral standards) created a context of benign inter-racial relations. Now miscegenation becomes the root of the country's 'natural democracy'. Heralded as a symbol of national identity, the *mestiço* embodies the synthesis of the country's diverse social configuration. In his veins flows the blood of both masters and slaves, merchants and servants, rural and urban populations. The myth of the Brazilian as a 'tri-ethnic race', characterised as 'friendly', 'happy', 'cordial', and 'industrious', was soon to become a common-sense category with the population at large. Concealing both racial and class distinctions, it allowed everyone to see themselves as Brazilian.

Just as Macunaíma's lack of character could hardly translate into this 'cordial *mestiço*', the *Ensaio* envisioned a more ambiguous 'essence' of the Brazilian musical psyche. At the moment of transition in which Mário de Andrade was writing, such an overtly populist national character had not yet emerged. In line with the thinking of his time, though, Mário accepted the myth of Brazilian tri-racial ethnicity, but his preoccupations centred around Brazil's process of musical nationalisation, that is, on how the contributions of the country's different racial groups had fused into original expressions of a Brazilian musicality. He was less concerned with dissecting the country's musical phenomenon than with showing the irreverent originality of the final outcome. Quite distinct from the evolutionary orientations of other researchers, which tended to organise material according to stratified ethnic origins, Mário de Andrade dealt with his material in relation to 'universal' elements of music, such as rhythm, melody, polyphony, instrumentation, and form, presenting the Brazilian solutions to these musical properties.

For example, he developed a theory of 'prosodic rhythm', based on what he saw as the conflicting rhythmic tendencies of the 'organised and square' Portuguese tradition on the one hand, and the Amerindian tendency toward a more speech-bound rhythmic conception on the other. The tropical fusion of these tendencies is to have resulted in a freer – or lazier – rhythmic sensibility among Brazilians, who had found a way of adhering to Portuguese quadrature while performing a true recitative. The Brazilian psyche was able to accommodate these diverse influences, turning them into elements of musical expression (Andrade 1962: 30–32). For Mário de Andrade the essence of Brazilian musicality resided in the interfaces of the different ethnic groups that inhabited the country, for none of them completely dominated Brazilian folk traditions. It could only be seen as the peculiar accommodation that had occurred in Brazil through the fusion of Amerindian, African, and European cultures. This synthesis was unique to Brazil, for no other nation in the world replicated the country's complex historic, ethnic, and ecological make-up. Precisely because of the ambiguity of Mário's 'fusionism', the *Ensaio* could be read – and was read – in the spirit of the emerging populist ideology of the 1930s; but it was also acceptable to those left-wing sectors that opposed the form of populist nationalism invading the country.

Mário de Andrade – the (Ethno)Musicologist

Although still very much in embryonic form, the *Ensaio Sobre a Música Brasileira* already hinted at some of the preoccupations that would dominate Mário de Andrade's ethnomusicological projects throughout his lifetime: Firstly, the genealogy of the Brazilian musical psyche; secondly, the musical manifestation of the Brazilian psyche; and thirdly, the role of the composer/intellectual in society. These issues were then elaborated in successive studies over the following decade.

The Genealogy of Brazilian Musicality

Mário's 'fusionist' approach to the study of folk music set him on a search for the musical manifestation of the unique psyche of the Brazilian 'race'. This search involved determining the ethnic origins of the elements he detected in specific musical phenomena, to show how the Brazilian psyche had acted upon them to produce something new. Although many of his conclusions in this sphere would be questioned today, here we are interested in understanding how his analyses relate to the logic of his project.

He contended that the Amerindian influence upon the national repertoire was rather insignificant, but this group had left its mark in 'prosodic rhythm' and in the 'typical nasality' of Brazilian vocal styles. Amerindians had also contributed a few instruments (primarily rattles) and certain poetic and dance forms to the national repertoire, such as the *cateretê*[12] and the *caboclinhos*[13] (1933: 17). He also claimed that certain 'magical-religious' traditions with restricted choreographic elements (e.g., *catimbós* and *pajelanças*[14]) were rooted in Amerindian practices (1983: 23–57).

African influences, on the other hand, were far more noticeable. This group was considered responsible for a wide variety of rhythms and instruments, many of which made their way into essentially Iberian dance forms (1933: 173). The 'fusion' was often so complete that some of these dances ended up acquiring African names (e.g., *Congadas* and *Moçambiques*[15]). Other African traditions showed little sign of syncretism, retaining their original African forms. Among these he cited the *lundu*[16] and the music of the 'fetishistic' possession cults with a marked choreographic element, such as *candomblé* and *macumba*[17] (1983: 23–57).

The Iberian heritage was by far the strongest, and from Portugal the Brazilian repertoire was to have received its harmonic structure, strophic quadrature, the basis for Brazilian syncopations, and a wide variety of instruments and musical genres (1933: 178–9; 1942: 148).

---

12. The *cateretê* is a social dance found throughout rural Brazil. It is distinguished by intricate clapping and stamping of feet during instrumental interludes. When he died, Mário was preparing a dictionary of Brazilian music. Working from the index cards he left, Oneyda Alvarenga and Flávia Camargo Toni have recently published the dictionary (Andrade 1989), which gives one a better idea of his understanding of the musical genres in his analyses.
13. *Caboclinhos* are dramatic dance groups that combine Amerindian, African and Portuguese elements. These troupes perform during patron saint festivals in various regions of the country.
14. Both the *catimbó* and the *pajelança* are possession cults common throughout northern and northeastern Brazil. The rituals of these cults are predominantly private affairs, held for the benefit of individual clients.
15. *Congadas* and *Moçambiques* are dramatic dance groups common throughout central and southeastern Brazil that combine African and Iberian influences. They often enact symbolic battles between Christians and Moors or Africans and slavers.
16. The *lundu* is a dance form that developed among Bantu slaves in the northeastern sugar cane plantations during the eighteenth century.
17. *Candomblé* and *macumba* are Afro-Brazilian possession cults of Yoruba origin involving elaborate public ceremonies. In Bahia the term *candomblé* was used while in Rio one spoke of *macumba*.

Precisely because the nationalist movement was attempting to combat European cultural domination, this prevalence had to be explained away. Thus, Mário de Andrade was at pains to demonstrate how the Portuguese heritage had been modified and adapted to the 'anthropo-geographic' reality of Brazil. The only sphere in which Portuguese genres had remained almost intact was in the innocuous realm of children's songs and games (1963c).

As Florestan Fernandes (1978a: 164) has observed, Mário also insisted on showing that Brazilian music had actually received a greater European than properly Portuguese input. Furthermore, Mário attempted to point out the 'reciprocity of influences' between the colony and the mother country. Brazil had not only contributed the *'modinha'*[18] to the Portuguese repertoire (1930: 5–7), the mother country also owed the colony for the ultimate symbol of Portuguese identity: the *fado* (1963a).

Brazilian Musical Ethnicity

Although Mário was clearly aware that the origins of Brazilian musical elements were diverse, producing a wide range of distinct musical forms throughout the country, the nationalist project required a discourse that would allow for the integration of the various regional genres. Mário was to find this unity in the way the national psyche had transformed European, African and Amerindian elements, a process which repeated itself all across the country, despite the diversity of the final products: 'From north to south the development of our national music is guided by the same lazy sweetness, the same throat, the same melancholy, the same fury, the same sticky sexuality, the same love cries' (1962: 65).

In a particularly detailed musical analysis of the 'magical-ritual' songs used in 'fetishistic' traditions of African and Amerindian origin, Mário de Andrade (1983) expounded upon the diverse ways in which the Brazilian psyche had structured available musical elements in its pursuit of hypnotic states. His first reflections derived from a personal experience of a *catimbó* ceremony in Natal (RN). In a style characteristic of his lyrical sensibility, Mário recounted his general impressions of the ritual event.

18. The *modinha* is a musical genre associated with the upper-class parlours of colonial Brazil. It developed in the late eighteenth century, and evinces the strong influence of Italian opera.

> It is impossible to describe everything that happened at that absurd ceremony, a mixture of sincerity and quackery: it was ridiculous, religious, comical, dramatic, enervating, repugnant, extremely moving, and profoundly poetic. Now recalling the folly in which I participated out of mere curiosity, it is no longer my disgust that is inscribed upon my memory; rather, I feel overcome by the lyricism of those unending songs, and more songs, heard in their natural form (1983: 32–3).

He continued his account with an explanation of how he and the ritual specialist (or *mestre*) were affected by the ceremonial music:

> The rhythm of the refrains, the monotony of the soft chants, the gentle 'sheeky-sheeky' of the rattle began to lull me; the music was entrancing me. Slowly my body began warming in a benumbing musicality, while simultaneously my powers of intellectual reaction were gradually abandoned. *Mestre* João was slowly fainting away; his gestures were becoming more careless and his diction mumbled . . . . But what I first took for despondency was actually a near state of hypnosis. This was caused by the excess of torporific music and by the monotony of the rhythms, which were played and repeated with maniacal insistence (1983: 37).

Extrapolating from this experience, Mário proposed that the musics used in such fetishistic cults were structured in special ways in order to bring about these hypnotic states. Somewhat predictably, he turned to rhythm to show how this musical feature acted psychosomatically upon the body, inducing an alteration of consciousness. For Brazilian fetishism he distinguished three different rhythmic modes which he believed to be responsible for inducing these states of torpidity: (1) repetitive rhythms, (2) free rhythms, and (3) rhythms with an occasional irregularity breaking an otherwise clearly-defined metrical system. Although one cannot be sure what exactly he meant by each of these modes since musical examples are not provided systematically, his descriptions and available information on the musics of Brazilian possession cults may allow the researcher to make certain inferences.

He contended that ritual musics using the repetitive mode occur when a short rhythmic motif is repeated hundreds of times, provoking obsession, such that the pieces acquire an 'eminently choreographic character' (1983: 37). Mário claimed that this kind of music is often accompanied by dance, which he saw as a further catalyst to the state of frenzied dizziness the music allegedly induces.

Although no specific example in the repetitive mode is given, one can infer that he was thinking primarily of the *candomblé* repertoire, particularly of the drumming styles of this Afro-Brazilian religious tradition. While *candomblé* canticles often present repetitive melodic phrases sung antiphonally between a soloist and a chorus, the drumming patterns are structured around short penetrating ostinatos. While Afro-Brazilian ritual traditions were seen to possess a strong repetitive rhythmic character, 'free rhythm' was thought to be more common to those religious cults with a stronger Amerindian input, such as the *catimbó*. Here he noted that the chants were presented almost in a recitative, or 'prosodically', inducing the state of drowsiness he described in the quotation above. Although this state also involves an alteration of consciousness, it was contrasted with the frenzy brought on by the violent repetitive character of the Afro-Brazilian traditions.

Afro-Brazilian traditions, however, were seen to utilise a form of free rhythm, but in this case it presented an 'incisive' character. To illustrate this contradiction in terms Mário de Andrade refers the reader to a canticle in honour of Xangô, the Yoruba god of fire and lightning, for which he presents a transcription in the *Ensaio* (1962: 55). While he obviously heard the tune accompanied by the twelve-pulse rhythmic cycle common to many pieces in the *candomblé* repertoire, mistakes in the transcription of the rhythm of the piece make it difficult to assess how the melody and the percussion accompaniment fit together. Regardless, his notion of 'incisive free rhythm' seems clear enough, alluding to what Richard Waterman (1952: 208–9) was later to call 'metronome sense': the participants' ability to retain rhythmic orientation within a context of contrasting pulse values.

The third rhythmic mode – rhythms with an occasional irregularity – was seen to lie between the repetitive and free rhythmic modes. Here the performers introduce sporadic temporal accretions, generally a single pulse, into an otherwise clearly-defined metrical system, creating disturbing displacements in the accentuation of the piece. Originally these occurrences were thought to be unintentional: the result of the performer's need to breathe or his/her desire to complete the text of a phrase, which would lead him/her to add a pulse to a measure here and there. The Brazilian psyche, however, had perceived their disorienting effect upon the senses, and had learned to use the technique more consciously (1983: 40).

In some styles these 'disturbing displacements' had even become highly systematised. Mário refers the reader to an unidentified canticle in honour of Ogum,[19] the Yoruba warrior god of metal, which he describes as being systematically structured by a sequence of two ternary measures followed by a binary measure. These systematic oscillations were thought to be particularly effective in provoking the physical perturbance needed to induce possession.

Still using this piece Mário continues his analysis by pointing out how the harmonic evolution of the melodic line acts as a further catalyst to this process. The final syllable of the piece – 'aê' – is sung to a leap from the second to the fourth degree of the scale, leaving one with the psychological need for one more note derived from the triad of the tonic. This note was provided by beginning the canticle once again; but in resuming the text, human psychology now required that the statement be completed, once again leaving the participants hanging at the end on the dominant-seventh chord. Thus, while at the beginning of the piece it is the text that demands completion, at the end it is the harmonic evolution that calls for repetition. 'But repetition is precisely what the national psyche desires, infinite repetition that hypnotises or intoxicates,' thus creating musical structures that are best suited to the pursuit of such 'physio-psychological' states (1983: 41–2).

Because Mário saw the search for torpidity as a trait of the Brazilian psychology, he found evidence to substantiate the theory in a wide range of musical practices throughout the country. He saw this as a way of explaining the Brazilian techniques of variation, in which only a few notes are changed or only a single accent is dislocated, leaving the participants in a state of uncertainty as they fluctuate between the actual performance and the virtual model underlying the variations. Other techniques of disorientation were noted in the way performers deliberately sang out of tune or used an extremely nasal vocal quality, so one could never be sure of the notes of the melodic sequence, were they to be sung with precision: 'Just as the Huitota or the fallen Inca's grandson always keeps coca leaves in his mouth, the Brazilian has a dancing melody in his mouth, which intoxicates and desensitises his whole being. . . . Oh, what laziness!' (1983: 43)

If at one moment the Brazilian psyche is seen to use music as a means of deadening sensibility, in another musical performance it

---

19. In her annotations to *Música de Feitiçaria* (Andrade 1983: 17), Oneyda Alvarenga has suggested that the piece might be a recorded example contained on one of the following records: Odeon 10690 or Parlofon 13254.

becomes the means for uniting – or 'generalising' – collective sentiments, giving them greater communicative force. In a short study conducted in 1930, Mário de Andrade analysed a series of political rally cries to show how the musical structures of the ditties were particularly suited to the expression of the 'same fury' that brought the crowd together in the first place. The study was based on examples he heard being used in São Paulo by a crowd awaiting the arrival of Getúlio Vargas. Soon afterwards Vargas was to achieve the presidency, consolidating his power by 1937, when he established an authoritarian populist regime, the *Estado Novo*.[20] Despite his personal distaste for certain aspects of the Vargas platform, Mário could not help feeling intense joy at seeing the crowds acting upon their 'national instincts'. In true Durkheimian spirit, Mário de Andrade relates his experiences as follows:

> What we saw ... was a crowd of certainly more than one hundred thousand people in procession screaming at the top of their lungs, all taken by a Dionysian rage, sanctified by their secure belief in someone. To forget they are made up of independent individuals, it is at such times that the people generalise their hymns, their marches, their songs, their rhythmic ditties. This smothers individualism and awakens the movement and consequently the common sentiment (1963b: 105).

He proceeded with a rhythmic and textual analysis of the ditties he collected at the rally, showing how rhythm and text worked together symbiotically to express the crowd's dissatisfaction with the country's state of affairs. For example, he went into great detail to show how the use of the rhythmic cell 'semi-quaver/dotted quaver' had been used by musicians 'whenever they wish[ed] to express aggrieved fatalism, slavery' (1963b: 109). Thus, following Wagner, Beethoven, Monteverdi, and other established composers, the crowd gathered to hail Vargas had instinctively chosen this 'universal' musical expression of the plight of the oppressed!

Although the analytic procedures of this study closely resemble those used for the 'magical-ritual' musics, the conclusions he reached are almost contradictory. While the experience of musical torpidity is essentially personal, the mobilisation of a crowd demanding respect for recognised social norms implies the existence of a collective

---

20. Even after the *Estado Novo* fell in 1945, Vargas remained popular, and managed to be elected president once again, remaining in power until he committed suicide in 1955.

consciousness that transcends hypnotic hedonism. Mário de Andrade was conscious of the ambiguity underlying the pleasure-seeking Brazilian psyche. If on the one hand it was presented as a positive Brazilian trait, distinguishing the national psyche from the dualistic morality of European culture, it also stood as an impediment to the development of a national 'moral culture', based on a recognised collective code of ethics that would take account of the whole of the population. Thus, when he saw the crowd collectively channelling their 'Dionysian rage' toward social injustices, he could only have become overjoyed at the thought of a possible reconciliation of the national dilemma.

The Composer/Intellectual in Society

As a music educationist[21] and as director of the São Paulo Department of Culture (1935–7), the role of the artist/intellectual in society was of major concern to Mário de Andrade. Throughout his life he was confronted with the problem of reconciling his commitment to 'dis-interested' art – art as individual expression – and 'interested' art – art at the service of society. Is one to view the efficacy of art in relation to the piece itself, or does it derive from the extra-aesthetic domains surrounding the piece? If it is in the piece, the artist expresses nothing by his/her own 'truths', which are unintelligible (or irrelevant) to anyone else; if it is outside the piece, the artist is reduced to exhibiting his/her technical proficiency, while the product would lack any sort of critical edge. How then is the artist to remain true to his/her personal 'truths' while simultaneously contributing to the construction of an authentic national 'moral culture'?

From his readings of 'historical materialism', Mário became progressively aware of the historical development of western 'individualism' and its relationship to high art ideology (Schelling 1991: 195). His project would be viable if artists took it upon themselves to 're-socialise' art by rediscovering their role as 'artisans' at the service of the 'spiritual progress' of the general public. 'Beauty and (leftist) ideology' could be fused without falling into 'didacticism' or 'socialist realism' if the artist's personal psychology had become fully nationalised. The artistic content would per force re-

---

21. He lectured in music history, piano, and aesthetics at the Conservatório Dramático e Musical de São Paulo during most of his life, having also taught for three years at the Instituto de Artes of the Universidade do Distrito Federal.

fer to 'secular truths', albeit mediated by the subjectivity of the artist's truths. Thus, a national artist would be able to speak critically to a wider audience, but the power of the message would depend upon the 'beauty' of the formal construction (Andrade n.d.). Thus, for Mário de Andrade the artist had an important social role in society by helping to 'generalise' a nationally-based code of ethics. Already in the *Ensaio* Mário was calling on composers to 'see beyond [their] desires for celebrity,' and assume 'a social function' in the country, by writing choral music, because 'choral singing unifies individuals; . . . [it] generalises sentiments' (1962: 65). Later when he began organising children's choirs in São Paulo that sang arrangements of Brazilian folk songs, he saw the enterprise as a way of developing a social commitment in the children that would help 're-organise the excessive individualism of the Brazilian psychology.'[22]

If in the first instance the artist/intellectual was to lead the debates involved in structuring a national cultural project, it was as the first director of the newly instituted Department of Culture in São Paulo that Mário de Andrade became aware of the potential role of government in the implementation of such a project (Castro 1989: 47). For three years he dedicated all his time and energy to the new Department, which finally allowed him to implement a visionary programme involving all sectors of the São Paulo population. While the various divisions within the Department were responsible for specific activities, the overriding philosophy was the democratisation of culture.[23]

True to his commitment to choral singing, he organised the 'Coral Paulistano' (City of São Paulo Choir), a more 'popular' municipal choir, and several neighbourhood choirs among the working classes.[24] In the various neighbourhood play centres that were created around the city, children were socialised through folk tunes and folk games. Along with furthering Mário de Andrade's social plans, this proliferation of musical activities created a demand for new compositions, and for the first time Brazilian composers were invited to produce works for a wide variety of musical ensembles.

22. Unpublished manuscript, quoted in Schelling (1991: 180).
23. On Mário de Andrade's activities at the Department of Culture, see Schelling (1991: 169-81).
24. He also created the Municipal Symphonic Orchestra, the Municipal String Quartet, the São Paulo Trio, and a madrigal group (Mariz 1983: 34).

Of particular interest to ethnomusicology are the activities organised by the Public Discotheque, placed under the directorship of Oneyda Alvarenga, one of Mário de Andrade's former students. First of its kind in Latin America, the Discotheque housed field and commercial recordings of Brazilian folk and serious music, recordings of regional dialects, collections of folk instruments, transcriptions of folk music, and films and photographs related to the recordings. Dina Lévi-Strauss was invited to organise a course in 'Ethnography and Folklore' to prepare teams of researchers to collect material for the archives.

The activities of the Discotheque were oriented by a view of the musical event as a totality. Musicologists and folklore researchers using the archives were provided with recordings of the music they wished to study as well as a wide range of complementary material related to the research topic. If, for example, a person was interested in the *babassuê*, a north-eastern Afro-Brazilian religious ritual, he/she would have access to cult artefacts, films, recordings, song texts, and lengthy descriptions of the informants and the context of the performance (Schelling 1991: 179). Even though these activities were suspended in 1938, the research teams gathered an impressive amount of material during their short-lived existence.

Soon after the institution of the *Estado Novo*, Mário de Andrade lost his administrative position because of his 'communist' sympathies. Although some of the programmes he created were maintained by his successor, the orientation of the Department was channelled to the populist project of the Vargas regime, which was primarily concerned with the promotion of events that would glorify the nation and the state. Disillusioned by this process, Mário began to question the basis of his previous arguments in relation to the artist's role in society: without state policies backing a cultural project the transformation of society through art was simply not feasible.

Mário de Andrade and Ethnomusicological Research in Brazil

Although today Mário de Andrade's research methods have become obsolete, we must acknowledge the ethnomusicological spirit of his perspectives. While he viewed the western musical system as the universal backdrop for all musics, he clearly attempted to relate his empirical data to Brazilian social reality. Already in the 1930s he was developing a methodology for explaining musical phenomena from a sociological perspective. Despite his Eurocentric bias, he was able to appreciate 'simpler' musical systems on their own terms: they had developed into performance practices that suited the nation's psychological pursuits. In this perspective he pre-empted the performative orientation we now consider a major breakthrough in contemporary ethnomusicology.

Indeed, Mário de Andrade set the foundations for the development of an anthropologically-oriented ethnomusicology in Brazil. Yet this did not happen. As Gerard Béhague (1991: 62–4) has pointed out, Brazilian ethnomusicology became essentially descriptive, and this is even true of the work of Mário's main pupil, Oneyda Alvarenga.[25] Thus, the perplexing question: what went wrong with Brazilian ethnomusicology? Was Mário too far ahead of his time to be properly appreciated? Is it only now with the benefit of hindsight that we are able to grasp the relevance of the directions he was pointing toward in his research? This is highly unlikely, given the intensity of public debate surrounding cultural issues that dominated Brazilian intellectual circles in the early twentieth century.

An understanding of the descriptive orientation taken by Brazilian ethnomusicology until recently can only be achieved by viewing the wider social context of the country during the 1930s. A patriotic wave was sweeping across Brazil, engulfing the upper and lower classes alike. Political nationalism split the intelligentsia of the art world down the middle, some waving the flag of right-wing fascism – a substantial sector of the music world among them – while others up-held Leninism as the solution to the country's problems. In all though, there was a general feeling that what was needed in the country was a strong centralised government that could unite the dispersed regions into a single nation-state. When Getúlio Vargas came to power, he robbed both sides of their discourses with his 'integralist' platform: his nationalistic right-wing regime modelled on Mussolini's Italy proposed an undeniably leftist programme.

Mário's views of the Brazilian psychology were drowned out by the populist current. Macunaíma – the irreverent, lazy trickster – did not conform to the hard-working cordial *mestiço* the Vargas regime wished to propagate. Once the *Estado Novo* was consolidated, Vargas's populist ideology dominated the public sphere, pushing alternative perspectives into isolated niches, particularly the new

25. It should not be forgotten that Oneyda Alvarenga dedicated a lifetime to the organisation and publication of Mário de Andrade's manuscripts on Brazilian music, making them readily available today.

universities (Levine 1989: 215–17). Prior to the Vargas era, cultural debates were conducted publicly in newspapers and editorials. Heated discussions animated night-life in the bars, restaurants, and social gatherings of local artists and intellectuals. Once censorship of the mass media became all-pervasive, these debates were confined to academic conferences and specialised journals, creating an 'ivory tower' culture that had little impact on the common-sense notions taking root in the greater society (Fernandes 1978b: 2; Ortiz 1986: 40–41).

The *Estado Novo* was particularly effective in co-opting the musical universe of the country. The most popular singers were contracted by the state-owned National Radio to sing the glories of Brazil. Lamartine Babo, Ary Barroso, Carmen Miranda, and many others became agents in the propaganda machine of the *Estado Novo*. Carnival in Rio was made official in 1934, and the state began to fund those samba schools willing to use their parades to glorify patriotic symbols and national heroes.

Serious music circles were faced with the dilemma of choosing whether or not to participate in the regime's cultural programme. They had no space in the more critical university culture, while symphonies and other musical ensembles could not subsist without state patronage (Squeff 1983: 37–8; Wisnik 1983: 152). Thus, the high art music world was compelled to embrace Mário's call for the development of a national repertoire based on the country's traditional styles to guarantee their access to state funds. In São Paulo the nationalist banner was carried religiously by Camargo Guarnieri, who saw himself as Mário's spokesman to the new generations of musicians, spearheading crusades against those who attempted to break out of the nationalist fold.

Co-opted into the Vargas political machine, Hector Villa-Lobos was hired by the Ministry of Education to organise a federal music education programme to be implemented in all state schools. He took it upon himself to devise an appropriate repertoire that could be sung by school choirs, which comprised his own arrangements of folk songs. In the populist mode of the times, he organised monumental choral concentrations in Rio de Janeiro, in which up to 40,000 youngsters could be heard singing these arrangements in two, three, or even four voices.[26]

---

26. Because of his commitment to choral singing, Mário was careful never to criticise even the most populist aspects of Villa-Lobos's choral programme.

The only group of musicians that openly rejected musical nationalism were the 'communists' associated with *Música Viva*. These composers congregated around Hans-Joachim Koellreutter, a German Jew who fled to Brazil to escape Nazi persecution, bringing with him the techniques of dodecaphonic composition. The exponents of *Música Viva* were to experience the full force of Guarnieri's wrath in the 1950s, and many reviewed their position toward the dominant trend.[27] This reassessment led to twelve-tone experiments by such composers as Claudio Santoro and César Guerra-Peixe which incorporated elements from the national repertoire, 'creat[ing] a new, modern expression of musical nationalism' (Béhague 1979: 280).

Consciously or unconsciously, the music intellectuals' collaboration with the state project helped obliterate the analytic dimension of Mário de Andrade's musical research. During the Vargas era the collection of folk material was no longer geared toward a critical understanding of Brazilian society. It was meant as a 'rescue operation' on the one hand, and as a source of raw material for the high arts on the other. Neither of these pursuits entailed sociological analysis, even when they did not contribute directly to the consolidation of the cordial *mestiço* ideology.

By dominating the country's most visible cultural spheres, the *Estado Novo* revealed the dark implications of Mário's astute perceptions: effective social transformation through art requires coherent state cultural policies. Indeed, the patronising state bred a league of patronising cultural élites with traditionalist folkloristic perspectives. The true face of this group would become evident when the military regime recruited the only available non-academic intellectuals as their cultural administrators and advisers in the mid-1960s.[28] Once again the state muffled the emergent cultural debates that had resurfaced during the short-lived democratic interim between the Vargas era and the military dictatorship.

The re-democratisation of the country (a process that began in the late 1970s), has again created an atmosphere for an open critical investigation of the nation's cultural heritage. Researchers interested in Brazil's musical repertoire have joined academics in other fields in the process of re-discovering the country. Since the mid-1970s there has been a steady increase in the number of competent studies

27. On the '*Música Viva*' movement, see Neves (1981: 84–146).
28. On cultural administration during the military regime, see Ortiz (1986: 90–108).

by local scholars in all realms of Brazilian music. An assessment of the impact of re-democratisation on the studies of ethnomusicological interest deserves an investigation of its own, given the diversity of theoretical approaches used and the variety of musical traditions to which they are being applied.[29]

Macunaíma's musical repertoire is vast, and we have hardly begun to scratch the surface. The present opening is an opportunity for researchers to begin fusing the fragments of available information into a clearer picture of the diversity of the whole. We are now faced with the difficult task of critically dismantling the tri-ethnic mythologies of the twentieth century if we are to understand what music means to those who perform it. The musical expressions of the diverse sectors of Brazilian society encapsulate the uniqueness of their experience of the wider social context. An ethnomusicology of Brazil today must look at how the country's Macunaímas are using the music they have created, and how it envisages the nation in which they want to live.

References

Ancona Lopez, T.P., (ed.), *Macunaíma – O Herói sem Nenhum Caráter. Edição Crítica*, Paris: Association Archives de la Littérature Latino-Américaine, des Caraïbes et Africaine du XXe Siécle, 1988.
Andrade, M. de, *O Baile das Quatro Artes*, São Paulo, Martins, n.d.
——, *Cartas a Manuel Bandeira*, Rio de Janeiro, Simões Editora, 1958.
——, *Compêndio da História da Música*, 2nd ed., São Paulo, Miranda, 1933.
——, *Danças Dramáticas do Brasil*, 3 vols., 2nd ed., Belo Horizonte, Itatiaia, 1982.
——, *Dicionário Musical Brasileiro*, Belo Horizonte, Itatiaia, 1989.
——, (1963b) 'Dinamogenias Políticas,' *Música, Doce Música*, São Paulo, Martins, 1963b, pp. 104–11.
——, *Ensaio Sobre a Música Brasileira*, São Paulo, Martins, 1962, [1st ed., 1928].
——, (1963c) 'Influência Portuguesa nas Rodas Infantis do Brasil,' *Música, Doce Música*, São Paulo, 1963c, Martins, pp. 81–94.
——, *Macunaíma*, Translated by E.A. Goodland, London, Quartet Books, 1984.
——, *Modinhas Imperiais*, São Paulo, Chiarato, 1930.
——, *Música de Feitiçaria no Brasil*, 2nd ed., Belo Horizonte, Itatiaia,

29. References to some of these recent studies can be found in Béhague (1991; 1985).

1983.

——, (1963a) 'As Origens do Fado,' *Música, Doce Música*, São Paulo, Martins, 1963, pp. 93–9.

——, *Pequena História da Música*, São Paulo, Martins, 1942.

Béhague, G., *Music in Latin America: An Introduction*, Englewood Cliffs, Prentice-Hall, 1979.

——, 'Popular Music,' H.E. Hinds, Jr., and C. M. Tatum, (eds), *Handbook of Latin American Popular Culture*, Westpoint, Greenwood Press, 1985.

——, 'Reflections on the Ideological History of Latin American Ethnomusicology,' in B. Nettl and P. V. Bohlman (eds), *Comparative Musicology and Anthropology of Music*, Chicago, University of Chicago Press, 1991.

Buarque de Holanda, S., *Raízes do Brasil*, 6th ed., Rio de Janeiro, José Olympio [1st ed, 1936].

Castro, M.W. de, *Mário de Andrade, Exílio no Rio*, Rio de Janeiro, Rocco, 1989.

Fernandes, F., 'Mário de Andrade e o Folclore Brasileiro,' *O Folclore em Questão*, São Paulo, Hucitec, 1978a, pp. 147–68.

——, 'Nota Explicativa,' *O Folclore em Questão*, São Paulo, Hucitec, 1978b, pp. 1–3.

Freyre, G., *The Masters and the Slaves,* Abridged, 2nd ed., Translated by S. Putman, New York, Alfred A Knopf, 1966 [1st ed, 1933].

Horta, L.P., *Villa-Lobos: Uma Introdução*, Rio de Janeiro, Jorge Zahar, 1987.

Levine, R.M., 'Elite Perceptions of the Povo,' M. L. Conniff and F. D. McCann, (eds), *Modern Brazil: Elites and Masses in Historical Perspective*, Lincoln, University of Nebraska Press, 1989.

Mariz, V., *Três Musicólogos Brasileiros: Mário de Andrade, Renato Almeida, Luiz Heitor Correa de Azevedo*, Rio de Janeiro, Civilização Brasileira, 1983.

Martins, Wilson, *The Modernist Idea: A Critical Survey of Brazilian Writing in the 20th Century*, Translated by J. E. Tomlins, New York, New York University Press, 1970.

Mello e Souza, G. de, *O Tupi e o Alaúde: Uma Interpretação de Macunaíma*, São Paulo, Duas Cidades, 1979.

Mello e Souza, L. de, *O Diabo e a Terra de Santa Cruz: Feitiçaria e Religiosidade Popular no Brasil*, São Paulo, Companhia das Letras, 1989.

Neves, J.M., *Música Contemporânea Brasileira*, São Paulo, Ricordi, 1981.

Ortiz, R., *Cultura Brasileira e Identidade Nacional*, 2nd ed., São Paulo, Brasiliense, 1986.

Proença, M.C., *Roteiro de Macunaíma*, 3rd ed., Rio de Janeiro, Civilização Brasileiro, 1981.

Schelling, V., *A Presença do Povo no Cultura Brasileira: Ensaio Sobre o*

Pensamento de Mário de Andrade e Paulo Freire, Translated by F. Carotti, Campinas, Editora da Universidade Estadual de Campinas, 1991.

Squeff, E., 'Reflexões Sobre um Mesmo Tema,' E. Squeff and J.M. Wisnik, (eds), *O Nacional e o Popular na Cultura Brasileira, Música*, São Paulo, Brasiliense, 1983.

Waterman, R., 'African Influence on the Music of the Americas', in S. Tax (ed.), *Acculturation in the Americas*, Chicago, University of Chicago Press, 1952.

Wisnik, J.M., 'Getúlio da Paixão Cearense (Villa-Lobos e o Estado Novo),' E. Squeff and J.M. Wisnik, (eds), *O Nacional e o Popular na Cultura Brasileira: Música*, São Paulo, Brasiliense, 1983.

6

Place, Exchange and Meaning: Black Sea Musicians in the West of Ireland

Martin Stokes

Performance does not simply convey cultural messages already 'known'. On the contrary, it reorganises and manipulates everyday experiences of social reality, blurs, elides, ironises and sometimes subverts commonsense categories and markers. Above all, performance is a vital tool in the hands of performers themselves in socially acknowledged games of prestige and power. The full force of these crucial insights has only relatively recently become a matter of mainstream social anthropological concern.[1] In the context of ethnomusicological study, nothing has hindered these insights more than the idea, propagated both within and outside the discipline, that ethnomusicology studies music 'in its social and cultural context'. In this formulation, music is simply a 'thing' slotted into a static social and cultural matrix existing outside and beyond the performance. If this seemingly innocuous formulation has been an obstacle to developing an understanding of music as a form of social performance,[2] it is perhaps also worth questioning some of the other assumptions hidden in it. This chapter therefore looks at what happens to music, musicians and musical meaning in a situation

---

1. See for example Herzfeld 1987. This chapter is based on research in Turkey funded by the ESRC between 1984 and 1987. I am also grateful to Kieran Carson and Sean Corcoran of the Northern Ireland Arts Council which funded the events described in the latter part of this paper.

2. For a more sustained critique of the notion of context and the scholarly reification of musicological objects, see Waterman 1990: 8, 214.

which we might hastily deem to be 'out of place'.

This suggestion raises issues which lie at the heart of the ways in which ethnomusicologists and social anthropologists construct locality, place and fields of meaning. It also reminds us that much of the Western experience of 'other musics' is, in a sense, of music out of context, a fact with which ethnomusicologists have been reluctant to engage. The two points are of course closely connected. As James Clifford points out, in a recent addition to what has now become an established critique of anthropological practice, the concern of anthropologists with 'local' meanings and practice tends to ignore the literary strategies through which 'locality' is evoked, and the political practices of which these strategies are an integral part (Clifford 1992). The problem is that social experience which is not tied to locality becomes difficult to grasp with the techniques of writing, and consequently analysis, at our disposal. The category of 'travel' is a case in point. Musicians often live in conspicuously translocal cultural worlds. They travel; their social skills are those of people capable of addressing varied and heterogeneous groups, and their value in a locality is often perceived to be precisely their ability to transcend the cultural boundaries of that locality.

However, it is not difficult for anybody involved in the music of 'other cultures' to think of uneasy moments in which the music we hear (on CD or on stage) appears to be nothing more than a model, a replica of some 'real' situation, with a real context and real meanings elsewhere. The World Music phenomenon presents the world as an exhibition of local styles in precisely this way, constructing truth and authenticity on one hand and models of those truths and authenticities on the other. It might be argued that the World Music phenomenon plays a vital role in mediating post-colonial structures of global domination today just as the nineteenth-century world exhibitions mediated a colonial order a century ago (Mitchell 1991). The problem is that this makes it difficult for us to think of transcultural music experiences as anything other than models of authenticities going on 'elsewhere'. Music out of place, we are too readily inclined to believe, is music without meaning.

Ethnomusicologists have only slowly begun to get to grips with this proliferation of new multicultural contexts. *World of Music* devoted an issue in 1978 to 'Musicultura' – a series of cross-cultural musical events organised by the Eduard van Beinum Foundation in Queekhoven, Holland. In 1986, the International Council for Traditional Music organised an international colloquium in Jamaica on the subject of 'The Impact of Tourism on Traditional Music and Dance'. Discussions of musical tourism have tended to look at situations where tourists come in as passive observers, and consequently much of the discussion has been concerned with illustrating or refuting Greenwood's thesis that tourism involves a commodification of traditional culture, which eventually destroys it (Greenwood 1978). Commodification is not the only problem. For John Blacking, the political context of international musical tourism totally overshadows the potential for a 'genuine' process of non-verbal communication. For him, what might subvert the ideological context in which such changes take place, is itself undermined by the ways in which events are staged:

> a great deal of our appreciation of world music confuses cultural chauvinism with musical taste. Performances of traditional music are too often associated with cultural bunfights, folklore festivals, and political jamborees in which various exotic musics, dances and associated arts are dished up for the promotion of national or ethnic causes. Many people's experiences of other worlds of music are derived entirely from such contexts, and there are two serious disadvantages. First, the music that is presented is not truly representative of the tradition that is advertised; and secondly, because of the context, the aims of musical exchange and mutual understanding are defeated (Blacking 1987: 133–4).

The aspect of this criticism that most interests me is the assumption that musical exchange and mutual understanding are compromised by the context, and that there is, quite simply, 'a context' in which exchange and understanding take place for any specific kind of music. Blacking's comments reinforce scholarly binarisms of musical authenticity and alienation (Adorno 1941), folklore and 'folklorismus' (Baumann 1976), folklore and 'fakelore' (Harker 1985), real and 'invented traditions' (Hobsbawm and Ranger 1983). As Stratton suggests (1983), binarisms contrasting authentic and debased experiences invariably have an ideological function, and it is always worth questioning them if only for this reason. This kind of globalising theory also makes it difficult to see certain events and processes for what they are, if one is able to 'see' them (i.e. determine them as relevant and legitimate subjects for research) at all. The remainder of this chapter looks at ways in which an ethnographic approach might provide some answers to the problem of cross-cultural musical experience. Turkey and Ireland provide the case studies.

Firstly, Blacking's comment lumps together a number of aspects of international music exchange and tourism. However, there are plenty of grounds for distinguishing carefully between these events on the basis of the groups and identities involved. The context of international World Music events are quite different from those in which particular supranational identities are celebrated, such as pan-Celtic or pan-Gaelic competitions and events, the Eurovision Song Contest, the Mediterranean Song Contest, the Balkan Dance Festival and so on. Organised musical tourism to Indonesia, on gamelan tours, or the influx of tourists from Scandinavia, Germany and France to the West Coast of Ireland constitutes a quite different category. Local level exchanges organised by, for example, town twinning organisations and tours of an educational nature sponsored by local Arts Councils are quite different again.

Secondly, there is an assumption in Blacking's comment that the representatives of national and regional identities for tourists at home or abroad become a formal professional élite, often with the aid and sponsorship of their governments. If and when this is so, it may be the case that they do not, or are not felt to represent the people that they claim to, and that their state sponsorship turns them into official agents of particular ideologies, mere flunkies with no claim to the authenticity we demand of musical 'others'. This assumption is born out to a limited extent in Turkey, where the state runs the *Milli Turizm Halk Müzik Orkestrası* (The National Tourism Folk Music Orchestra). Its members are largely graduates from the State Folk Music conservatories who have not qualified for, or not chosen a career in the Turkish Radio and Television. These are urban musicians who give staged performances of both music and dances from rural regions of which in many cases they have no direct experience and receive a salary from the state for doing so.

To see these as representative of the huge number of Turks involved in international competitions throughout Western and Eastern Europe and the Middle East would be to miss an opportunity to observe and understand a significant phenomenon in Turkish cities, namely the small private music and folk dance clubs known as *dernek* or *cemiyet*, and the state-run *Halk Eğitim Merkezleri* (People's Education Centres). These provide the most important focus of amateur urban music making, offering organised courses, usually in the evenings or on Sundays, and places in which both young men and women can meet. The two *dernek* in which I conducted surveys in Istanbul in 1990 were typical in their size and constitution. Both contained about 200 members attending classes and using the facilities, and both sustained a small number of regular teachers (who also taught and played elsewhere) and an administrator as well as providing a small income for their owners.

The facilities they offered differed, reflecting their position in the city. That in the old city centre, close to the public transport routes leading to the *gecekondu* (squatter town) districts, gave classes exclusively in the long-necked lute (*bağlama*), with sporadic classes in *folklor* (regional folk dancing). The ages of the members ranged from sixteen to thirty-six, largely male (69 per cent), and single (80 per cent). Their occupations ranged fairly evenly from professional (accountants, teachers, lawyers) to skilled and semi-skilled labourers (cooks, secretaries, workers and attendants in shops and small businesses). There was also a high proportion of students living in *gecekondu* districts or in the old city area close to the universities. The parents of the majority were semi-skilled or unskilled labourers and first generation migrants from the South East of Turkey, living in the *gecekondu* to the west of the city walls.

Courses were structured in such a way that a year could be spent in each of three classes, but no formal qualifications were to be gained, and in practice most people promoted themselves from one class to another when they, or their friends, felt the urge, and usually did not stay for more than two years. Since the cost of membership was low, a certain informality prevailed and the emphasis in the clubs was on respectable socialising. This meant that young unmarried women could participate without worrying their parents. If people wanted to socialise in mixed company, they would stay in the club and not leave the premises to go and drink tea or soft drinks elsewhere, since to do so would compromise the female *dernek* members. As a result, these clubs become an important social focus, in which members might spend an entire afternoon and evening if they had nothing else to do. This is not to say that the quality of tuition available was not extremely high. Many Turkish Radio and Television star singers and performers run *dernek* as a sideline, and as well as providing a social meeting place for people whose involvement with music was casual, *dernek* provide a first-rate network of teachers and contacts for more seriously committed musicians. Regular attendance at *dernek* run by such *bağlama* players as Arif Sağ or Yavuz Top in Istanbul ensured at least some contact with them, and very few professional musicians I met had no involvement with this kind of organisation.

The focus of activity for most clubs is participation in national competitions, in which the winners compete at an international level. For others, less successful in domestic competition, efforts are made by any members who are capable of doing so to contact organisers of folk festivals and competitions who would pay expenses enabling the group to travel. So the particular attraction of this is that it provides people who would not normally have the opportunity or means to travel outside Turkey – particularly young women – with a chance to do so. For young men it is quite unambiguously an opportunity for *zamparalık*, for sexual adventure. For this, and other reasons, the ideal is travel to a folk festival in Western Europe, with the former states of Eastern Europe a close second, although in my experience many of the opportunities that offered themselves were to places then considered more mundane destinations closer to home: Yugoslavia, Egypt, Northern Cyprus.

The attraction of these occasions, apart from the opportunity for travel and adventure, is the frequent success of Turkish, and particularly Black Sea groups in competitive events. Turkey's failure in the Eurovision Song Contest in 1987 (scoring no points whatsoever) was widely perceived as a humiliating failure on the world stage. Without doubt, this perception of humiliation, echoed in international sporting events, increases the commitment that the *dernek* participants have to what they are doing, and partly explains the tremendous investment of time and effort that is channelled into performances of military discipline and precision. I often heard the sentiment that if only Turkey were to enter one of its *Halk* ('Folk') music singers for the Eurovision Song Contest, such as Arif Sağ, Turkey would either win outright, or would succeed in demonstrating that there was no need to compete on terms laid down by others in a musical language which was entirely alien to them. The support upon which these organisations rely therefore draws upon a perception of cultural powerlessness. Whatever its causes, participation in the *dernek* was frequently explained to me by members of these clubs in terms of this perception of powerlessness. The clubs were a way of doing something with one's time, other than hanging around at home (for women) or in the café (for men). They enabled people to travel and to meet members of the opposite sex, which they could not do otherwise. The language of the competition provides young people leading uncertain lives on the peripheries of urban Turkish society with the means by which they could associate themselves unambiguously with official discourses of Turkishness. Finally the clubs provide what its members perceive as a world stage upon which these feelings of powerlessness could be expiated. Turkish performers at international competitions are not then members of a privileged élite, and their participation must be understood in terms of an urban experience which undoubtedly overlaps in some ways with an officially promoted 'cultural chauvinism', but cannot be entirely reduced to it.

This leads to the question of how these events are staged, and how new fields of meaning are constructed and organised in relation to them. A trip to Ireland by three Black Sea Turks in 1989 provided me with an opportunity to observe these processes at first hand. In this case, meanings were constructed and transacted by Irish and Turkish musicians in relation to distinct ideas concerning regional identity. When Black Sea musicians or dance groups perform they have recourse to a large and sometimes contradictory fund of representations of Black Sea identity. Even though their own language of self-presentation evokes notions of the authentic (*otantik*)[3] in order to privilege certain groups at the expense of others, there is absolutely no level of 'prior' Black Sea cultural experience to which they can refer. It is worth looking at these representational forms in some detail, in order to see how they were mobilised in the case of one particular group on tour in Ireland.

Black Sea musicians in Turkey see their genealogy stretching back to Piçoğlu Osman at the beginning of the twentieth century, performing to a community which consisted of both Greeks and Turks, before the 'population exchanges' of 1923 removed the Pontic Greeks in their entirety to Greece. The establishment of the Turkish Republic forced musicians to orient themselves to cultural policy emanating from Istanbul and Ankara and obliged them to see themselves as a particular and 'remote' kind of Turk in the modern state. Intense rural–urban migration to Western Turkey and Germany following uneven industrialisation, intensive cash cropping of tobacco, tea, and hazelnuts, and the economic hardships of the late 1940s and early 1950s compounded the process. This created a Black Sea diaspora, in which highly regionalised differences had to be recast by musi-

---

3. Irony would seldom be far from the surface whenever I heard TRT musicians using the term. Holding the floor in a tea break at a recording session in Istanbul, I once heard Ibrahim Can pronounce on authenticity with a simple pun. Parodying an Istanbulian notion of the 'Laz' (see note 4) accent, he commented '*otantik, o dandik*' (the 'd's and 't's in this dialect being phonetically very close). *Dandik* was metropolitan slang (from a Kurdish word meaning 'sunflower seed'), which might be translated as 'crap'. His comment, which meant 'authenticity – that's crap', cleverly juxtaposed the notion of TRT authenticity with demeaning Istanbulian notions of regional 'others'.

cians as well as everybody else to suit the wider groupings typical of Black Sea life in Istanbul and Berlin. Small Black Sea recording companies in Istanbul such as Harika consolidated this process, at the same time, encouraging singers to think in terms of a number of discrete songs, rather than the long improvisations over *kayde* (riffs) typical of the area. This aspect of performance has fed back into the practice of musicians at Black Sea weddings and evenings at Black Sea *lokal* (clubs), the bread-and-butter activity of these musicians today. It is impossible to identify any distinct rural Black Sea musical practice to oppose to an urban practice: people, and musicians in particular, move around across the country, from village to city, with great regularity. Their natal village, or father's natal village, is a matter of great emotional significance, as in most societies dominated by a patrilineal ideology. For most purposes though the identities that matter are one's place in an extended family that might be spread across a number of individual households in the Black Sea area, Istanbul and Germany, and to an abstract idea of 'the Black Sea'. So when Black Sea people refer to the 'real' Black Sea in the context of their own discourse of authenticity, they are of course referring to a situation which has changed, and is continuing to change rapidly, although change is never, and can never, be acknowledged.

There is one other important agent in the ever mutating relationship between musicians, the audience and their perceptions of identity. The patronage of the official state-run radio stations at the Turkish Radio and Television (TRT) has been of paramount importance to Black Sea musicians. Black Sea performance in the east Black Sea area involves one player of the *kemençe*, a small, bowed box fiddle, and one or more singers taking turns to improvise over a fixed *kayde*. At the TRT on the other hand, all solo singers perform to the accompaniment of the central Anatolian *saz* or *bağlama*. These are now played in groups of various sizes of about ten players, all accompanying one singer. Various solo regional instruments are, as it were, framed against this, indicating regional identity. A *mey* (a small double reed aerophone) represents the South East, a *kabak kemane* (a gourd fiddle) represents the Aegean, the accordion represents the North East, and so on. In the same way, the *kemençe* represents the Black Sea. Its use is in a sense iconic, in that its complex textures are often played down in the mix, but it figures heavily as an image in the televised broadcasts of these programmes featuring 'regional' singers. The TRT therefore has its own distinct vision

Place, Exchange and Meaning 105

of the Black Sea as one regional musical style amongst a number of others. Like them, the Black Sea can be reduced in musical performance to an element in an orderly vision of a regionally diverse yet culturally unified state.

The Black Sea musicians I knew in Istanbul played at Black Sea *lokal* to Black Sea people whose spoken Turkish they might scarcely understand, provided the music for dancing classes at Black Sea clubs, played brief spots in city centre night-clubs, sandwiched between belly dancers and magicians for Western and Eastern European tourists, and went back to the Black Sea on public holidays and for the high pasture migrations in the Black Sea area for 'research'. Most were highly articulate about the differing contexts in which their Black Sea identity was being expressed. In one case it might be entertainment and an expression of solidarity with an urban Black Sea diaspora; in another, a contribution to Turkey's national self-renewal through preservation of its traditional – as opposed to pan-Islamic culture; in another, pursuing a career within the TRT; and in yet another, the need to earn money from tourists by presenting them something in a format that they could understand. It is not difficult therefore to dismiss the idea that traditional music making takes place in one context, in which musician and audience alike can take the transaction of meaning entirely for granted. In the case of Black Sea musicians in Turkey, multiple contexts exist, defined by the migration from the Black Sea to Istanbul, by the *dernek*, by international and internal tourism, and by the TRT. The skill of the good regional musician involves an ability to manipulate these quite distinct representations of region in a variety of distinct performance contexts.

Outside these relatively familiar situations, the problem of constructing and managing meaning merely becomes more accentuated. How can agreement between hosts, guests, audiences and performers be reached, or, at least, disagreements be managed? Who defines and then occupies the new performance space? How are questions of exchange managed? What happens when the musical expectations of the host society problematise for the visitors some hitherto 'invisible' aspect of the visitors' musical habitus? These kinds of question are routine for an emerging class of 'world music' musicians, and their resolution in some form is necessary if an event can take place at all. The three Black Sea Turkish musicians visited Ireland in a trip organised and financed by the Arts Council of Northern Ireland, involving workshops, concerts and pub sessions in Belfast, Westport, Galway and Dublin. What the organisers intended was an exchange of ideas, in which the Turkish musicians would leave knowing something about Ireland and Irish music, and that the local musicians would have some direct experience of Turkey and Turkish music. However, the organisers, the Turkish musicians and the audiences that listened to them and participated in the workshops had different expectations, resulting in a series of musical events which were the outcome of quite different interpretations of what was happening. As the week progressed, the interpretations and consequently the events changed. The internal dynamics and a particular hierarchy of musical and social relations of the Turkish group had been transformed as a result by the end of the week.

Finance permitted inviting only three musicians – a singer, a *bağlama* player and a *kemençe* player. This was a useful combination from the point of view of the dynamics of a Turkish *Halk* music ensemble, in that the basic structure of a singer backed by a band, or group, could be maintained. The distinction between the artist (*sanatçı*) and players (*müzisiyen*) pervades all aspects of urban music making in Turkey. A *sanatçı* is hired for an occasion (such as a concert, a wedding, or a circumcision ceremony), or for the making of a commercial cassette, who then in turn hires *müzisiyen* to support him or her. A relatively well-known singer might command fees of about TL 2 million (about £2,000 in 1990) for a night's work, of which up to TL 1 million might be distributed among the *müzisiyen* by the singer, depending upon the age and seniority of the musicians involved. This relationship is expressed not just in the arrangement of pay, but in the spatial organisation of the performance: *müzisiyen* invariably sit, whilst singers stand and move about in front of the players, addressing the audience.

Amongst the musicians themselves a strict hierarchy prevails. In larger ensembles for popular music (*Arabesk*), a lead violin player is responsible for organising the musicians, working out the arrangements (*partisiyon*) and distributing the pay amongst them. In performances of popular folk music (in which the violin is absent) this role is assumed by the leader of the group of *bağlama*, who is also responsible for getting the band in tune, and for sorting out arrangements. The *kemençe* therefore becomes a kind of optional extra, whose impact is largely visual. What is important is that it is there, and not necessarily that it is clearly heard. In fact the complexities of the texture and playing style of the instrument are such that most *bağlama* players, even if they are from the Black Sea, regard the *kemençe* as an unnecessary and problematic encumbrance.

Needless to say, this view is not shared by *kemençe* players. In most bands organised to support a Black Sea *sanatçı* there is consequently a constant antagonism between the *bağlama* and *kemençe* player. Numbers are very much on the side of the *bağlama*. *Halk* music singers in clubs use about four *bağlama*, with one or two different melody instruments, such as a *kaval* (flute) or a *kabak kemane* (gourd-fiddle). Undoubtedly more important is an argument of an explicitly ideological nature, that all rural folk music is ultimately reducible to that which can be played on the *bağlama*. This instrument is held to have a particular 'ethnic' association with the Turks of Asia as well as Asia Minor. It is considered to be simple and logical, and, most importantly, capable of being developed in a scientific and rational way (Stokes 1992: 70–81). The *kemençe* on the other hand is widely considered to be a difficult instrument, with an uncompromising sound meaningful only to Black Sea people, whose fingering and performance is not reducible to a simple, teachable form. For some, the instrument palpably lacks what the *bağlama* is considered to possess in abundance: *mantık* (logic).

The *sanatçı* who came to Ireland was a close friend of mine and the whole trip had been organised through him. He had asked along a *kemençe* player with whom he had been working on several projects in Istanbul that summer. The *kemençe* player had not travelled, and had to be lent a moderately large sum of money to pay for his visa and contribution to the *konut fonu* (a housing fund), which all Turks are required to pay on leaving Turkey. The money was repaid by the Arts Council on their arrival, but repaid through the *sanatçı* (who had made the initial payment), who thereby maintained a tight control of the command structure of the group. The *kemençe* player had even less say in the formal proceedings than the *bağlama* player, another musician who had worked frequently with the *sanatçı* , and who also had to be lent money by him. However, he was a graduate of the state conservatory, making a good living playing popular and folk music in Istanbul, and at the highest level of prestige in *müzisiyen* circles. Following performance practice in Istanbul, the *bağlama* player worked out reduced *partisiyon*, providing the kind of framework that would normally be supplied by a group of three or four *bağlama*, whilst the *kemençe* player played quietly in the background, using one string only in the manner of the *kabak kemane*, an instrument closer to commercial and TRT aesthetics, and was only wheeled out for particular 'numbers' during the formal performances. The musical dynamics of the group then initially exhibited a clear hierarchy between the *sanatçı* and *müzisiyen*, and between the two *müzisiyen* themselves.

Only one of the musicians, the *sanatçı*, had travelled out of Turkey before on a trip to a festival in Italy. He had some familiarity with the idea of performing to foreigners interested in Turkish music, although in this case he was aware, through his contact with me over a period of four years, that something a little more serious was required. It became clear to me that the musicians understood through him that they would be expected to give concerts and workshops introducing Turkish folk music in its entirety to an audience of interested Irish musicians. In the first concerts, they arrived at a format which was a compromise between a typical stage performance (at, for example a wedding, or a performance in a club), and an international festival-type demonstration of representative genres and styles from all regions of Anatolia. In this compromise, a sequence of songs began with slow and serious songs from Central Anatolia, and ended with more rapid, light-hearted songs, interspersed with jokes, stories and quick solo dances from the Black Sea area. The *kemençe* player played quietly, using one string only, for 'standard' Anatolian songs. As the Black Sea section began, in the second half of the programme, he began to play in the style characteristic of the *kemençe*, alternating passages with the *bağlama* in carefully worked out *partisiyon*, and played two solo pieces, singing and accompanying himself on the instrument. Left to their own devices, on the concert stage, cut off from the audience not only by the stage and lights, but a laborious (and not always accurate) process of simultaneous translation provided by myself, the Turks performed according to what they felt was expected from them, preserving the command structure and hierarchy of instruments within the group typical of a Turkish Radio and Television ensemble.

The organisers of the tour however had something quite different in mind. Far from seeing the week as a series of concerts and formal presentations, they had intended a series of events which were collaborative and participative, in which local musicians would not only have a direct experience of Turkish *musicians* (rather than just music), but that the Turks would have an experience of Irish music and musicians. This imposed significant conditions upon the kind of interaction that eventually took place. The brief of the Traditional Music section of the Northern Ireland Arts Council is to sustain the practice of Traditional Irish music in Northern Ireland. This is principally through active involvement in music teaching in schools, the organisation of concerts and media events to raise the profile of traditional Irish music, and through the sponsorship of musicians for work in what is determined to be their own local community. One difficulty faced by the Traditional Music section is the widespread association, among both Protestant and Catholic communities, of 'Traditional Music' with the Republican cause. Although predominantly Catholic in its personnel, the Traditional Music section of the Northern Ireland Arts Council maintains that both Protestant and Catholic communities in the North used to share the same musical tradition, and should continue to see their cultural heritage as having the same roots. It is also engaged in a bitter struggle with the Dublin based Traditional Music organisation, *Comhaltas Ceolteori Eireann* which is also active in the north. *Comhaltas* was founded in 1951 to continue the cultural aims of the Gaelic League (1893) in a musical arena. Apart from the perceived political agenda of *Comhaltas*, the Traditional Music section of the Northern Ireland Arts Council takes exception to the bureaucratic apparatus of the organisation, and the heavy emphasis on competition (through local and all Ireland Fleadhs) rather than participation. Opposition to *Comhaltas* has resulted in a tendency for the Northern Ireland Arts Council to stress the role of the musician in the community, rather than in organised competitions, concerts and staged ceilis.

The focus for this is 'the session' in pubs, bars and clubs, of the kind which takes place in cities and towns across Ireland, but with a particular intensity at many locations in Belfast. These require a certain kind of informal organisation, without which a session could not take place. Once they begin to take place in certain bars at certain times of the week or month, with the encouragement (or at the very least toleration) of the landlord, they acquire a certain dynamic of their own. The emphasis however is very much on an idealised spontaneity. Some kind of leadership is in fact involved, in that certain musicians are 'in the driving seat', beginning sets of reels, jigs and hornpipes, but an ethos of egalitarianism prevails. Rounds of drinks are shared out, everybody can join in, the musicians usually form an inward-facing circle, and once the session has got going, the musicians play for themselves rather than for the benefit of non-musicians in the bar. Musicians have a way of freezing out players who are too obtrusive, or confusing the playing, but no clear hierarchy of instruments or instrumental functions exists; any number of melody instruments can participate in the melodic line. The only clear division of labour is that of accompaniment (bozoukis, guitars) and percussion (*bodhran*, bones, spoons). A corollary of this egalitarian ethos is the view that non-Irish music can be incorporated into the session repertoire – not as Irish music as such – but as something that can be performed as if it were. It is not uncommon to hear Bulgarian, Romanian and Macedonian tunes (learned from holidays abroad, recordings or other exchanges), and particularly French and Breton tunes, in bars in Belfast and elsewhere.

Sessions were arranged for the Turks by the Irish musicians in which the intention was clearly that interaction would take place in terms of the conventions of the pub session. For a number of reasons, this never quite happened. Whilst bearing a family resemblance to Bulgarian and Macedonian music, Turkish music is slower. This made the complex irregular rhythms actually more difficult for the Irish musicians to perceive – even though there was a certain familiarity with irregular rhythms from a widespread awareness of Balkan music. The intervallic and modal structure of Turkish music revolves around small groups of tones and non-tempered intervals, whereas that of traditional Irish music is equally tempered, rapidly performed and covers a wide range. Even though they were reluctant to admit this – constantly asserting that Irish music was 'simple' – the Turkish musicians could not grasp the jigs and reels. While both Turks and Irish musicians were determined to trade tunes, the musical material proved too complex for the time available. This side of the intended interaction remained unfulfilled. There were a number of reasons for this beyond the tonal and rhythmic properties of the tunes.

For a start, the Turks were unfamiliar with the conventions of the pub session, demanding total silence when they played, and complaining when other musicians tried to join in. I found myself in the excruciatingly embarrassing position of having to ask people to be quiet and listen. Perhaps more problematic was their unfamiliarity with the egalitarian ethos of the session. With the high value accorded to fiddle playing in Ireland, the *kemençe* player found his skills much in demand, whilst the *sanatçı* and the *bağlama* player found themselves in the unusual position of being at the fringes of the event. Questions in workshops, and in the sessions themselves focused heavily on the *kemençe*. The *sanatçı* and the *bağlama* player were extremely uneasy about this, a fact which the Irish musicians were not slow to notice, and keen to explore. The *kemençe* moved slowly but surely to the centre of the events. In discussions and more particularly jokes the Black Sea emerged as a region possessing qualities of 'remoteness' analogous to those of the West coast of Ireland. The *kemençe* (as an object) and Temel the *kemençe* player (as a person) became unshakeably entrenched in a distinctly Irish discourse of place, 'remoteness' and identity.

In formal presentations and sessions, the Black Sea therefore came to predominate. As the week progressed the *kemençe* began to feature more heavily in solo spots in the programme, and to participate more actively in the ensemble, playing in its characteristic polyphonic style. If the initial impetus for this came from the hosts, the Turkish musicians responded to the situation in a variety of ways. As far as the *kemençe* player was concerned, the situation was undoubtedly a source of quiet but intense satisfaction. Unlike the other two musicians, he was not a high school or conservatory graduate. He was accustomed to spending his time as a professional musician within Black Sea communities in Istanbul, and was neither obliged, nor remotely concerned with impressing others. He spoke Black Sea Turkish with little regard for Istanbulian notions of conversational refinement. His blunt comments about the ways of 'the infidel' (*gavur*) and the peculiarities of farming practices in Ireland observed through the windows of the minibus emerged as the object of somewhat unkind banter on the part of the other musicians.

Nonetheless, his emergence as the star of the show could not have happened without the active collusion of the lead singer, since he controlled the purse strings on this particular trip, and on their return to Turkey, Temel was going to remain dependent upon the singer for prestigious (if occasional) work. The singer was also from the Black Sea, and had expressed to me on many occasions a frustration with the ambiguous role of the *kemençe* in TRT and other official performance contexts at home. The *bağlamas* dominated TRT practice in the performance of a music constructed around the peculiar characteristics of the *kemençe*. Its iconic use by TRT (rather than 'authentic' Black Sea players – who could not read music and therefore could not qualify for the TRT entrance examination) did not satisfy him. He felt it was artificial, and the difficulty of integrating the *kemençe* with the *bağlama* was a constant irritation. A private campaign directed at television programme directors bore fruit last year with a number of Black Sea music programmes featuring only himself and one *kemençe* player – in 'traditional' style, with no *bağlamas*. Another set of 'official' media performance conventions are thus emerging from a protracted and complex debate in Turkey, in which the *kemençe* is being redefined and reintegrated into TRT practice.

Irish interest in the *kemençe* pushed it to the front of the group's performance. Despite the collusion of the singer, this necessitated a number of adjustments on both his and the *bağlama* player's part. The singer was obliged to play up the notion of the Black Sea, which he did by relating it, in comments between numbers, to his perceptions of the West Coast of Ireland. Jokes played a more important part in the proceedings. Kerry jokes could easily be transformed into 'Laz'[4] jokes, and vice versa, since both played on notions of cunning masquerading as stupidity, and relations between remote areas and the city. The singer was an accomplished joke teller, and was extremely quick to make the connection. Black Sea repertoire predominated in the last concerts: the *kemençe* player was offered more solo spots. The *bağlama* player, for his part, played in a way which allowed more space for the rhythmic and textural peculiarities of the *kemençe*. Quicker and sparser *bağlama* playing was required. The *bağlama* player was able to oblige, since it enabled him to reinforce his own self image, and present himself to the singer (upon whom he also was occasionally dependent for jobs in Istanbul) as a competent, workaday musician, able to adapt to the most peculiar of demands. The musicians quickly developed strategies for coping with this unforeseen situation in ways which would not sour their relations of dependence upon the singer once they returned to Istanbul.

However, a certain tension inevitably emerged in relation to performances and workshops. The *bağlama* player suddenly snapped that he felt the trip had been a waste of time. He had only come, he said, because the singer had promised him that they would be able to find an amplifier to buy and take back to Turkey. The result was an irritable afternoon walking round music shops in Galway looking for and eventually buying a large valve amplifier. Performing to an audience which presented the Turkish musicians with unexpected demands did create a certain amount of stress on top of the strain of constantly travelling and meeting new people. The speed with which the singer and musicians adapted and developed strategies for coping with the situation was particularly striking.

The ability to deal with unfamiliar performance situations is a basic resource for professional musicians in many societies. The musician is not simply a cipher representing a culture to and for it-

---

4. The term 'Laz' is used inaccurately, and in a somewhat derogatory fashion for all inhabitants of the area between the Pontic Alps and the Black Sea coast between Samsun and Artvin. Actual speakers of the Laz language now only inhabit a few valleys in Rize and Artvin.

self: musicians travel and are frequently skilled intermediaries. In spite of this, the problems of dealing with an event which all of the participants would regard as inter-cultural were substantial. They included the unexpected demands of the hosts, the reconciliation of ideologically loaded conflicts within host and guest musical groups, and the need to cooperate in such a way that the complex relations between singer and musicians could be picked up upon return. A plurality of meanings and strategies predominated, each one with implications for the others. The event as a whole was however provided with a common frame by two strikingly congruent representations of regional identity.

The language and rhetoric of regional identity has much in common in the West of Ireland and in North East Turkey, even though the experience of participation on the margins of new nation-states is in both cases different. For the Irish musicians, the West coast is the true home of Irish music, the home of the Irish language and the focus of moral values which constitute the essence of Irishness. The North East of Turkey focuses analogous values for Turks for quite different reasons. Its geographical location confers on it both a remoteness and a proximity. It is the closest part of the modern Turkish republic to Central Asia, which had been identified by early Turkist ideologues as the home of a Turkishness uncorrupted by Arabs and by Islam (see Stokes 1992: 25–33). On the other hand, its very distance from the urban centres, and its long history of hostility to the 'Kurds' and Alevis[5] the other side of the Pontic Alps, attest to a vigorous, uncorrupted and assertive Turkishness. In both the East Black Sea coast of Turkey and the West Coast of Ireland, topography is an important metaphor of moral integrity, both as an explanation for the absence of corrupting urbanism and as a trope in which a certain 'wild' machismo and vigour are constantly evoked. Both representations of a pristine periphery have a precise and definable place in Republican ideologies in both Ireland and Turkey. If the language and rhetoric of national culture is shaped by a common set of political and economic imperatives, this common fund of representations is perhaps not surprising.

The relationship of music to these remote regions can perhaps be accounted for in other ways. Both Ireland and Turkey are identified in and outside both countries as peripheral economies on the fringes

---

5. Alevis (Alawites) are heterodox Muslims who revere Ali rather than Muhammed as the bearer of God's final message.

of capitalist Europe. Labour migration plays a vital role in both economies, and the long history of migration both inwards into Europe and outwards to America (in the case of Ireland) and the Middle East (in the case of Turkey) has led to an intense cultural elaboration of the migrant situation. In both societies, music is credited with powers of bringing people together and engendering the moral cohesion of the community, evoking collective and private memory. Place, for many migrant communities, is something which is constructed through music with an intensity not found elsewhere in their social lives. It is no coincidence that the heroes of Irish traditional music should have made their names, and their records, in migrant communities in the United States, and that many of the stars of Turkish popular or regional musics should have made their names in Istanbul or in Germany.[6] Musicians in Turkey and Ireland today experience place and identity in ways which embrace many of the characteristic contradictions and ambiguities of modernity and its legacy. More often than not they are separated from 'their' cultural locus by a gulf of time and space: the discourses in which place is constructed and celebrated in relation to music have never before had to permit such flexibility and ingenuity. 'Traditional' musicians involved in the kinds of experiences detailed above need to be peculiarly good at managing these discourses. Without doubt, their expertise is a vital resource for the rest of us.

References

Adorno, T.W., 'On Popular Music', *Zeitschrift für Sozialforschung 9,* 1941, pp. 17–49.
Baumann, M.P., *Folklor und Folklorismus,* Winterhur, Amadeus Verlag, 1976.
Blacking, J., *'A Common-sense View of All Music': Reflections on Percy Grainger's Contribution to Ethnomusicology and Music Education,* Cambridge, Cambridge University Press, 1987.
Clifford, J., 'Traveling Cultures' in L. Grossberg, C. Nelson and P. Treichler (eds), *Cultural Studies,* London, Routledge, 1992.
Greenwood, D., 'Culture By The Pound: An Anthropological Perspective

---

6. The Sligo fiddle player Michael Coleman established a definitive performance style, which musicians in many parts of Ireland still seek to emulate, from New York in the 1920s. Bülent Ersoy, the transexual transvestite *Arabesk* singer became one of the icons of this genre whilst in virtual exile in (former) West Germany (see Stokes 1992: 172–3). The most well-known Black Sea singers operate in Istanbul (Ibrahim Can, Mustafa Topaloğlu, Erkan Ocaklı) and Ankara (Süreyya Davulcuoğlu).

on Tourism as Cultural Commodification', in V.L. Smith (ed.), *Host and Guests: The Anthropology of Tourism*, Oxford, Blackwell, 1978.
Harker, D., 'Fakesong' in *Popular Music Perspectives 2*, Göteborg, IASPM, 1985, pp. 346–59.
Helm, E., 'Musicultura: Three Orient–Occident Encounters', *World of Music*, vol. 20, no. 2, 1978, pp. 1–17.
Herzfeld, M., *The Poetics of Manhood: Contest and Identity in a Cretan Village*, Princeton, Princeton University Press, 1987.
Hobsbawm, E. and T. Ranger (eds), *The Invention of Tradition*, Cambridge, Cambridge University Press, 1983.
Mitchell, T., *Colonising Egypt*, Berkeley, University of California Press, 1991.
Stokes, M.H., *The Arabesk Debate: Music and Musicians in Modern Turkey*, Oxford, Clarendon Press, 1992.
Stratton J., 'Capitalism and Romantic Ideology in the Record Business', *Popular Music*, vol. 3, 1983, pp. 143–56.
Waterman, C., *Jújù: A Social History and Ethnography of an African Popular Music*, Chicago, The University of Chicago Press, 1990.

7

Identity, Place and the 'Liverpool Sound'

Sara Cohen

The 'Liverpool Sound' is a term that has been commonly used within and outside of the Merseyside region over the past twenty-five to thirty years. It implies a certain relationship between the city and its music. This paper examines the way in which the 'Liverpool Sound' is currently being described and discussed by groups of young rock musicians, journalists, and others living in the city, and considers the social and economic factors that might be involved. In doing so, it highlights the discourses of place and authenticity surrounding the notion of an identifiable Liverpool Sound. These discourses involve a series of oppositions, whereby Liverpool and its music is contrasted with Manchester and London, and distinctions are made with regard to music within the Merseyside region. The construction of a 'Liverpool Sound' is revealed as a political strategy, a resource through which relations of power at local, regional, national, and international levels can be addressed.

Liverpool's popular music incorporates a variety of regional, national and international influences, but it is also particular to Liverpool, reflecting a range of social, economic and political factors peculiar to the city. Local issues of ethnicity, religion and gender, patterns of immigration and intermarriage, kinship networks, and the geographical distribution of musical instruments and equipment, are closely bound up with the production of musical sounds and structures.

Geographical variations in the background, culture and influences of musicians, although reflected in their music, also help to construct particular places and the ways in which people conceptualise them. This relationship between music and locality is constantly changing.

Political and economic developments are continually shifting the way in which particular cities and regions are represented and marketed, and altering relationships between them. This obviously affects cultural production and consumption within those areas.

The relationship of the record industry with locality also varies. Whilst many companies are concerned with the transnational market, others are more likely to be concerned with the creation and marketing of 'local' scenes and sounds for 'local' audiences. In Britain for example, major record companies based in London view some areas, such as Liverpool, as more culturally significant than others, and consequently focus attention upon them which affects self-presentation and categorisation of artists within them. If an artist from a particular place achieves success, it is common for that area to be consequently deluged with visits and correspondence from company representatives anxious to cash in on that success and to beat rival companies to it. This can result in the signing of a number of artists from one area and contribute to a media construction, promotion and marketing of a local 'scene' or 'sound', as with the so-called 'Liverpool Sound' in the 1960s, the 'Coventry Sound' in the 1970s, and the 'Manchester Sound' in the 1980s.

This situation is reflected in the press and the media. Local media stations have a different relationship with places than do national ones. Meanwhile journalists write about popular music within conventions and constraints imposed by particular magazines or papers aimed at specific types of readers. Whilst a British magazine like *Smash Hits* is likely to emphasise the global star appeal of Kylie Minogue or Michael Jackson, music papers such as *New Musical Express* are more likely to focus upon 'local scenes' because of their concern with notions of authenticity. The linking of particular artists with particular places identifies them with roots and presents them as real people embodying artistic integrity and honesty, rather than glitzy stars representing an unreal world of glamour, commerce and marketing strategies. Finally, there is also some evidence of regional variations within Britain regarding record sales and tastes in music.[1]

There are many ways of investigating music in relation to place, and it is with the issue of identity and the construction of locality through music that this paper is primarily concerned. Liverpool iden-

---

1. An article in *Music Week* (17 November 1990) for example pointed to a north/south divide in Britain involving tastes in dance music.

tity was placed on the world map by the *Beatles* and the so-called Liverpool or 'Mersey sound', a label applied to the music of many Liverpool bands when some of them achieved notoriety during the 1960s. However, although Liverpool might be famous for its rock bands, its football teams, and for other performance arts, since the early 1960s it has lost a third of its population and nearly half of its jobs. It has little employment generating industry of its own. In 1985, the unemployment rate in Liverpool was double the national average, and it remains well above that of other northern cities, rising to 70–80 per cent in some areas. The population continues to fall, decreasing by at least 50,000 (10 per cent) over the past ten years, and the city has been continually used by the press and the media as a colourful backdrop to inner-city decline.

This is just one dimension of the city's high but not very flattering media profile. The national press and media have exhibited almost an obsession, and certainly a fascination with Liverpool, attributing to it exoticism, alongside sensationalised qualities of aggression and trouble-making, and continually resorting to it as a provider of headlines. This national media image has built upon a general sense of oppression and of being 'hard-done by' within the city, and emphasised a sense of local identity, loyalty and defiance or adversity to the outside world which is reflected in the humour for which the city is so well known. This sense of identity is also fuelled by the local media, which strive to engender pride in Liverpool and its achievements.

This, alongside Liverpool's role as a seaport, has contributed to a sense of detachment and difference from the rest of the country, and has influenced in many other ways the social, political and economic characteristics of the city. Lane (1987), for example, points out that the traditions of the port have given rise to a reputation for masculine exuberance, assertiveness, flamboyancy and a fierce sense of individualism, existing alongside deep-rooted traditions of egalitarianism and democracy. These rather contradictory tendencies are apparent in different aspects of the city. The media image of unity and solidarity often associated with Liverpool might to some extent reflect its crews of sailors, its large close-knit families, its football supporters and its rock bands. Whilst the latter often exhibit strong ambitions directed outside the city, thriving upon challenge and attention, they display at the same time a democratic structure and inspire strong feelings of loyalty among members.

The strength of such ties might have contributed to the deep rifts and barriers that exist, resulting in family rivalries and strong ethnic, religious and gender divisions. One characteristic of the city, for example, is the noticeable segregation of its black population within the boundaries of an area known as Toxteth or Liverpool 8. Few blacks are seen working or shopping in the city centre less than one mile away. The Gifford Enquiry set up by Liverpool City Council to investigate race relations within the city, documented overwhelming racism within the police, educational and other establishments. It concluded in its report (published in 1989) that the situation regarding racism in Liverpool was 'uniquely horrific', despite the fact that Liverpool's black population is probably the oldest in Europe, and despite the high incidence of racial intermarriage.

Spatial boundaries within the region are also determined by non-racial factors. Each of Merseyside's districts is seen to have its own particular character and even, locals often insist, its own distinctive accent. Those within the city centre often talk of those living only a few miles outside of it in a derogatory fashion as 'woonlybacks', 'country-folk' (and therefore associated with sheep), and make such remarks as 'You'll need a passport to get there.' Boundaries determined by religion, which were once strongly demarcated, are now blurred, but their overtones remain.[2] Spatial divisions are reinforced by the fact that many working class extended families have remained in the same district, neighbourhood, or even street over the course of the century, thus establishing their identity with that area and often expressing strong parochialism. This is further heightened by the high levels of unemployment and by the fact that Merseyside has the lowest car ownership rate in the country,[3] which has restricted geographical mobility within the region.

Although Liverpool people represent a complex mix of religion, ethnicity and other factors, they may nevertheless have a common view of themselves and of 'Liverpool' in relation to wider society, based on local and national media constructions, a sense of common history or fate, collective symbols such as the liver bird, the *Beatles*, the local football teams and other factors. This identity may be enhanced by a concern with kinship relations, strong collective memories, recent political crises and tragedies such as Hillsborough and Heysel, which are constructed as local to Liverpool, and not to

2. The Catholic/Protestant divide, for example, is still implicated in the boundaries between different districts and in the marching bands. Until fairly recently it was also reflected in the rivalry between Liverpool and Everton football clubs.
3. Over 62 per cent of Liverpool residents, for example, have no car.

one particular team or to a wider region.[4] The complexities of this Liverpool identity are reflected in the popular music culture of the region, and, not surprisingly, expressions of local identity often focus upon popular music.

The linking of particular musical styles, instruments, voices or sounds with particular places, and with various characteristics and stereotypes associated with those places is fairly common. A Sunday *Observer* article (24 February 1991) about a band from Bristol stated that 'Bristol's character, particularly its pace, does seem to have influenced the music produced there', and a Bristol musician was quoted as saying, 'Unlike many musicians in London we've never been rushed, we have time to make music and, more importantly, simply think about it. Bristol is friendly, slow-paced and relaxed'. A music journalist wrote of the Manchester band *New Order*: 'In their late seventies incarnation as *Joy Division* they captured the alienated, terrible glee of a decayed city.' He quoted a member of the band as saying, 'Manchester is more spacious than London, where you can't see more than 200 yards in front of you', and he wrote, 'This freedom of movement is all important to the Manchester groups: you can hear it in the slowed down James Brown backbeat which . . . has become the year's dominant rhythm' *(Observer Magazine,* 7 July 1990). A music entrepreneur from Manchester said that there was a 'Scottish dimension' to the music of Scottish bands, which was hard to describe but consisted of a 'swirling thing' at the back of the music which made it sound Scottish. Similarly, a Liverpool student pointed out to me 'There is a relatively recognisable Scottish sound – but don't ask me to try and quantify it . . . There is something in there.'

In Liverpool, the preoccupation with a 'Liverpool Sound' has continued since the 1960s, not just in the press, but among musicians and non-musicians from Liverpool and elsewhere. During autumn 1990, about 15–20 young Liverpool rock musicians and others particularly interested in or involved with music were invited on a weekly basis to form an informal discussion group as part of a project set up to investigate notions of locality in relation to music and music making. Some meetings were organised at Liverpool University, but most took place at Merseyside Trade Union Community and

---

4. Ninety-five Liverpool football fans were killed during a match at the Hillsborough football ground in Sheffield in 1985 as a result of crowd pressure. At Belgium's Heysel stadium in 1989, thirty-six Italian football supporters were killed when a wall collapsed after disturbances involving Liverpool supporters.

Unemployed Resource Centre. In relation to the 'Liverpool Sound', participants were asked to consider if there was such a thing, and if so, what it was. Even if there isn't, participants were asked, music must reflect aspects of the culture in which it is created, so how does this process manifest itself, and how does a city become associated with a particular sound? Several individuals were invited to present their opinions on the subject to the group and played selected music recordings. The discussions were tape-recorded and they were complemented by unstructured interviews with individual group members, and by comments made by such individuals in the press, statements about music were related to the life histories of the individuals making them, involving particular configurations of social, economic and political groups and institutions at a local and national level.[5]

Regarding dance music, one musician pointed out that 'Manchester has more of a Latin feel to it, but the Liverpool sound is different, it's harder. Radio DJs say they can't even categorise our music. That's probably because it is unique' *(Liverpool Echo* 26 February 1990). Another said, 'Liverpool bands have always written songs whereas Manchester has always gone for grooves' *(New Musical Express* 12 January 1991). Of his own music, one band member said, 'We're aiming for this to be a Liverpool Sound' *(Sounds* 6 January 1990). One reviewer of that band described it as having a 'sometimes hard-edged, distinctly Liverpool sound' *(New Musical Express* 24 March 1990), and another described the band as one of the groups of 'exciting young scouse guitar bands' that have emerged from the 'drug/dole culture' of rundown council estates and 'carry its values with them'. All of them, he stated

> wrote proper songs, chock full of vibrant melodies and glorious harmonies... Liverpool kids were, for the first time in ages, making their own music. Too often in the past, the musical voice of the city has come from unrepresentative arty outfits made up of weirdoes, students and Wirral[6] rich kids with synthesisers. But now... the true organic sound was at last making itself heard *(ID* February 1991).

Definitions and descriptions of the 'Liverpool Sound', are wide-rang-

---

5. It should be pointed out that whilst many participants began by denying the existence of a 'Liverpool Sound', talking of it as a media construction, or denied that the knowledge of where a band or artist came from influenced their reception of the music, in subsequent discussion they usually contradicted those statements.

6. An area lying opposite Liverpool across the River Mersey.

ing and often contradictory. These contradictions give rise to debate and scepticism as to its distinctiveness or even existence. Many believe that it is melodic and harmonious, suggesting a romantic, emotional music that contrasts with the masculine, tough image usually associated with the city. The lack of bands performing in a more aggressive, punk or political style has often been noted. Some however, point to a certain 'attitude' in Liverpool which comes through in the music and could be described as individualist, blunt, combative. 'There's more of a Liverpool attitude than a Liverpool sound' said one musician, 'but most people smoke loads of pot', he added, 'so there's a sort of dreamy element to the music'. A local black musician said, 'When people talk about a Liverpool sound, they're talking about the white rock sound. They're not talking about the black Liverpool sound... There is a distinctive black sound, but... it's never really been given a chance.' He described this sound as 'heavy', 'aggressive' and 'anti-social', reflecting the problems experienced by those in Liverpool 8.

The construction of the Liverpool Sound today is, of course, often influenced by the success of the *Beatles*. Some are embarrassed or worried by that success and find it restrictive because it affects the way in which people perceive their music. Others acknowledge that the music that so dominated their childhood or the lives of people around them, has inevitably influenced their own creativity. Many of those who performed alongside the *Beatles* in the 1960s now teach or manage their musician sons or daughters. Whatever they feel about the *Beatles*, a lot of musicians reveal a strong sense of local tradition and heritage when they talk about their music, alongside the common preoccupation with tracing, acknowledging and denying the particular influences of other non-local bands within it. This is of course a selective process. Some musical influences are seen to have a resonance in the popular music of today, but not others.

Recently, there has been much publicity surrounding the so-called 'Manchester Sound', and local and national media have played upon a long-standing rivalry between Manchester and Liverpool. This surfaced frequently during discussion of the 'Liverpool Sound' at Liverpool University and the Merseyside Trade Union and Unemployed Resource Centre. Manchester was depicted as wealthier than Liverpool, and some suggested that its population tended to be better travelled, less isolated and wary and more open-minded. Consequently, its music reveals a variety of influences, unlike the 'Liverpool Sound', which displays a paucity of influences, a certain parochialism and an obsession with the past. Manchester's wealth was also seen to be reflected in technological and synthesised sounds in contrast to the Liverpool Sound which is more 'acoustic' and 'raw'.

Differences between Liverpool and Manchester were also attributed to their physical characteristics. One Liverpool musician suggested:

> Maybe it's the space in Manchester and the size... Liverpool was described to me as a big village... Maybe that restricts artists from being experimental, because people in Liverpool are... more likely to put you down or criticise you for being what they would see as, I suppose, pretentious. And in Manchester, you've got space to... do things... and not circulate as much with people on a day-to-day basis. You have that creative space as well as a sort of physical space to arse around or become pretentious or... creative.

Many, of course, deny that Liverpool bands reflect a restricted range of influences. 'All the bands sound different', claimed one musician, 'and there's no real competition because there's room for us all. It's not like the Manchester scene... which was contrived, with everybody jumping on the backs of the *Stone Roses* and *Happy Mondays*' (*ID* February 1991). A Liverpool journalist wrote: 'Some of the Manchester bands obviously use the same influences (as Liverpool bands)... but tend to disguise them in contemporary trappings and grooves, whereas the scouse beat combos go out of their way to capture that raw, pure 60s feel... But now the world is ready, and after the Manchester burnout comes the Liverpool blitzkrieg' (ibid.)

'At last', wrote another Liverpool journalist *(Liverpool Echo* 12 May 1990), 'Liverpool music is fighting back against the dominance of Manchester and against its own history.'

Distinctions made between Manchester and Liverpool through popular music thus encompass binarisms such as technological and synthesised vs. acoustic and raw; rich vs. poor; hospitable and open vs. closed and wary; creative vs. restricted. Similar oppositions were implied in distinctions between the music of other places, for example Wirral vs. Liverpool, north Liverpool vs. south Liverpool, Liverpool city centre vs. the outskirts. One musician for example, referred to the cliques of bands existing in different districts of Merseyside, each of which he described as 'a very closed shop' resistant to infiltration from outside musicians. He and others agreed that there existed a north/south divide in Liverpool and some depicted the north as more 'introverted' and 'inward looking' due to 'upbringing and social class'. One said of musicians in the North End, 'they've known each other for years. You don't get that down south', and he said it was harder to travel in and out of town from the North End: buses to the South End are more frequent and people in the South tend to be wealthier. He, like others, related this to the prevalence of students in the South End and to its greater cultural mix. One said that within the Liverpool music 'scene' there existed a 'snobbishness towards North End bands'. Another said of his family and friends in Kirkby, 'they really don't like the idea of south Liverpool . . . you never hear a scouse accent down there, they're all frigging cockneys'.

Whilst London record companies tend to focus attention upon city centres, associating creativity with urban as opposed to rural areas, some in Liverpool insist that bands on the fringes tend to be more adventurous and creative than those in the city centre. A few journalists have noted that such bands lack local role models to follow and emulate, and are less oriented towards the record industry and less confident than Liverpool bands in their ability to 'make it'. The latter, they complain, tend to be overly ambitious, with high expectations, whilst those from the outskirts are more relaxed about their music making, and less competitive. Some of them believe that their distance from the city gives them a better chance of creating a different, more original sound. The owner of a Liverpool record label believes that music in the region gets 'freer' the further you go outside the city centre. Likewise, a cultural geographer has suggested regarding certain musical styles, that innovation tends to come from outside city centres (Glasgow 1987: 251). A Liverpool journalist reporting on the current group of bands from working-class overspill estates on the outskirts of Liverpool city centre wrote that these estates remain 'a world apart with a language and scally street culture all of its own. Although the groups themselves would probably deny it, the quirky distinctive nature of this particular environment has helped set them apart from the Mersey musical mainstream and aided their confident separatism' (*ID* February 1991).

At one of the meetings, a local radio disc jockey presented his views on the 'Liverpool Sound', or what he termed 'the localness of local music', or the 'character sound' of Liverpool. He entitled his talk 'The Train and The River', suggesting that these represented two tendencies that 'mix and match and cross in various ways as contemporary Liverpool music'. The train represented the Lime Street to Euston trip undertaken by Liverpool bands in their struggle for commercial success. It was reflected in their music which the DJ described as 'beatish', pointing out musical features such as 'propulsive drumming'. It was not, he said, the 'natural' music of the city: 'The train sounds express Liverpool now . . . the dilemma of an economically isolated region which cannot support its own music and propel its own music to economic success . . . The beat is also the beat of history and of economics . . . And there is the sense that the beat has left Liverpool behind.'

On the other hand, he said, 'riverine music' is 'beatless', 'romantic' and 'local', and is bound up with the 'roots' and 'soul' of Liverpool. He described one song reflecting that riverine sound as having just enough instrumental accompaniment 'for the voice to ride over, like waves'. Underneath the tune of another, the music 'rotated' in a circle, thus reflecting the physics of waves with their circular movements of water. A record entitled *Christian* by the local band *China Crisis,* who achieved international success in the 1980s, was described as 'the definitive riverine sound in the sense that it has perfected drift', a lack of beat, words and ideas 'get nowhere. The music rotates and crashes. The word emotion sounds like "ocean".'

The roots of these two musical tendencies, the DJ suggested, lay in the city's geographical position. Liverpool is caught between southern Mediterranean and Irish music coming from the west and across to Liverpool from the Wirral[7], and plain syllabic northern music from the east. Whilst trainish music is about being away from home and 'taking the beat elsewhere', riverine music reflects the tendency, said the DJ, to 'stay at home and lose the beat . . . face up to the fact that the place is in a sense economically isolated, and just find what music is there'. He suggested that a record by another local band, *Echo and the Bunnymen,* reflected this, with characteristics of an Irish lament, a 'rotating harmony' and a 'local feeling of home'. Behind this, the DJ suggested, are feelings of loss and regret expressed through particular diatonic structures, cadences, falling melodies and 'big sighs'.

This description of Liverpool music, like some of those mentioned earlier, obviously reflects notions of 'authenticity'. Train music is depicted as commercial, emulated and fake, whilst riverine music is non-commercial, a cathartic and honest expression of the true feelings and situation of the city, and thus, by implication, natural and real. Similarly, the owner of a local record label bemoans the

---

7. 'Much of the riverine music is', he said, 'interestingly, Wirral music'.

'conservative' nature of local music, which, he believes, reflects the bands' strong desire to be commercial and successful, and to use music as a way out. Music should instead, he insists, reflect 'the real Liverpool character'.

A Liverpool university student was taken with some of the DJs ideas and said that for him, *China Crisis* were 'the quintessential Liverpool band of the 1980s', and one that definitely embodied the 'Liverpool Sound'. As a newcomer to Liverpool, he was struck by certain geographical features such as broad expanses of sky, a sense of space and a changeable climate. This, for him, was conjured up by the music and lyrics of *China Crisis*. Titles of their songs included 'No More Blue' 'Horizons', 'Comes a Raincloud', 'Blue Sea', 'Jean Walks in Fresh Fields', 'Hampton Beach', 'Northern Sky'. In addition, he said, the music was 'full of gaps ... it's not an intense claustrophobic music ... it's almost ambient ... very drifty'. He described the vocal as 'dreamy and faraway' and pointed to the 'washy synths', along with other sonic and lyrical references to the sea. 'I always get this sense', he said of *China Crisis,* 'that they are off on their own ... in their own little world'. They conjure up a feeling of 'looking outwards rather than back into the rock mainstream'. He related this to what he termed the 'self-isolating' mood and humour of Liverpool, and related that in turn to Liverpool's geographic position *vis-à-vis* the rest of Britain, describing it as 'out on a limb'. He also noted the religious imagery in the music. Song titles included 'Christian', 'The Soul Awakening', 'Wall of God', 'Sweet Charity and Adoration', 'All my Prayers', 'Singing the Praises of Finer Things', 'The Highest High', 'Gift of Freedom', 'Strength of Character', 'King in a Catholic Style'.

Later, one of the two main members and songwriters of *China Crisis* explained that he and his partner came from large catholic families in Kirkby, a district lying a few miles outside of Liverpool city centre. They left school with no qualifications living at home on the dole until, in their late teens, the band achieved success. Up until then their geographical world consisted of 'just Kirkby and "Crokky".'[8] The lead singer explained: 'I'm really surprised people even think we are a Liverpool group ... I mean Kirkby was like so isolated ... growing up in Kirkby it was like ... growing up on the other side of the moon ... You didn't even go into town. I don't think I even knew me way home from town.' He insisted that at the time he wrote them the lyrics didn't mean anything - much to the

8. Croxteth is a district which borders Kirkby.

frustration of those who kept questioning him about them. In retrospect however, he can see how they did relate to certain events in his life, such as the birth of his first child. On the religious imagery in his lyrics, he explained:

> I was a catholic. I went to church for years and years . . . I was brought up in St. Joseph's school . . . looking back and thinking about it, it is definitely an important language. If I was to say anything that was important, it was usually religious . . . because they had all the fabulous words . . . There was a guilt thing in there as well because when you're brought up that way . . . you're wrong to kick off with . . . That's how I interpreted it. And I suppose . . . whenever I was in a position where I was doing fine, there would always be this side . . . 'why are you feeling like this?'. . . Because a lot of time I wasn't feeling that great in the group, but we were having, you know, this success so . . . I suppose the words would come to mind then and I would use them.

He thought that the suggestion of wide open spaces in his music and lyrics might also have something to do with the way he was brought up, and he described visits to the beach as a child:

> They had such an impact. Because you'd be cooped up in this tiny little council house sharing a bed . . . I didn't get a bed until I was 14 or 15, and I don't think Ed got one until he'd left home . . . it's a real big contrast isn't it, to the way we were living – how we would really like to live. And . . . Kirkby . . . is a green belt thing . . . it was a matter of . . . all the kids in your street walking for 25 minutes and you were in the woods you know, and it was like superb, it was like you were set free.

He also mentioned the language of the docks which was 'there all the time', and hearing about people in the American mid-west who never saw the sea, and how unimaginable that was. More recently, when he visited Hawaii, he thought he could never live in a place where there was so little seasonal change.

The attitudes and upbringing of this musician were similar to those of others involved in the research project. Many of them said that religion had been very significant in their lives, but until someone raised the issue in relation to their music they didn't realise how prevalent it was in lyrics, song titles, and perhaps even the music itself (in the form of 'orchestrated harmonies' for example). One musician from the North End of Liverpool said that its districts were still referred to as 'parishes' and named according to the church associated with that parish: 'I think it's very subconscious in Liverpool because of the religious situation that existed here a while back . . . the morals of that religion – like Catholicism – still prevail.' Discussions of the 'Liverpool Sound' could imply imagined differences between sounds from different places, although such debates might influence the creation of sounds in subtle ways. Alternatively, as indicated earlier, a complex relationship does exist between music and the socio-economic context in which it is made. It may well be, therefore, that the music of a band like *China Crisis,* in its use of echo, timbres and vocal qualities for example, is coded in such a way that it expresses the social and biographical context of the band members, with its particular configuration of factors such as religion, kinship, ethnicity and class. For consumers open to such suggestion, such music may indeed encourage particular images and emotions, such as those linked with open spaces or Catholicism. What *is* apparent however, is that the notion of a local sound, like the 'Liverpool Sound', does reflect the desire to symbolically assert difference and a sense of local identity.

Liverpool identity was described earlier as revolving around particular issues: money (or rather the lack of it) and class, specific dimensions of time (involving kinship and tradition, heritage and local history), specific dimensions of space (such as the way in which the city was conceptually divided into specific districts determined by categories of ethnicity and religion) and media constructions of the city. All these issues involve distinctions between 'us' and 'them' relating to Liverpool vs. the rest of Britain, or to divisions within Liverpool and the Merseyside region. They were reflected in the discussions of the 'Liverpool Sound' implicated in the debates over the 'Manchester' vs. the 'Liverpool Sound', the 'Wirral' vs. the 'Liverpool Sound', the 'North Liverpool' vs. the 'South Liverpool Sound'.

The research on music and locality in Liverpool has thus indicated various ways in which people create an image or sense of place in the production and consumption of music. This may be revealed in processes of musical composition and rehearsal, in the collective memories embodied in the music, in patterns of buying and use, and in discourse surrounding the music which can involve territorial negotiation and conflict over sound and meaning. It may reflect political motivations and geopolitical assertions of affiliation, roots or ethnicity,[9] economic motivations (such as protectionist strategies

9. Hence the reflexive politics of minority groups and marginalised countries often incorporate references to place. (See Berland 1988 on Canadian music and Carney 1987 on American Country music.)

surrounding local cultures threatened by national or international culture), ideological motivations (such as the notion of authenticity), or social motivations resulting in other assertions of difference.

Conclusion

This emphasis upon place and local images, traditions and heritage contrasts with the way in which popular music is often depicted. Rock music, for example, has frequently been presented through the media and in academic literature as a symbol of modernity, situated at the forefront of a process of cultural globalisation, imperialism and homogenisation, breaking through international barriers more effectively than any other medium, and perceived as a universal language. It was then associated with fast-changing trends, rising consumerism, and Americanisation. These are again characteristics of modernity and modernism, involving the domination of world markets by multinational conglomerates and cartels, and the 'shrinking' of the world through expanding networks of increasingly sophisticated communication technologies. Which have brought into existence McLuhan's 'Global Village'.[10]

The world record industry is now concentrated in the hands of five multinational companies, and major record companies based in particular countries, such as Britain, can no longer rely upon national sales alone, but are concerned with international sales and thus with the international appeal, exportability or 'geographical agility' (Berland 1988) of their artists. This has contributed to a discourse of transnationalism within the industry, and it is often in the vested interests of the major companies to obscure and overcome subnational or national boundaries in order to market their products as widely as possible.

In recent years much academic literature has addressed what has been termed the 'crisis' of modernity and resulting 'post-modern' era or condition. The confusions and ambiguities of post-modernism have been noted, yet many have focused upon its spatial and temporal dimensions. They disagree as to whether the condition of post-modernity marks an end of modernism[11] and perhaps a recog-

---

10. See for example Meyrowitz 1985.
11. See for example Davis 1984 and Cooke 1988.

nition of its limitations; or a crisis within, and a new phase of, modernism.[12] Many are agreed however, that post-modernism does embody a shift in the experience and representation of space and time, and various writers have described the identity crisis which this has involved.

Some depict this crisis as a condition of 'placelessness'. Berland wrote on the Canadian experience of electronic media: 'Situated in many places at the same time, tuned in, hooked up, wired into, we know how to see ourselves as part of a global village and to see its boundarylessness as the essence of who we are' (1988: 347). Meyrowitz (1985) asserts that such media have abolished both space and time and 'destroyed' their 'specialness'. They have blurred traditional distinctions between individuals and groups, social situations, and physical places, leading to a homogenisation of places and group identities and experiences, and to 'no sense of place'. More and more people, he concludes (ibid.: 146), 'are living in a national (or international) information system rather than a local town or city'.

Timelessness, or the substitution of spatial for temporal co-ordinates, is also emphasised. Berland (1988), for example, illustrated the way in which 'the accelerating conquest of space through the media is inseparable from the increasing disunity of our place in it', and suppresses time. Post-modernism has been said to involve a loss of historical continuity and memory, and a preoccupation with instantaneity and with surfaces disconnected from the meanings behind them[13] or, as Harvey (1989) put it, an emphasis upon universalism and upon divergent possibilities of escape, fantasy, disposability and, consequently, the production of images rather than commodities.

These descriptions of modernism and post-modernism are accompanied by discourses in the press, media, and everyday language, and they pervade much popular and academic writing on rock and pop music. Recently we have seen the category of 'world music', television programmes such as *Rhythms of the World* and *Big World Café*,

12. See for example Harvey 1989 and Jameson 1984.
13. Grossberg, seeking to explain the declining political relevance of rock music, has asserted that the condition of post-modernity is characterised by change, but:

> no sense of progress which can provide meaning or depth and a sense of inheritance. Both the future and the past appear increasingly irrelevant; history has collapsed into the present . . . As history loses its sense, it can no longer be a source for the values by which one chooses and validates one's actions . . . As history becomes mere change – discontinuous, directionless and meaningless – it is replaced by a sense of fragmentation and rupture, of oppressive materiality, of powerlessness and relativism (1984: 229).

and 'global' events like Band Aid, with the associated song 'We are the World'. At the same time, some writers on popular music delight in focusing on the current politics of musical 'theft', whereby new cultural and aesthetic attitudes, and new technologies, have supposedly resulted in the plundering of different cultures or eras and the bringing together of rhythms, sounds and images from a multitude of sources 'which often bear no apparent 'natural' historical or geographical relation to one another' (Hebdige 1988). The result is 'a constant collage of unexpected proximities' (Chambers 1985), 'bricolage' or 'cut and mix', achieved by techniques such as 'scratching' and 'sampling'. Everything in this process is seen to be 'up for grabs'. 'Musical and cultural styles ripped out of other contexts, stripped of their initial referents, circulate in such a manner that they represent nothing other than their own transitory presence', wrote Chambers, which, he asserts, signifies the end of the logic of origins and the romantic 'moment of authenticity' (1985: 199). Hebdige has celebrated the increasing recognition of otherness and difference, 'abolishing boundaries of race and nation in the interests of a different kind of internationalism' (1988: 216).

Meanwhile Reynolds (1990: 138–9) discusses what he terms 'schizoid music' which represents the loss of a sense of past and future, spurns narrative and takes us 'nowhere . . . no place'. Hip Hop, for example, is described as a 'perpetual now', 'shallow, an array of surfaces', whilst House music represents the end of biography and location. 'It's difficult', writes Reynolds, 'to imagine a genre more place-less or hostile to an infusion of ethnicity. Although it comes from a place (Chicago) it does not draw anything from its environment' (ibid.). Similarly Reynolds constructs the category 'oceanic' music, a style which is again placeless and timeless, representing 'an end of history and an end of geography' (ibid.).

To many of those traditionally concerned with classification and difference involving the construction of identity and meaning, this focus upon a blurring of levels and categories, of places, spaces, times and identities might seem rather naive[14], and it does seem to contradict research data on the production and consumption of rock music in Liverpool. Yet, as Harvey pointed out (1989), place and

14. Earlier arguments asserting the eclipse of community and the single stranded anonymity resulting from the modernisation of society have likewise been criticised (see A. Cohen 1985).

placelessness, the particular and the universal, are part of the same process. The globalisation of cultural forms has been accompanied by a localisation of cultural identity and claims to authenticity, resulting in a tension or dialectic between the two trends. Transnational trends or styles are received, mediated and appropriated within a local context, and although popular music's communication networks are not restricted to local or national boundaries, they increasingly enable cultural production within localities and the expression of local identity defined, or perhaps emphasised, in relation to the 'non-local'. 'Locality' (representing a district, city, region) can thus be seen as a political strategy within a global, plural system. Within this strategy, music exercises territorialising power, framing public and private spaces or domains.

Musicians embroiled in the competitive, factional Liverpool 'scene' struggle for the success that would enable them to leave the city and achieve fame on a national or transnational level. At the same time they are embedded in webs of kinship and collective memory, located within a cognitive map defined by factors such as ethnicity and religion, within a city marginalised and ostracised in terms of power and resources on a national level. Consequently, the music they are involved in, far from being 'placeless' or 'timeless', often resonates with the breadth of space and the depth of time. The networks of technology that envelop the world and shrink it, supposedly distorting our sense of space and time so successfully, are at the same time rich with the patterns of intersecting group identities, local and historical significance.

Liverpool's popular music is thus closely bound up with its social and economic context. The label, 'The Liverpool Sound' may have been used to market some of that music to an international audience, yet the label is at the same time contested and debated and used by many within Liverpool itself, to construct a sense of difference and distinctiveness, a sense of Liverpool-ness.

References

Berland, J., 'Locating Listening: Technological Space, Popular Music, Canadian Meditations', *Cultural Studies,* vol. 2, no. 3, 1988, pp. 343–58.
Carney, G.O., 'Bluegrass Grows All Around: The Spatial Dimensions of a Country Music Style', in G.O. Carney (ed.), *The Sounds of People and Places: Readings in the Geography of American Folk and Popular Music,* Lanham, University Press of America, 1987.

Chambers, I., *Urban Rhythms: Pop Music and Popular Culture,* London, Macmillan, 1985.

Cohen, A., *The Symbolic Construction of Community,* London, Tavistock, 1985.

Cooke, P., 'Modernity and Postmodernity and the City', *Theory, Culture and Society,* vol. 5,1988, pp. 475–92.

Davis, M., 'The Political Economy of Late-Imperial America', *New Left Review,* 143, 1984, pp. 6–38.

Gifford, Lord, Brown, W. and Bundy, R., *Loosen the Shackles: First Report of the Liverpool 8 Enquiry into Race Relations in Liverpool,* London, Karia Press, 1989.

Glasgow, J., 'An Example of Spatial Diffusion: Jazz Music', in G.O. Carney (ed.), *The Sounds of People and Places,* Lanham, University Press of America, 1987.

Grossberg, L., 'Another Boring Day in Paradise: Rock and Roll and the Empowerment of Everyday Life', *Popular Music* 4, 1984, pp. 225–58.

Harvey, D., *The Condition of Postmodernity,* Oxford, Basil Blackwell, 1989.

Hebdige, D., *Hiding in the Light,* London, Routledge, 1988.

Jameson, F., 'Postmodernism or the Cultural Logic of Late Capitalism', *New Left Review,* vol. 146, 1984.

Lane, A., *Liverpool Gateway of Empire,* London, Lawrence and Wishart, 1987.

Meyrowitz, J., *No Sense of Place: The Impact of Electronic Media on Social Behaviour,* New York, Oxford University Press, 1985.

Reynolds, S., *Blissed Out: The Raptures of Rock,* London, Serpents Tail, 1990.

8

'The Land is Our *Märr* (Essence), It Stays Forever'[1]: The *Yothu—Yindi* Relationship in Australian Aboriginal Traditional and Popular Musics

Fiona Magowan

In the Northern Territory of Aboriginal Australia relations between musical performance, rights to geographical place and social identity are strongly marked. Aboriginal identity is formulated through access to knowledge of the Ancestral Law which relates spirit creator ancestor beings to individuals and clans by rights to land through mythological links. These rights are asserted in paintings, songs, dances and the production of sacred objects, all of which associate people with places.

As components of Aboriginal life traditional ritual music and dance[2] communicate a complex of relationships, identities and social realities structured internally – as elements of similarity or

---

1. Stephen Yunupingu, Gumatj clan member of the *Soft Sands* band of Galiwin'ku.
2. 'Traditional ritual' performance is based on a number of songs series and their accompanying dances which narrate mythological events said to have occurred in the distant past. It is these traditional songs that have been used prior to colonial contact to which I refer by the terms 'traditional' and 'ritual' although other non-ritual traditional genres do exist such as children's songs and young men's songs which will not concern us here.

135

difference within a clan or between clans – and externally – as a communal ideology of Aboriginal cultural values to inform Euro-Australians. Following fifty years of colonisation in North East Arnhem Land, the introduction of media and commercialism have led to the genesis of an Aboriginal popular music in which processes of accommodation and resistance[3] to colonial influences are being expressed in a new Aboriginal musical identity related to ritual forms. Ritual song texts and their meanings are being adapted to popular music forms. These 'new' musics are part of a process of creating an Aboriginal ethnicity by which Yolngu[4] present a unified front to the West.

This chapter deals with the internal and external structuring of Aboriginal identity as expressed by the mother–child or *yothu–yindi* link (as I shall refer to it from now on) which is an organisational feature of traditional ritual song and popular music. Internal and external perspectives are analysed using the concepts that Myers terms 'relatedness' and 'differentiation' in Pintupi social structuring, where rights in, and the exploitation of, Pintupi knowledge control the dramatisation of social and cultural life.[5]

I consider how *yothu–yindi* ideology is articulated in two spheres, the traditional and the popular. The objective and subjective values of the *yothu–yindi* link are separable and separated in the traditional and modern secular domains. In traditional song ideology *yothu–yindi* represents part of a sacred permanent timeless core,[6] the

---

3. In his book, *Whitefella' Comin*, Trigger discusses the impact of missionary influences on the people of Doomadgee in North Queensland from perspectives of domination or affinity within the colonial system. Here I use the concepts of 'accommodation' and 'resistance' to illustrate how textual meanings are being transformed from their traditional values to be adapted for the Western music industry (Trigger 1992: 219).
4. The Aboriginal or Yolngu people of the North East Arnhem region is the term which they use to identify themselves.
5. Myers discusses 'structure' in Pintupi society from two angles as an 'objective order outside themselves to which they must adapt through knowledge of the Dreaming'. He also examines the internal aspects of social life which he says, 'consist of the opposition between overall relatedness and differentiation'. Here I apply his terms, 'relatedness' and 'differentiation' to internal performance practice rather than, as Myers does, to social and political decision-making. (Myers, 1986: 288)
6. Stanner, Maddock, Morphy, Rudder, and others have detailed the complexity of the religious component of the Dreamtime. Stanner describes the permanent nature of the Ancestral Law of the Dreamtime which he says instigates 'the fixation or instituting of things in an enduring form with good and bad properties'. (Charlesworth, Morphy, Bell, & Maddock (eds), 1984: 146)

totality of which consists of the internal events of the Ancestral Law known as the Dreamtime[7] and constitutes the essence of Aboriginal identity.[8] In practice however, the concepts of the Dreamtime are adapted for each circumstance and context, constantly being redefined as necessity to external pressure dictates. The concept of *yothu–yindi* may be isolated as part of Aboriginal identity which can then be adjusted and negotiated as an ideology to structure songs for commercial use in the popular music industry. Thus, the value of Aboriginal music in the traditional and popular spheres is accorded varying significance as a result of the confluence of two cosmologies and value systems. From an Aboriginal perspective *yothu–yindi* ideology has distinctive meaning and importance in the two contexts. Its value is then, 'at one and the same time both "objective", that is external to or independent of the actor, and "subjective", that is, internal to the actor, a perception of the self' (Epstein 1978: 14). In order to understand how these objective and subjective perceptions are expressed through Aboriginal music, I will first discuss the principles underlying the *yothu–yindi* concept in its social context in the North East Arnhem Land region.

Yothu—Yindi as Social Ideology

Yolngu identity is first established on the basis of clan membership. Clans belong to one of the two exogamous patrilineal moieties, Dhuwa and Yirritja. On Galiwin'ku the exact number of resident clans are disputed due to the mobility of the community. Yolngu identify sixteen clans as being represented at Galiwin'ku. These sixteen clans interact on a relationship basis for ceremonial as well as social and political purposes. Funerals are the most frequent ceremonial events. When a death is announced three or four clans will meet to determine the songs and dances appropriate to the deceased which

---

7. The Dreamtime or Dreaming refers specifically to the creating acts of Ancestral beings who wandered across the landscape in the distant past transforming its geographical features, creating and naming clans and land at every place they came to.
8. In the beginning the creator Ancestral beings were humans although they took the form of animals as they crossed each clan's territory.

will structure the ritual performance.[9] Specific individuals will hold rights in organising the events of each ritual occasion. Rights in singing distinguish clans who belong to a particular place from those who share the same songs about that place although resident elsewhere. Performance rights may apply either to individuals or clans. These are partially determined by Yolngu notions of skill in singing and dancing which illustrate the different levels of ritual knowledge held by men and women. Skills are then reflected through those organising, leading and participating in the ritual singing and dancing.

Kinship relations[10] form the basis of asserting rights[11] in organising the ritual participants. One of these relations is the *yothu–yindi* mother–child dyad which can be analysed from both egocentric and sociocentric perspectives. Egocentrically the term is used to refer to the relationship between

a) A child (*yothu* or *waku* S/D) and its mother,

b) A child and its MB, *ngapipi*.

Sociocentrically it implies the relationship between,

a) A child's clan group, *wakupulu* and its mother clan, *ngandipulu*,

b) A small area of land, and a larger area of land, its *ngandiwänga*.

Egocentric and sociocentric relations affect rights to ritual knowledge and performance. Inheritance of ritual knowledge is patrilineal

---

9. Turner identifies the elements of performance as concerned with 'social drama', 'multivocality' and 'the polarisation of ritual symbols'. In Yolngu ritual multivocality may apply to song texts which bring different images, sentiments, values and ideas into a metaphorical relationship between the performer, listener and their environment. These symbols are enacted through dance with varying levels of interpretation which are reflected by or are implicit in the social structure. (Turner 1974: 23)

10. The Yolngu kinship system allows each person in the North East Arnhem Land region to relate to one another as either actual or classificatory kin. The terminology applies to both egocentric links between individuals or to sociocentric networking between clans. Kin terms operate in reciprocal pairs. For example, *märi* (MM/MMB) and *gutharra* ZDC or *ngandi* (M) and *waku* (C) are reciprocal referents. The system is further divided by eight subsections which delineate marriageable couples (See Williams, 1986: 53 and Shapiro 1969).

11. Morphy (1991) discusses in detail the distribution of rights in 'sacred law' at neighbouring Yirrkala, which, though similar to the Galwin'ku case, shows differences in emphasis.

although men and women have rights in learning their mother's ancestral law and its manifestations in the form of paintings, songs, dances and sacred objects. Senior males in each clan control the use and performance of clan songs although senior women have authority to negotiate in the ceremonial proceedings. In performance a woman may sing songs belonging to her own clan which are 'owned' by members of her clan and through Ancestral Law she shares rights in singing songs owned by other related clans in her moiety. She also has rights in singing her mother's clan songs (songs of the opposite moiety) through the *yothu-yindi* relationship. Women's rights in singing depend on their status and age within lineages. Women acquire song knowledge and status by a process of public performance and private teaching. Fathers and mothers narrate the ancestral stories through songs at home while boys experiment together with ritual singing in the bush. Girls also learn crying songs from their mothers and grandmothers during times of mourning. Elderly senior women may have the authority to advise their sisters' daughters' sons, *gutharra*,[12] on the appropriate order of songs at a ritual when no senior male members of the clan are still alive, or when the clan is nearing extinction. In this case, a woman may have authority in ritual decision-making although the songs will have been given to her sisters' daughters' sons, *gutharra*, for safekeeping as the caretaker of her clan's ritual knowledge (Keen 1978: 140). Sisters' sons, *waku*, have rights in approving the final structure of the ritual events. These rights are balanced by their obligations to serve as *djunggaya* or 'workers'[13] for their mothers' clan by playing the didjeridoo, dancing, producing sacred objects and paintings and constructing the shade and performance area.

Yothu—Yindi as Arnhem Land Topography

Land and its ecological components of plants, animals, seasons and waters provide a metaphorical medium to express the complexities of human relationships. The properties of contours and locations

---

12. The mother's mother's (brother) (*märi*) stands in a reciprocal relationship to the sister's daughter's sons (*gutharra*) who are in the same moiety. *Märi* have primary rights in holding the Ancestral Law and organising each stage of the funeral proceedings.
13. Keen refers to sister's sons as both 'workers' and 'helpers' (Keen 1978: 164)

reflect analogous relationships between individuals, clans and their Ancestral past. Songs manifest the power of the Ancestral world in the present establishing links between spiritual and physical realities. Meanings of song texts are analogues connecting people with places. Features of land and water in song texts represent human body parts, human relationships, life cycles and clan interrelations (Williams 1986).

In North East Arnhem Land Yolngu think of clan homelands as being organised in *yothu–yindi* pairs. A child's (*yothu*) land is located next to its mother's (*ngandi*) land within close proximity of its mother's mother's brother's (*märi*) land. Large clans may divide land between lineages in different areas (Keen 1978: 21). In this case lineages may have different mother lands, either actual or classificatory, adjacent to their own clan land. The land is thus seen as embodying both male and female aspects of identity. People are thought of as coming from, merging with and returning to the land. Djiniyini,[14] leader of the Golumala clan on Galiwin'ku, commented, 'The land is my mother. Like a human mother the land gives us protection, enjoyment and provides for our needs – economic, social and religious. We have a human relationship with the land: Mother-daughter, son. When the land is taken from us or destroyed, we feel hurt because we belong to the land and we are part of it' (Yule 1982: 8).

Waters connect *yothu–yindi* lands and represent the spiritual essence of each clan's identity. This has been illustrated in the bubbling froth of two streams of fresh and salt water meeting as an analogue with troubles flaring in a marriage relationship where each stream represents the identity of husband or wife. The editor of Yirrkala Literature Production Centre, Michael Christie puts it this way: 'The floodwater has come down to the sea but the sea water is refusing to give way to it' (Christie 1989: 10). 'Resistance' is encountered in the symbolic conflict between fresh and salt waters as metaphors of personal identities. In another context the symbolism may also be used as one of 'accommodation' incorporating members of other clans of the opposite moiety into the one source. *Yothu–yindi* ideology here implies a peaceful marriage link between the exogamous moieties in Yolngu society. This concept was used in 1988 as part of a maths workshop to inform Europeans about the basis of Yolngu relationships. Two swirling streams meeting in the middle symbolised

---

14. Rev. Dr. Djiniyini Gondarra is also the Aboriginal representative for the World Council of Churches and the Australian Church Congress.

at one level the strands of parental ties allowing an individual to be both Dhuwa and Yirritja while, at another level, it symbolised the confluence of the two moieties. With reference to the waters, a female teacher at Yirrkala, Dhanggal, commented, 'It is the strands, the *gurrkurr* that ties all the people together' (Dhanggal 1991: 11). The confluence of two rivers may unite different clans of the same moiety through the meanings of the song texts. Where the rivers of one clan meet they are said to be in one *ringgitj* (sacred area shared by several clans related by Ancestral Law). In water songs of the Yirritja moiety this area is known as Ganma[15] linking the Yirritja clans and their sacred land. In the case of the Gumatj and Wangurri clans the confluence of two rivers unites their homelands at Biranybirany and Dhälinybuy.

Yothu—Yindi Ideology in Traditional Performance

The conjoining of Dhuwa and Yirritja moieties' homelands via coastal and inland waterways is an important socialising feature in ritual organisation, dance and the construction of song texts. Yolngu concepts of the cosmos are derived from knowledge of their foundational identity, *Djalkiri*, which is contained in the land providing the basis for ritual negotiations. In the decision process prior to a funeral men will discuss the starting point of the singing for the deceased through all the connections made with other clans in the individual's lifetime. The clans who will be singing at a funeral are those which relate to the deceased as,

1) mother's mother's brother's clans, *märipulu*,

2) the sister's daughter's sons' clans, *gutharra*,

3) the deceased's sister's clan, *yapapulu*,

4) the sister's son's clan, *wakupulu*,

5) the deceased's own clan,

6) the deceased's mother's clan, *ngandipulu*.

---

15. Ganma is the intermingling of two currents where foam is created on the surface of the water symbolic of the meeting of two separate identities, usually of clans (Marika, Ngurruwuttun, and White (eds) 1989).

Families will sit together in *yothu–yindi* groups at the ceremony ready to join together in the dancing for the men who are leading the singing. The senior men in each clan will decide the order of the songs relating to the deceased and his or her land. The songs will metaphorically transport the body of the deceased back along a pre-determined route of the Ancestral Dreaming track to which it is related. Song orders are decided by those who have rights at each place in the mythological journey and they are determined prior to the ceremony proper although other clans may use songs and song series to vie for ritual domination over the organising clan during the proceedings. Competition for status may be subtly played out in the construction of the song series through the manipulation of texts and their meanings. For example, if a clan of lesser ritual importance omits some of the songs that are usually performed in their song series and finishes singing before the leading clan, conflicts and tensions may disrupt the proceedings until apologies are publicly expressed and acknowledged. Those clans who may claim rights in directing part of the performance can then make a political statement through song structuring (Morphy 1984).

Gurwanawuy, a senior man of the Djambarrpuyngu clan, explained how the song associations between the deceased and their land might be envisaged.

> If a person of the ngurruyurrtjurr Djambarrpuyngu clan passes away you (Datiwuy -mother's mother's brother (*märi*) for Djambarrpuyngu) start singing at Djarraya and go away from it. So Manydjarri may start singing at Djarraya and sing (about the ancestral shark) up to Rorru creek, the (the shark turns to travel) to Gonguruy and eventually to ngurruyurrtjurr
> F: How long would this take?
> G: On the first day you sing from Djarraya to Rorru. On the second day you start at Gonguruy and sing to Rorru and back to Gonguruy, or go inland from Rorru to the bush side and back to Rorru. On the third day you must end up at ngurruyurrtjurr.

Datiwuy and Djambarrpuyngu clans will aim to sing songs that will take them to Rorruwuy. They may approach the creek at Rorruwuy from different directions, but both must reach Rorruwuy to begin the second day's singing with the appropriate song subject identifying the deceased at Rorruwuy itself. Gurwanawuy puts it this way: 'You would never start the thunderman song far away from the deceased's homeland. It is a close song. I would get into trouble with other people if I started singing the thunderman when Manydjarri was singing the East wind. He would be far away and it would take him a long time to finish singing and we would finish first.'

Clan members who take the final responsibility in ritual singing are sister's sons, *waku*. As actual or classificatory children of the deceased they consolidate the bond between their physical existence and the origins of their spiritual identity as sacred objects from their mother. Children are important as they represent part of the essence of the 'spiritual inside'[16] coming from the physical water of their mother's womb and its metaphorical association with the water at her clan land. This alliance is illustrated in the meanings of song texts. While sister's daughter's sons (*gutharra*) may sing songs of their own clan and moiety they may not sing the melodies of clan songs belonging to the opposite moiety such as those of their sister's son's clan, *wakupulu*. However, names of ancestral beings reflecting the identity of the deceased from the opposite moiety may be incorporated into their own melodies and song texts. For example, in the Dhuwa moiety song of the shark the Datiwuy clan singer may incorporate the names of the Gumatj clan water, *Rramgura* if the Gumatj canoe, *Matjala* crosses the Dhuwa current where the ancestral shark being is lying. These two clans are *yothu–yindi* for each other, Datiwuy being children of their Gumatj mother.

In song, rivers may be called by the powerful surnames or *bundurr* of the clans who own them. These names embody the spiritual essence of the clan and their foundational knowledge, *djalkiri*. Different lineages within a clan may occupy more than one area of water and are recognised by their water names. For example, in the case of the Wangurri clan of the Yirritja moiety, two subsets are called Munyarryun water and Dhurrkay water. Different lineages within clans sharing the same water will distinguish themselves by separate water names, melodic contours and rhythmic motifs to indicate the differing strengths and natures of the currents. This technique is also used to distinguish between clans who share the same song text. For example, the concept of Ganma, whereby two clans come together at a sacred area as noted earlier, is illustrated in the following

---

16. While the distinction between the Aboriginal religion and daily experience is not clearly divided, Yolngu themselves determine degrees that are more or less sacred in terms of restricted Ancestral knowledge. The 'spiritual inside' refers to the sacred inner core of the Dreamtime mythology and has been identified by Morphy as 'linking the individual directly within a wider cosmological scheme in which the power of the Ancestral world is transferred from one generation to the next' (Morphy 1984: 217).

song of the merging Wangurri and Warramiri clans' water which is cried by women in this way:

> *lalalalalalalala Gularri ngarra ngunhi dhuniya ngarkalama Guninyirryirriwuy*
> Rippling and gurgling water I there go down water names
> I am travelling down the fast flowing Wangurri water called Gularri, ngarkalama, Guninyirryirriwuy
>
> *Dhurrwalapamurru*
> Through the Dhurrwalapa freshwater (going from Dhäliny to the sea)
>
> *Guniniyirryirri Djambalmurrunguru ngarkalama*
> Names of the freshwater at the Wangurri clan land, Dhälinybuy
> (I am in) the water, my foundation
>
> *Djinaku ngunha ngarra Muwatji Bandjurruwu*
> Inside there I Warramiri water tree
> I am inside the tree in the Warramiri clan waters.
>
> *nuku Mirrarrwirrarrwi Djalathun*
> Foot foundation anchor
> These waters are the foundation of my Ancestral Law.

The singer is Murukun, a woman of the Djambarrpuyngu clan, the *wakupulu*, or sister's child's clan for Warramiri and she is singing her mother's clan song. In this text the two waters merge in a rushing whirlpool at Mindharr, an island opposite the Wangurri outstation, Muthamul. While the Wangurri freshwater begins at Dhäliny and flows out to the sea, the Warramiri water comes from Dholtji around the coast to Mindharr point where the fresh and the salt waters join together.

Water is one element of the environment which is used as an analogue with male and female body functions. It symbolises a medium of protection in the act of procreation, a nest for the next generation and is the vehicle through which clans physically and spiritually interact. It is most frequently used to convey the production, transportation and interaction of individuals from life to death.

Song Knowledge as Commercial Exchange

So far, I have considered the *yothu–yindi* principle as an internal ideology that structures the content and form of ritual and social interaction through a series of controls over knowledge, representation, performance and space. The controls placed on the acquisition and expression of Ancestral knowledge as determined by seniority and status have been seen to affect the construction of song meanings and their dramatisation in performance time and space. Thus, an understanding of personal identity is intimately associated with the degree of freedom or limitation on individuals' access to, use and appreciation of mythological knowledge as experienced in ritual. I have shown how traditional songs are composed within a cultural framework based on Ancestral identity articulated by shared perceptions of the system of restrictions upon knowledge and performance.

I shall now examine how the meanings and structuring of traditional song texts are being translated into a popular music genre through a process of adapting *yothu–yindi* ideology as part of an international Aboriginal identity. As knowledge of Ancestral Law is valued for social gain – since all Yolngu law is to some lesser or greater degree restricted – the control of singing, both ritually and for commercial purposes, is politically advantageous. Morphy notes that, 'Not only is it (knowledge) related to differential control and participation in religious events on the basis of an individual's status and group affiliation, but it is also integrated within the political structure of society' (Morphy 1983: 110). Controlling knowledge is a vital force in mediating political power outside the structure of Yolngu society as well as within it. If the control of Ancestral knowledge is to be used in another arena as a component of cross-cultural exchange, there is always the danger that it will contradict its indigenous value. Ritual knowledge must be regulated to establish rights over land, access to women, clan and individual identities. It is through the idea that Ancestral mythology provides a concrete symbolic core that Yolngu are able to maintain a separate identity which must be controlled in order to resist colonial influence.

The international music industry involves a complex set of institutions, relationships and practices. Where financial remuneration is received for producing albums, Yolngu have sought indigenous means of mediating payment distribution from record sales. In Yolngu spheres of exchange the obligations of kin ties in social and ceremonial events regulate the system of giving and reciprocating. In ritual, performances are determined by relationships where duties to relatives are mandatory. Profit and loss in terms of time, effort, virtuosity and performance practice are not calculated as ends in themselves. Payment is usually in kind. The host clan will provide the performers with food and drink. Thus, when money is given as payment for recording popular music the allocation of that reward operates on a system of redistribution through social obligations. For Yolngu, money acquires the role of fulfilling social bonding by payments to specific kin. Popular music provides a mode by which its performers may gain support from key individuals or clans in the community affecting their own prestige and social status. Hence, popular music carries a symbolic load that is not equivalent to a specific economic goal, as is the case in ritual music.

One of the strategies of the Western music industry has been to view non-Western song as a financially negotiable 'alienable commodity' (Gregory 1982). However, when Yolngu perform they are not embarking on an exchange of music for music's sake but offering an inalienable gift of what it means to be Yolngu. In determining the value system of Yolngu popular music we need to consider how it has come to convey indigenous meaning through the place and purpose of Yolngu ritual music in the past and the changing state of Yolngu perceptions of music today. My aim, in the remainder of this paper, is to show how Yolngu reconcile the demands of the music industry with the social demands of the *yothu–yindi* ideology outlined above.

The Politics of Resistance in an Aboriginal Music Identity

As Yolngu are seeking to establish popular music as the 'traditional voice of the people' it is necessary to examine the qualitative differences between the form, meaning and content of songs in the ceremonial and commercial spheres. The formation of Aboriginal popular music groups in the 1970s initiated interest in the Australian music industry to produce marketable recordings for national distribution. Amongst these early groups was the Galiwin'ku pop group, *Soft Sands*, which, like several others, accommodated familiar Western music styles by playing a mixture of Country and Western and Gospel songs. The conversion from ritual musical forms to a commercialised music industry saw the introduction of guitars, keyboards, and equally tempered fixed pitch. The meanings of these songs were not part of the traditional Yolngu worldview but were governed instead by full-scale adaptation to demands of the popular music industry. Although some of these songs were performed in Aboriginal dialects, with a hybrid form of Yolngu and Western rhythms, some Gospel songs are the result of missionary contact, while other texts ultimately refer to the colonial context of 1970s Australia and are influenced by American singing and texts heard on the radio.

Today this early form of Aboriginal pop music has undergone a shift in emphasis through innovations in meaning and content. The impact of the pop group, *Yothu-Yindi*, whose members are drawn from both Galiwin'ku and Yirrkala, has resulted in changes in the nature of Aboriginal pop music by transferring entire concepts of Yolngu worldview into the meaning of their songs. These recent innovations were heralded by the international acclaim of their album *Tribal Voice*. This second album, produced in 1991, differed radically from the first album in music and text, by using traditional songs with their original form and words. Prior to this The Homeland Movement album used a mixture of song texts in English and Yolngu dialect underlining Yolngu political and social concerns. Social solidarity is reflected in the name of the pop group *Yothu-Yindi* who have directly adopted the *yothu-yindi* concept as evidence of a unified Aboriginal identity through the organisation of the band and the meaning of the song texts. The band is composed of members of the Gumatj and Rirratjingu clans who stand in the relationship of mother–child for one another. During concert tours the sister's son's, *djunggaya,* may sing as well as dance, and play instruments. The responsibilities allocated between clan members as singers or accompanists on the album, *Tribal Voice*, show that the *wakupulu*, Rirratjingu, are workers for their Gumatj mother clan, *ngandipulu*. The earlier processes of accommodation within a Western music framework are being replaced by resistance through an explicitly indigenous identity.

Resistance to European musical values are also expressed in the restructuring of song texts by incorporating a mixture of ritual symbolism and concern with colonial hegemony. Stephen Yunupingu, singer of the *Soft Sands* band, commented, 'We have to protect the background and be strong because our ancestors fought for their rights. Through words and feelings in the songs we show our political history. We claim the rivers and the land through song. You can change the song but not the land. The land is our *märr* (essence) – it stays forever.'

Adapted song texts emphasise a Yolngu identity from clan origins, the Ancestral history that underpins their rights to the land. The song, 'Tribal Voice' expresses the fight for equal recognition between Aboriginals and Euro-Australians presenting equality as a communal concern for all clans. It is a cry to unite in the face of encroaching values and Australian government policies.

> So you better get up and fight for your rights
> Don't be afraid of the move you make
> You better listen to your tribal voice – voice!
> Well I wonder if it's part of history
> Full of influential mystery
> From the spirits of my people
> Who have just gone before

In the text, fourteen of the thirty-two clans of the North East Arnhem Land region are then called upon to unite and account for their struggle to survive.

> You better listen to you Gumatj voice
> You better listen to you Rirratjingu voice
> You better listen to your Wanguri voice . . .
> You better listen to your Warramiri voice

The concept of 'land' forms an insistent refrain in these songs, which can best be understood in the context of ongoing changes between Aboriginal and Euro-Australians.

The threat of losing land to mining companies has been a continual battle since the first victory for Yolngu rights in the Gove bauxite mining case in 1974. Recognition of Aboriginal rights does not just involve identifying the people but also their homelands and the songs, dances, rituals and paintings associated with them. The song 'Treaty' highlights the importance of land by reflecting on the Australian bicentennial tensions that arose over the celebrations of the ownership of Terra Nullius in 1988. Feelings of mistrust were intensified by the threat of losing land to more mining companies.

> Back in 1988 all those talking politicians
> Words are easy, words are cheap.
> Much cheaper than our priceless land.
> But promises can disappear . . .
> This land was never given up

This land was never bought and sold
The planting of the Union Jack
Never changed our law at all

('Treaty' from the album *Tribal Voice*)

The desire for unity based on equality and understanding is also emphasised later in this song text. Water metaphors are used to imply the meeting, co-operation and future unity of European and Aboriginals. The concept of Ganma, referred to earlier in the ritual context, is adopted here to illustrate the negotiations between Yolngu and European relations. In this way, we can see how 'the language of song is a vehicle for bringing comprehension and autonomous social action to bear upon forces so often beyond the singer's control' (Coplan 1990: 367).

Now two rivers run their course
Separated for so long
I'm dreaming of a brighter day
When the waters will be one
Treaty Yeh Treaty Now

('Treaty' from the album *Tribal Voice*)

Unity is considered possible if Europeans will follow the pattern of what is imagined as 'the *yothu–yindi* lifestyle'. The song '*Matjala*, Driftwood', is sung entirely in Yolngu language and adapts the principle of working and caring for each other, made explicit through *yothu–yindi* ideology, as the way forward for peace and reconciliation between Euro-Australians and Aboriginals. Here the rules of traditional song composition have been reconstructed for commercial purposes. The imagery of the song text uses a mixture of different clan Ancestral identities belonging to the Gumatj and Rirratjingu clans. The Rirratjingu song of the Morning Star is incorporated alongside images of the Yirritja Driftwood and Sunset. In ritual each image would constitute a complete song item. Here they are combined in the complete text which is also modified musically to suit a Western pitch, melody and rhythm.

In this popular version the driftwood does not float past the ancestral shark being of the Datiwuy clan but instead unites the identity of the Rirratjingu clan by analogy with their Ancestral essence as the Morning Star Pole, *Banumbirr*. Within ritual the driftwood has several levels of symbolic imagery. It represents the Gumatj canoe in which the body of a dead person travels to the Land of the Dead and is also representative of the body of the deceased inside a coffin. It suggests a return to the Ancestral homeland and thus to the identity of the Gumatj clan which it also symbolises. In a similar way, the Morning Star imagery of the Rirratjingu clan comprises a wooden pole to which feathers are attached representing the backbone or foundation of the clan's identity. Rirratjingu are one of several Dhuwa clans sharing the same Ancestral origin, the branches of the pole symbolising the interrelatedness of clans through marriage descendants. The pole, like the driftwood is symbolic of each clan's foundational knowledge linking themselves with their homeland and Ancestral spiritual realm.

> *Gumatj Rirratjingu nhina mala wanggany*
> Gumatj and Rirratjingu sit together as one people
>
> *– Miyaman manikay. ngaraca Maypurrumburr*
> They sing the song of the Morning Star pole called Maypurrumburr
>
> *– ngäthi miyaman Gunda Rirraliny*
> They cry of the stony gravel path (taken by their ancestors)
>
> *– Dhiyala nhina. Mala wanggany*
> Here they sit. One people.
>
> ('*Matjala* Driftwood' from the album *Tribal Voice*)

The interlocking fabric of Yolngu physical and spiritual identities are used as a symbolic model to create an interwoven structure of an idealised Yolngu and Euro-Australian political and social understanding which allows them to maintain their own ethnic independence. Later in this song of the Driftwood the symbol of the sunset is used with a double meaning. In ritual singing, the deep red glow represents the death of a relative, their blood having coloured the clouds and the sky. Sorrow at the loss of the deceased is poignantly projected by the colours. Stephen Yunupingu expressed the sentiment to me in this way: 'It's not just the sunset on the west side but at the deceased's homeland itself and the *warwu* (worry, anxiety) within it. By singing we send the message through the sunset.' In the pop song, *'Matjala'*, reference to the sunset evokes memories of the blood of Yolngu ancestors who have been killed through unrests of Australia's troubled history. They mourn those who are gone and are united with them through the feelings and emotions aroused by the need to fight for recognition of their indigenous rights.

Djapana warwu
The sunset carries our worries

Lithara Wartjapa
It burns a deep red pink and orange

Miny'tjinydja Garrumara
The colours of the vibrant red glow

(*Matjala* Driftwood from the album, Tribal Voice)

By listing names of the sunset, the panorama of intermingling colours is also envisaged as a symbol of the interaction between Yolngu and Euro-Australians since the early 1900s.

Textual symbols are not the only form of expressing Yolngu identity. The album also includes traditional songs with traditional music structures. Two of these are *'Dhumdhum'*, a song of the Wallaby, and *'Yindjapana'*, the Dolphin. As in ritual performance the didjeridoo and clapsticks accompany the melody, pitch and rhythmic text of the songs. On the record sleeve and in live performances, each performer is covered in white clay, *gapan*, a ritual requirement for participation, and loincloths are worn which are usually reserved for special ceremonial occasions. The aesthetics of appearance are as important as the quality of the sound and the emotive associations of textual imagery. Since the majority of Euro-Australian and international audiences are excluded from an appreciation of textual symbolism Yolngu ritual values are conveyed through the stylised use of dance space, the energy of the visual display and the articulation of instruments and voices as if in conversation with one another. These performance techniques are employed specifically to engage a Euro-Australian appreciation and understanding of Yolngu culture. The sensory dimension of performance reinforces the ideology of the song texts. The emotional and ideational message is communicated at a number of different levels to non-Aboriginal listeners which is reflected in the languages used. The songs in Yolngu dialect employing ritual language exclude all audiences except those with an existing knowledge and concern for Yolngu culture. Songs with a mix of ritual text and English aim to inform and raise awareness of cultural characteristics while texts in English not only carry overtly political messages for governments and politicians within but also outside Australia.

Today Yolngu popular music is adopting a political tone as a strategy for attaining justice in all Aboriginal communities. The musical medium is however the last of the artistic forms to be used in this manner. Yolngu popular music is a relatively recent innovation and lags behind similar advances in the commercial sphere of the Yolngu art market. Unlike music, Yolngu art has been used as a means of asserting and explaining Yolngu identity within Australia and internationally for thirty years. In 1963 the Yolngu of Yirrkala sent a bark petition[17] to the Commonwealth Parliament as a statement of their rights to the land. This was used to dissuade the government from granting a permit for bauxite mining on Gove Peninsula.[18] In 1957 Galiwin'ku Yolngu revealed previously restricted and sacred objects as symbols of Aboriginal identity to mediate between Christianity and Aboriginal religion in what came to be known as the Elcho Adjustment Movement.[19]

Nowadays Yolngu traditional music and dance is sometimes used as a symbol of identity in welcoming government officials and saying farewell to Euro-Australians. When these symbols are transferred to a popular music genre they reach a huge local and international audience. Yolngu pop songs highlight social anxiety and concern for attaining cultural respect. By grading levels of textual intelligibility, audiences who know little or nothing of the words receive a semi-stereotypical image of traditional Aboriginal culture through their dress, dance, performance and painted bodies, by which they can feel part of the tribal situation.

Understanding texts is not an *a priori* necessity for inducing

---

17. Paintings are made for ritual and personal use depicting the relationship of clans and individuals to their land. Today they are more commonly produced on canvas although bark is the traditional medium. In this case the bark painting was presented as a legal document of rights to land at Yirrkala.
18. See Morphy 1983b and Morphy and Layton 1981.
19. See Morphy 1983b and Berndt 1962.

empathy for a cause. The ethnoaesthetics of display through performance content and structure create an atmosphere that evokes feelings of what it means to be Yolngu. Whether the song is understood or not does not detract from aesthetic value. As Jakobson notes, 'performance and context actively constitute one another and are not empirically divisible' (Jakobson 1960: 371). Sound in itself may be aesthetically pleasing. Communal appreciation of that sound reinforces agreement amongst listeners of a shared pleasure. This translates into a shared comprehension or concern for the welfare of the individuals and the cause behind its initiation. Thus, both dramatic effect and sound quality actively reconstitute the social 'force' of Aboriginal cultural identity. By creating multivocal symbols from which international audiences may interpret Aboriginal identity they are communicating, simultaneously and to a hugely varied audience, the multifarious orders of meaning that exist in Yolngu life.

I have argued that the way in which Yolngu popular music has been and is being constructed is dependent on the political and historical factors affecting Euro-Australian and Aboriginal relations. I do not want to suggest that an Aboriginal identity is wholly self-determined and unchanging but is rather a reaction to external influences fluctuating and adapting to the changing nature of internal social relations. Identity is based on Yolngu shared values of ancestral law, land, clan interrelations, and a performance ethos. As I have shown, relatedness is the basis of negotiations in ritual and in the politics between Aboriginal and European as it is in the construction of song texts and the performance of music.

With the expansion of the commercial music industry worldwide and the growing interest in non-Western musics in the 'world music' scene of the 1990s, the market for Yolngu pop music is more accessible to Yolngu performers and economically more viable than previously. Undoubtedly the world music phenomenon has constructed global musical 'difference' in ways which suit the strategies of multinational corporate industry, but it has also been successful to some small extent in contributing to an awareness of the very real imbalances that exist in the distribution of power and resources in the world today. *Yothu–Yindi* have constructed an influential and successful way of using an indigenous aesthetic of performance, with its demands for political and cultural space and appeals to primordial relationships between social groups, individuals and lands, to articulate the new demands of Aboriginal groups as a whole. These demands are addressed to Euro-Australians and also to the world beyond them in ways which they hope will put pressure on them to recognise their rights. A key element of this has been the adaption of the *yothu–yindi* element of their own cultural identity as the symbol of Yolngu interrelations to serve as a model for parallel discourse between all Aboriginal communities and the global music industry.

References

Berndt, R., *An Adjustment Movement in Arnhem Land*, Paris, Mouton, 1962.
Charlesworth, M., Morphy, H., Bell, D., & Maddock, K. (eds), *Religion in Aboriginal Australia*, Queensland, University of Queensland Press, 1984.
Christie, M., *Galtha Workshop, Vol. 2*, Nhulunbuy, Yirrkala Community Education Centre, 1989.
Coplan, D., 'Musical Understanding: The Ethnoaesthetics of Migrant Workers' Poetic Song in Lesotho', *Ethnomusicology*, vol. 34, 1990, pp. 337–68.
Dhanggal, *Garma Maths Workshop*, Yutana Dhäwu, Nhulunbuy, Yirrkala Literature Production Centre, 1991.
Epstein, A. L., *Ethos and Identity*, London, Tavistock Publications, 1978.
Geertz, C., *Local Knowledge*, New York, Basic Books, 1983.
Gregory, C., *Gifts and Commodities*, London and San Diego, Academic Press, 1982.
Jakobson, R., 'Linguistics and Poetics', in T. Sebeok (ed.), *Style in Language*, Cambridge, M.I.T. Press, 1960, pp. 350–77.
Keen, I., 'One Ceremony, One Song', D.Phil thesis, Australian National University, Canberra, 1978.
Marika, R., Ngurruwutthun, D. & White, L. 'Always Together, Yaka Gäna': Participatory Research at Yirrkala as part of the development of a Yolngu Education, Paper Presented at the Participatory Research Conference in University of Calgary, June 1989.
Morphy, H., *Ancestral Connections: Art and an Aboriginal System of Knowledge*, Chicago, University of Chicago Press, 1991.
——, *Journey to the Crocodile's Nest*, Canberra, Australian Institute of Aboriginal Studies, 1984.
——, '"Now you understand": An Analysis of the way Yolngu have used sacred knowledge to retain their autonomy', in M. Langton and N. Peterson (eds), *Aborigines, Land and Land Rights*, Canberra: Australian Institute of Aboriginal Studies, 1983, pp. 110–33.
——, & Layton, R., 'Choosing among Alternatives: Cultural Transformation and Social Change in Aboriginal Australia and the French Jura', *Mankind*, vol. 13, 1981, pp. 56–73.
Myers, F., *Pintupi Country, Pintupi Self*, Washington, Smithsonian Institution Press, 1986.
Shapiro, W., 'Miwuyt Marriage: Social Structural Aspects of the Bestowal

of Females in N.E. Arnhem Land', Ph.D thesis, Australian National University, Canberra, 1969.

Trigger, D., *Whitefella' Comin'*, Cambridge, Cambridge University Press, 1992.

Turner, V., *Dramas, Fields and Metaphors: Symbolic Action in Human Society*, Ithaca & London, Cornell Press, 1974.

Williams, N., *The Yolngu and their Land: A System of Land Tenure and its Fight for Recognition*, Canberra, Australian Institute of Aboriginal Studies, 1986.

Yothu-Yindi, *Tribal Voice*, Mushroom Records, 1991.

Yule, I., (ed.) *My Mother The Land and I, Galiwin'ku*, Elcho Island Literature Production Centre, 1982.

9

Personal and Collective Identity in Kalasha Song Performance: The Significance of Music-making in a Minority Enclave

Peter Parkes

In this essay I examine the significance of song performance in articulating personal, group and collective identities among the Kalasha of Chitral, a unique non-Islamic minority of northwest Pakistan.[1] As a peculiar religious enclave, the Kalasha appear to have few overt problems of self-definition. A distinctive identity is presupposed by their status as non-Muslim, whose ritual, social and moral institutions are all evidently very different from those of their Islamic neighbours. Music, which is equally distinctive of Kalasha culture, need not therefore have any especially privileged status as a performative 'emblem' of symbolic differentiation. Yet I shall argue that song performance has been more crucially integral to the historical constitution and perpetuation of Kalasha society. The orchestration of song and dance in festival

---

1. I am grateful to the Leverhulme Trust for a research fellowship at the Queen's University of Belfast (1988–90) on 'Kalasha Language, Music and Performance' under the direction of Professor Rembrandt Wolpert. Fieldwork among the Kalasha was conducted in 1972, 1974, 1975–7, 1989 and 1990, supported by grants from the SSRC (3930/2) and ESRC (R000 22 1087). My understanding of Kalasha song has especially benefited from transcriptions and analyses by Dr Jonathon Stock (Parkes and Stock n.d.; see Parkes 1994: appendix) together with suggestions from Dr Suzel Reily. I am, as always, indebted to Saifullah Jan and Ķazi Khosh Nawaz of Rumbur for their painstaking ethnographic assistance.

celebration is a focal expressive medium for interrelating personal and collective identities, representing individual achievements as corporative acts of collective allegiance, and hence dramatically displaying in performance a solidary moral community that appears expressly united in the face of external oppression as well as internal animosities. Kalasha song performance thus manages to resolve inherent tensions concerning the recognition of interpersonal competition and differential status within a communitarian context of collective enclavement. In the informal organisation and implicit etiquette of singing together, as well as in the explicit verbal content of their lyrics, Kalasha define for themselves a 'heterophonous' political order of segmentary identities, creating a resonant ensemble whose constituent self, group and community allegiances become vocally and experientially fused in musical celebration.

Kalasha Collective Identity: Enclavement and Ethnicity

Just under 4,000 non-Muslim Kalasha inhabit three small valleys of the Hindu Kush mountains in the southwest corner of Chitral District in northern Pakistan. The unique survival of this minority enclave within Islamic South Asia can be initially explained as a chance conjuncture of geographical isolation and historical accident. Until the final decade of the nineteenth century, several other non-Muslim or 'Kafir' peoples were known to inhabit adjacent mountain valleys in eastern Afghanistan. These were the 'Káfirs of the Hindu-Kush' observed by Robertson (1896) just prior to their military invasion and forced conversion to Islam under Amir Abdur Rahman Khan of Afghanistan. By 1900, however, Kafiristan, the enigmatic 'Land of Unbelievers', could be renamed Nuristan, the 'Land of Illumination', whose pre-Islamic culture had been eradicated. Only the so-called 'Little Kafiristan' of the Kalasha in Chitral managed to escape the Amir's proselytising zeal, for their territory then lay just within the administrative borders of British India. This accident of frontier demarcation evidently protected the Kalasha from forced conversion by the Afghans in the late nineteenth century; yet the earlier survival of their traditional culture, and its persistence to the present, appears to be more problematic. For unlike the relatively independent Afghan Kafirs, Kalasha communities have been subject to dominant Islamic powers ruling Chitral for over four centuries. It has therefore been through their persistent negotiation of subjection to such alien powers, as well as through their continued cultural resistance to Islamic assimilation, that the Kalasha have managed to perpetuate themselves as a non-Islamic enclave.

After the conquest of the last Kalasha rulers of southern Chitral, probably by the late fifteenth century, Kalasha communities were reduced to tributary serfdom under the Katur Mehtars or princes of Chitral. Tolerated as a subject people, their valleys were afforded some protection as dependencies of the Mehtar against the predatory raids of the Afghan Kafirs, as well as against proselytising Islamic missionaries. But like other reduced minorities, all Kalasha households were obliged to pay substantial annual taxes in subsistence products and to provide arduous corvée labour services for their overlords, while young women and children were periodically sold into slavery. These oppressive exactions are still bitterly recalled by many elder people, who were performing such feudal dues barely forty years ago (cf. Saifullah Jan 1994). Following enfranchisement from serfdom in the early 1950s, Kalasha communities continued to be subject to heavy taxation, as well as recurrent attempts at forced conversion by their Muslim neighbours; and even nowadays, despite improvements in their welfare, Kalasha continue to suffer relative oppression and disadvantage as a non-Muslim or 'Kafir' minority. It is therefore within this historical context of subordination to a politically dominant and culturally alien Islamic environment that we need to assess the resilience of Kalasha cultural identity, and the crucial significance of musical performance in its perpetuation.

The political ethos of Kalasha communities, shaped by this chronic experience of oppressive subordination, has several characteristic features of what Mary Douglas (1993) has recently diagnosed as an 'enclave culture' (cf. Castile & Cushner 1981). The societal institutions of enclaves are expressly modified to ensure communal solidarity in the face of an encompassing and alien social universe, being particularly adapted to discourage the 'defection' of internal members to this more dominant exterior environment, as irrevocably occurs through Kalasha conversions to Islam. The religious culture of enclaves also tends to be preoccupied with exacting ritual criteria of purity and pollution (Parkes 1987), serving to demarcate a distinctive group boundary that defines insiders from outsiders; and the political institutions of enclaved societies are similarly instituted in contrastive opposition to the 'hierarchical' polities in which their communities are encapsulated. In other words, enclaves are determinedly *egalitarian* in principle, where all members are supposedly alike in status and moral evaluation. Yet it is this egalitarian ethic of enclaves that poses a crucial institutional dilemma according to Douglas, undermining the establishment of consensual leadership, necessary to protect communal interests against external coercion and internal defection, which receive little institutional support in a political culture where any expression of authority, entailing social differentiation, is inherently distrusted. Hence the internal politics of enclaves is recurrently factional or 'sectarian', where popular resentment of leadership always threatens to unravel the solidarity and consensus in terms of which such communities are morally instituted.

Douglas's vivid portrayal of the 'enclave culture' and its sectarian contradictions does have resonance in Kalasha indigenous conceptions of their own communal identity (Saifullah Jan 1994), where it is repeatedly emphasised that 'all Kalasha are poor, all are equal' in contrast to the hereditary status grading characteristic of surrounding Muslim peoples in Chitral. Kalasha local politics in recent decades has also been marked by recurrent factional conflicts concerning collective leadership. Yet these 'sectarian' animosities appear to be episodic and contextually circumscribed modalities of social action, coexisting with alternative 'ceremonial' social performances that rather serve to coordinate particularist political interests within broader group and community projects of collective 'renown' (*namūs*). It is the special significance of musical performance in inter-orchestrating personal and group interests in this 'ceremonial' manner that I examine in this essay.

Equality, Eldership and Segmentary Identity

Kalasha festival song performance is focused upon a small circle of recognised 'elders' (*gaḍērak*, pl. *gaḍerakān*) representing lineage and valley-community constituencies. Such elders inaugurate a recurrent cycle of three song-and-dance genres, taking turns as soloists in introducing new songs within each genre, which are then taken up in chorus by other male and female participants to the accompaniment of drumming and communal dancing. Kalasha musical culture is thus largely identified with the vocal performances of male elders. If Kalasha society is properly characterised as egalitarian, its 'sound structure' therefore seems scarcely expressive of either its normal social practice or ideology (cf. Feld 1984), being rather hierarchically organised as a celebration of the 'traditional authority' of senior elders (Bloch 1974). Yet we should briefly consider how Kalasha eldership is effectively articulated with personal identity and group representation in quotidian contexts.

As in many other 'egalitarian' societies (Woodburn 1982: 446), the fraternal community of political equals emphasised in Kalasha rhetoric is essentially a community of male household heads or 'house elders' (*dūrä gaḍērak*), who are not of course all equally endowed with material resources. Dependent upon a mixed agropastoral economy of small-scale agriculture and transhumant livestock husbandry, relative prosperity largely emerges from the increased labour power of expanding households over the course of the normal domestic cycle. But such accumulated wealth in land and livestock is generally dispersed in each generation through equal male inheritance. Exceptional wealth is therefore a transient product of successful eldership, achieved by only a few senior patriarchs who have managed to dissuade their children from premature separation, and whose surplus yields of livestock and grain should be ceremonially distributed in public feasts as well as in assistance afforded to less fortunate kinspeople (Parkes n.d.). Kalasha may therefore reasonably maintain that all households are potentially 'equal', while still recognising differential status among elders in ceremonial feast-giving and informal patronage. Within each household, however, there is a clear allocation of authority (*čit*) over wives and dependents under the jurisdiction of its 'house elder' (*dūrä gaḍērak*), who represents his family's interests in lineage and community meetings.

The metaphorical extension of this acknowledged 'hierarchical' authority of house eldership to wider lineage, village and community constituencies is, however, less easily established. Kalasha terms of eldership are markedly informal and ambiguous in normal speech: the honorific *gaḍērak*, literally senior or elder, may be used to address any adult man on formal occasions. Eldership only begins to denote a political personage when attached to some group term, implying a constituency of dependents who recognise a senior elder's ability to represent their collective interests on public occasions: e.g. 'lineage elder' (*kam gaḍērak*), 'village elder' (*grom gaḍērak*) or 'community elder' (*dēšä gaḍērak*). But even these nominal epithets of progressive authority scarcely amount to an unequivocal hierarchy of political status, since there are likely to be several men competing for dominance in any situation by vociferously demonstrating their influence on public affairs. Seniority and leadership beyond the level of the household are therefore perpetually contested by rival elders, attempting to mobilise their own networks of support through disparate ties of kinship and patronage from one political situation to the next. Hence the practical politics of Kalasha communities is characteristically factional, occasionally erupting into polarised bloc formations behind dominant leaders that may divide each valley, village, lineage and even household into opposed parties.

It is in the quotidian context of such recurrent animosities, inevitably engendered by competitive leadership in the egalitarian enclave, that we need to evaluate the rhetorically corrective influence of Kalasha ceremonial performance. I shall argue here that it is through musically manifesting an otherwise *implicit schema of segmentary self-representation* through ceremonial eldership that song performance on festal occasions derives its ideological power as an illocutionary enactment of Kalasha collective identity. This 'ceremonial' representation of social order has many of the attributes of a classic segmentary system of patrilineal descent, where each valley-community (*deš*) is comprised of discrete exogamous patrilineages (*kam*), tracing seven or more generations of descent from an eponymous ancestor (Parkes 1984). Lineages congregate as distinct associations for ritual celebrations, and lineage members are expected to assist one another in contributing to group marriage payments and prestige feasts. Yet it should be noted that outside of these ritual or 'ceremonial' contexts that signify the collective prestige of the group, Kalasha lineages have a negligible or indeed negative role in the organisation of everyday subsistence.

Yet Kalasha lineage organisation is not simply an idealised 'fiction' of ritual and ceremonial representations. Lineages are actively mobilised as solidary groups in all of the distinctive societal institutions of the Kalasha, and most notably in their 'three great customs' (*tre ghōna dastūr*) of wife-elopement, prestige feasting and festival celebration. Each of these highly dramatised occasions creates a clear-cut segmentary alignment of opposed lineage allegiances, in terms of which a relatively stable symbolic order of ceremonial eldership may be expressed (cf. Galaty 1981). In wife-elopement (*alaṣiŋ*), for example, extramarital adultery among youths instigates the elopement of a married woman to a new husband, which polarises the two lineages of the ex-husband and abductor into a state of quasi-feud, vigorously pursued by their respective lineage elders.

After several weeks or months of such hostilities, peace-making is gradually initiated by other elders acting as mediators from lineages unrelated to the belligerent parties, who should then help arbitrate the payment of 'compensation' (*doṇḍ*) in the form of a double bridewealth. After the histrionic bargaining of group elders, negotiating the always disputed payment of this compensation wealth, senior community elders (*gāḍa baṣāra*), who have otherwise retired from active politics, are ultimately called to impose an impartial settlement on behalf of the entire *deš* community. Elopement thus successively calls into play a tripartite structure of opposition and mediation among three male age-grades – those of youths (*ǰuān*), active elders (*gaḍērak*) and senior or ceremonial elders (*gāḍa baṣāra*) – whose antagonisms are performatively enacted and resolved at successively higher levels of seniority (Parkes in press: chs. 10–11).

This performative template of competitive opposition and collective mediation, differentiating successive grades of eldership along a sliding segmentary axis of personal–group identities, is equally manifest in the organisation of Kalasha prestige and mortuary feasts (Parkes 1992). Here the initial ambitions of household members to honour a deceased or living elder critically depend upon a successive mobilisation of descent group and lineage support through subsidiary feasting, where their individual enterprise will be progressively adopted by representative elders in competitive rivalry with those of other lineages. Again, the seniormost elders of the community – the *gāḍa baṣāra* – play a symbolically prominent role in impartially orchestrating and supervising prestige feasts in conformity with community traditions (*dēšä dastūr*). In summary, I suggest that Kalasha 'ceremonial' (*dasturī*) institutions enact a recurrent performative schema of segmentary identities (Table 1): a highly dramatised representation of social action that initially renders personal ambition and particularist domestic interests into corporative embodiments of competitive lineage prestige, and further transmutes such interlineage competition into a collective assertion of communal achievement – the 'work of the community' (*dēšä krom*) – under the symbolic authority of senior community elders, the 'great old men' (*gāḍa baṣāra*).

In Kalasha song performance on festal occasions we witness a strikingly similar structuring of segmentary identities, although it must be noted that this ceremonial schema of collective integration through the competitive juxtaposition of lineage rivalries is only implicitly manifest as an organising principle of performance, rather

Table 1. Schema of Segmentary Social Action in Kalasha 'Ceremonial' Performance

I. **Personal-Household Identities** (*dur*), represented by house elders (*dūrä gaḍērak*) and juniors (*juān*). Interdomestic rivalries instigated by personal ambition (*niāt*) and enthusiam (*šāuk*) in wife-elopment and feasting are mediated and resolved in terms of:

II. **Corporate-Lineal Identities** (*kam*), represented by active lineage elders (*kam gaḍērak*). Interlineage competition in feasting and quasi-feud or 'revenge' (*badelā*) in wife-elopement are mediated and resolved in terms of:

III. **Valley-Community Identities** (*deš*), represented by senior ceremonial elders (*gāḍa baṣāra*). Collective approbation of personal and lineage 'renown' (*namūs*), emblematised in festal rank emblems and commemorated in oratory and praise songs.

than being an explicitly stated 'script' for vocal and choreographic expression. Representations of eldership in Kalasha ceremonial performance always entail an ambivalent rhetorical negotiation of personal and collective identities, depending upon a tense dialogue of mutual recognition from other rival elders as well as from dependent supporters (cf. Herzfeld 1985: 11-12, 72-91).

Kalasha Song Performance

Kalasha festival music may be easily distinguished from that of any surrounding Islamic peoples by its singular emphasis upon vocal rather than instrumental expression; its simple monodic style of recitative chant within a narrow tonal register of two basic pitches; and its collective choral accompaniment, together with drumming and group dancing, in the context of seasonal festivals and prestige feasts.

Kalasha song and dance is predominantly manifest in the celebration of three seasonal festivals associated with community rituals that inaugurate the annual subsistence cycle of sexually divided agropastoral activities. This begins with the spring Joshi (*Žoši*) festival in mid-May, celebrating the vernal regeneration of nature and the 'awakening' of each valley community from the idle months of winter, comprising three full days of collective celebration before herdsmen leave with their goats for distant mountain pastures and women move out of the main villages to tend their fields in dispersed summer hamlets. Shortly after Joshi, rites dedicated to the god Mahandeu initiate the 'night dances' (*rat-nat*) of the summer season, which are held on alternate evenings by young people as explicit occasions for sexual flirtation, as well as offering an informal opportunity to practise and perfect the public song performances of their elders. These night dances culminate in the late summer festival of Uchao (*Učáu*), a single-day festival held in late August which celebrates the peak of pastoral production in the mountain pastures. Following the return of the goat herds to the valleys in October, there is a further month of lineage sacrifices and prestige feasting before preparations for the midwinter festival of Chaomos (*Čāomos*) in December. The Chaomos festival, lasting over two weeks and reaching its dramatic climax at the winter solstice, is the central religious performance of the Kalasha, characterised by a distinctive musical culture of agonistic and obscene chanting between the sexes as well as the recitation of lengthy religious hymns (cf. Loude & Lièvre 1984). In this essay, however, I shall concentrate upon the more prevalent manner of musical celebration characteristic of other seasonal festivals and prestige feasts. Song examples are mainly taken from the Joshi spring festival of the northern Kalasha valley of Rumbur, recorded in May 1976, 1989 and 1990 (Shepherd 1990; Parkes 1990; cf. Kojima 1991).

All Kalasha festal celebrations take place within a circular dancing-ground (*naṭikāin*) that can accommodate total valley communities of some five to eight hundred people. In Rumbur valley, for example, the dancing-ground for the Joshi and Uchao festivals is an elevated ridge (*gri*) forming the village plaza of its ancestral settlement of Grom. Onlookers form a ragged circle around the edge of this dancing-ground, its focal point being a compact inner circle of singing elders (*gaḍerakān*) with two drummers standing nearby (Figure 1). Apart from the droning chorus of male and female dancers, musical accompaniment to dancing is created entirely by the rhythmical combination of two double-headed drums: a large bass barrel-drum (*dahù*), struck alternatively with the palm of the left hand and a curved stick in the right hand, and a small hour-glass shaped drum (*waj̓*) beaten rapidly on either side with both hands. The tempo of drumming orchestrates three distinct styles of communal dancing, which all proceed in a counter-clockwise movement (*drāc̨ūři gehēnao* 'to the right') around the central circle of elders.

Kalasha festival performance consists of an indefinitely repeated series of just three genres (*rāu*) of song-and-dance: *čā*, *dūšak*, and *dražaīlak*. Most festivals begin with a prescribed order of seven traditional songs of each genre in turn (*sat rāu*), after which their successive performance becomes open to compromise between the respective demands of singers and dancers. Elders prefer the lyrically elaborate *dražaīlak* genre, which is most appropriate for their prolonged mutual panegyrics, while younger people are keener to display their personal skills in enthusiastic *čā* dancing; so these two contrastive genres commonly alternate for several rounds, with the intermediate *dūšak* being performed less frequently. Yet all three genres should ideally succeed in rotation (*gherēk*), and singers are specifically requested to recite in the less popular *dūšak* genre if this has been under-represented for several turns.

The distinctive features of these three genres of song (*grū*) and dance (*naṭ*) may be outlined as follows:

I. Firstly, the fast *čā* or 'clapping' style of song-and-dance has minimal emphasis upon song composition and maximal emphasis upon virtuosity in performance and dancing. *Čā* songs have a fixed repertoire of traditional lyrics, usually consisting of short refrains of just one or two lines of verse, although this style includes two peculiarly elaborate narrative lyrics of the Joshi spring festival: its Daginai and Luli songs (Morgenstierne 1973: 50–65). After initial recitation by a senior elder, immediately followed by loud whistling and rapid drumming, successive lines of verse are taken up in turn by most members of the inner circle of male singers, clapping in time to the fast tempo of drumming while others are dancing. In the *čā naṭ* dance, partners of either sex form groups of three to four, which rotate rapidly three times in either direction before leaping off in a counter-clockwise direction to begin pivoting again on a new site (see Figure 1). As the dance develops, with the tempo of drumming becoming faster, individuals often disengage to demonstrate their inspired virtuosity: women twirl around with sinuous hand gestures, opening and closing their fists (*bāzuŋ kai*), while men perform more vigorous hops and leaps, whistling with their fingers and brandishing sticks or dancing-axes.

II. The *dūšak* genre of singing is intermediate between *čā* and *dražaīlak* in both form and expression. Most songs of this style again belong to a fixed repertoire of traditional lyrics rather than being original compositions. Yet the *dūšak* style may also be used for the composition of short panegyrics of four to six lines. Dancing begins immediately after two brief renditions of the song by a soloist, in plain and ornamental form; and dancers sing sepa-

Identity in Kalasha Song Performance 167

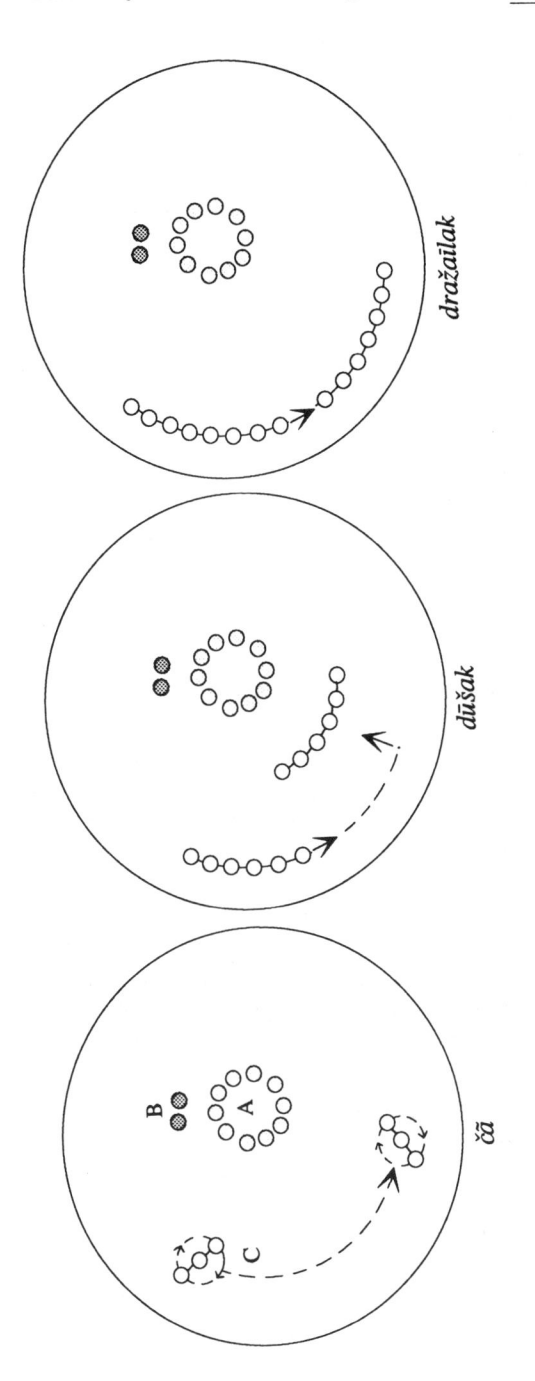

Figure 1. Choreography of Kalasha Festival Dances Styles. A: Elders, B: Drummers, C: Dancers

čā

dūšak

dražailak

rate refrains, or simply drone on sustained notes, rather than repeat the original song. The *dūšak naṭ* 'confrontation dance' is also a vigorous performance, accompanied by fast drumming (see Figure 1). It consists of short chains of four to eight people linked shoulder to shoulder, shuffling sideways around the dancing-ground at a quick pace for eight or nine steps before sharply retreating to the edge of the ground in order to stampede forward and collide into another chain of male or female dancers with the excited shout *dusiā ha! ha! ha!* 'We confront, ha! ha! ha!' Expressing male group-rivalry as well as mock sexual aggression, the dance movements supposedly represent the butting combat of wild goats (ibex and markhor) in the mountains.

III. Finally, the *draẑaīlak* style of singing, which may be translated as 'prolonged' recitation (from the verbal root *draẑ-* 'to stretch out'), is the most textually as well as vocally elaborate genre of Kalasha song performance. A *draẑaīlak* song typically consists of ten or more lines of verse, each composed in a regular seventeen-syllable metre and sung in a prolonged, predominantly two-tonal chant (Parkes 1993: appendix; cf. Kojima 1986). Although there are many traditional songs of this genre, appropriate for particular festivals or rites of passage, all are recognised to be the historical composition of known ancestors rather than being anonymous lyrics. After repeated solo recitation by a singer, in alternative plain and ornamental renditions, allowing a large audience to memorise the verse, the song is gradually taken up by male and female singers, crowded around the soloist and the inner circle of elders, before being recited again in dance. The *draẑaīlak naṭ* dance consists of a stately procession of long chains or lines (*tren, šaŋgřāyak*) of either male or female dancers linked shoulder to shoulder, shuffling in a very slow side-step around the central circle of elders in concentric arcs (see Figure 1). The performative emphasis is thus upon collective memorisation and recitation of song compositions rather than upon personal display in dancing.

These three separate genres of song-and-dance seem expressly designed to provide a contrasting succession of aesthetic variety, including a notable shift in the pace of dancing and tempo of drumming from fast to slow, as well as providing distinct opportunities for the display of both personal and collectively orchestrated skills of dancing and singing. All male and female participants thus have an opportunity to sing together while dancing, and most adult men can contribute at least one or two lines of traditional verse as brief solo performances in *čā* songs; elder men may compose short panegyrics for their peers in the *dūšak* style, while senior elders may have more carefully prepared and elaborated praise songs collectively memorised in prolonged *dražailak* performance. There is also a congruent shift of performative focus, from 'personal' to 'group' to 'collective-impersonal' dance display, as one proceeds through these three successive genres; indeed, there is an evident correspondence between these contrastive features of song and dance display and our earlier tripartite schema of segmentary identities (cf. Table 1).

This homology of musical and choreographical expression with other social processes of segmentary representation may appear unremarkable in view of the very basic categories of personal and group identity that it comprises. With just three performative genres, some contrastive thematic clustering of differential kinaesthetic and vocal attributes, congruently structured according to relative tempo, might seem inevitable. Yet their repetitive order of succession – from personal enthusiasm in *čā* dance performance to mock group-antagonism in *dūšak* 'confrontation' and to collective choral orchestration in the sedate *dražailak* line dance – does overtly enact, in a multi-sensually manifest experience, a pervasive segmentary scheme of collective mobilisation: one that cumulatively focuses upon senior elders as synecdochal representatives of competitively integrated communities, whose emblematic renown is foregrounded as the respectful subject of collective memorisation in *dražailak* performance.

A similar orchestration of personal and collective identities is also implicitly manifest in the solo performances of singers within the inner circle of elders, in the reciprocal responses of other elders, as well as in the heterophonic musical effects of collective choral singing in each of these three genres. All Kalash songs are repeated at least twice by a soloist, in a plain and ornamental fashion: firstly outlining a simple two-tonal framework of ryhthmic motifs, and then decorating sustained notes with melismatic voice breaks and vibrato. But this cumulative structuring of solo performances is especially elaborated in *dražailak* songs, which are respectfully attended by a hushed crowd of all participants densely massed around the inner circle of elders. Here there are at least three separate renditions of an originally composed song: firstly recited in a very quiet and expressly modest fashion, then repeated more boldly for choral accompaniment, and then again recited in a highly elaborate 'name-naming' (*nom-nomēk*) display rendition, accompanied by dramatic flourishes of a stick or dancing-axe pointing out places or peoples alluded to in the verse. Each of these performances is also characterised by distinctive patterns of vocalisation: initially with pitch largely restricted to a single tonal axis, then with a more distinctive two-tonal framework, and finally employing a fuller pentatonic scale, with elaborately decorated sustained notes employing complex melismatic figures and rapid voice break ornamentation (Parkes 1993: appendix). Also distinctive of *dražaīlak* performance is its choral accompaniment in the second rendition, where female singers notably duplicate the predominantly two-tonal pattern of the soloist in parallel fourths. A slightly delayed staggering of song parts between the soloist and both male and female chorus further displaces such intervals to minor thirds and fifths, creating a resonant heterophony of canonically layered voices. Finally, after completion of the song in display rendition, when it is also being repeated in staggered choruses by slowly circulating lines of dancers, senior elders will be prompted to compose 'name-naming' songs in honour of the original singer, again in an ornamental fashion accompanied by histrionic gestures with a stick or dancing-axe, evoking shouts of encouragement from other elders at the end of each line of verse. Such reciprocal praise songs should properly be sung by a senior elder of the lineage initially praised by the original singer, readdressing his eulogy to the comparable renown of the singer's own lineage ancestors, which should provoke a further recitation of the original song in display rendition, followed by another reciprocal 'name-naming' composition by a third elder, and so on. At major festivals and prestige feasts, where senior elders from all three Kalasha communities are likely to be present, such escalating cycles of mutual eulogy may be prolonged for over an hour.

The heterophonous musical effects of choral accompaniment to Kalasha song performance might also be regarded as a communal vocalisation of the same underlying structure of segmentary representations. As we have already noted in the choral accompaniment to *dražaīlak* singing, a slight staggering of song parts, usually delayed by two or three seconds, creates a dense heterophonous texture of overlapping tonal and rhythmical motifs that is further enhanced by female singers duplicating the tonal contours of male voices in parallel fourths; and this quasi-polyphonous effect of unevenly stacked male and female voices, within an otherwise narrow tonal register, is especially marked in the *dražailak* dance, where separate lines of slowly circulating singers repeat the same verses with a variable time-lag of up to twenty seconds. A more cacophonous but still resonant heterophony of predominantly two-tonal drones is also created by the swirling movements of chanting male and female dancers in the *čā* and *dūšak* genres, as noted by Brandl (1977: 18). The Japanese ethnomusicologist Kojima (1986: 106) also refers to the 'polyphonic' effects of Kalasha heterophony, suggesting that this may be an unintentional consequence of discrepant vocal coordination, associated with a libertarian 'individualism' and lack of strong leadership (ibid.:111); but her further suggestion that Kalasha are *unable* to sing the same melody in unison' seems refuted by the prevalence of unison singing of more complex melodies during the Chaomos festival, as well as in the occasional group singing of women's lullabies (treated below). Indeed, there is strong evidence that heterophonous effects are both appreciated and intentionally exploited in Kalasha festival performance, their peculiar vibratory resonance (*Schwebungsdiaphonie*) being related to a narrow tonal emphasis on two dominant pitches separated by a minor second interval (in contrast to unison melodies that employ a heptatonic scale). Kalasha informants do sometimes refer to such echoing effects of choral resonance as 'rebounding voice' (*awāz piṣṭyāk gherēlä*, literally 'voice turning around on itself'): an image of reflective sound that perhaps more broadly evokes the entire performative dramatisation of festival song recitation, i.e. as a collective recapitulation of ancestral tradition and lineage renown (*namūs*), metaphorically embodied in the leading voices of prominent elders and echoed in choral approbation.

Whether or not these heterophonous effects are an intentional or a felicitous accidental disposition of staggered choral singing, the carefully choreographed vocal orchestration of Kalasha festivals scarcely supports Kojima's overall analysis of their musical performance as simply reflecting an 'acephalous' social order of discordant individualism. I have rather suggested that an implicit hierarchical structure of representative eldership is ceremonially constructed through song performance, even if political leadership is often keenly contested in practical life. Rather than reflecting the sometimes anarchic antagonisms of everyday life within the egalitarian enclave of Kalasha communities, such festival performances conversely present an aesthetically coherent experience of segmentary integration under the benign symbolic dominance of senior 'ceremonial' elders.

The Pragmatics of Panegyric: Dialogic Eulogy

The prolonged recitation of praise songs in the *dražaílak* style, foregrounded by its musical and choreographical restraint and coordination in contrast to other song and dance genres, thus creates a recurrent dramatic focus on the ceremonial personality of senior elders at Kalasha festivals. This focalisation upon individual personalities as collective emblems does, however, raise inevitable contradictions inherent in synecdochal segmentary identity: concerning group identification with the very particular achievements of representative elders; and these symbolic problems of self-presentation are further exacerbated by the competitive nature of practical politics within the egalitarian enclave, where any assertion of authority or token of self-aggrandisement tends to be mistrusted. These social-pragmatic problems of personal eulogy are partly resolved through the ceremonial staging of Kalasha song performance: an elder praises others in order to evoke reciprocal 'name-naming' praise for himself, within a self-congratulatory circle of mutual (albeit rival) admirers. Praise should also properly address the collective lineage 'renown' (*namūs*) of an elder, represented by allusions to the historical achievements of lineal ancestors whose glory can be comparably shared by other descendants present; and this renown needs to be expressed in appropriately formulaic language, itself paying intertextual tribute to a cumulative tradition of ancestral praise recitations (cf. Opland 1983; Barber 1991). But despite these performative demands for indirection, elision and extreme stylisation, sung panegyric may presume an extensive shared knowledge of historical and personal events to implicate its allusive intentions of interpretation by means of formulaic imagery.

Historical knowledge or 'memory' (*yat*) is indeed thought to be a critical and sufficient poetic quality for competent song composition in Kalasha opinion. Many fine *dražaílak* singers seem even unaware of the exacting isosyllabic structure of their prosody and its musical articulation in vocal enunciation. Singers simply reflect that words, whether short or long, may be easily fashioned to 'fit into the tune' (*hāŋuna sāus hīu*) of *dražaílak* recitation; but it is the verbal choice of theme or 'meaning' (*mahanā*) that requires special knowledge and experience. Singers may be noted for the fine tonal quality of their voice (*pruṣṭ awāz*); but such expressive musical features are always treated as aesthetically subordinate to the expressed verbal content of their lyrics. Knowledge of extensive lineage histories is certainly a prerequisite for the composition of effective praise songs. Such knowledge is transmitted in the form of prose narratives known as *wasiāt*, which may be translated as both 'testaments' and 'precepts' (conflating the Arabic-Persian loanwords *wasiāt* and *nasiāt*), consisting of lineage legends that recount the famous activities of *kam* patrilines of ancestors, over seven or more generations, down to living elders (Parkes 1975; 1991). Only a handful of men in each community are considered to have comprehensive knowledge of such *wasiāt* traditions, and elders commonly resort to these acknowledged experts in order to prepare composed praise songs prior to a festival or funeral celebration. Many praise songs simply sketch out the narrative outlines of such legends in allusive verse, advertising a singer's respectful interest in the renowned achievements of an elder's predecessors; but nuanced compositions, which are more likely to be memorised, should ideally suggest some thematic continuity between the memorable deeds of a line of ancestors and their living descendants.

Primary themes of renown (*namūs*) concern the prosperity of elders and their prominent personal achievements as leaders, including their sponsorship of prestigious feasts and their successes in outwitting neighbouring enemies. These attributes are poetically heightened by the use of an extensive repertoire of honorific epithets for renown: the patriarch of a large extended household, for example, is referred to as a 'king bee' (*machērik ṣa*) commanding a prosperous 'beehive' (*machērik mřū*) of married sons. Such epithets are furthermore elements of recurrent 'formulas' or formulaic phrases (Lord 1960), which provide both metrically appropriate segments of verse for *dražaīlak* recitation, and especially for 'name-naming' composition-in-performance, as well as familiar mnemonic bridges of easily recognised verse for choral repetition (cf. Finnegan 1977: 58–87). Opening lines of praise, for example, follow a stereotypical exclamation of eulogy (*ṣabāṣ!* bravo!) followed by the lineage identity of the elder addressed, named as 'grandchild' (*nawāu*) or descendant of an apical ancestor, and usually the singer's kinship relationship to the elder, thus inscribing an authorial 'signature' on the song text. Surrounding peoples and places are also alluded to by conventional formulaic idioms: Chitrali peoples, for example, are invariably a 'white butterfly army' (*ghōra pachōřik bāu*), ironically connoting their spotless cotton clothing, and Chitral town is always a 'golden bazaar' (*sūřā bazār*) or a 'great court' (*ghōna šarān*). Many such idioms and formulaic phrases are evident in the following short praise song, recited in honour of a senior elder of Rumbur at its Joshi festival in 1976 (Appendix: Song 1):

> Bravo to you oh Kalasha king, grandson of Mutimir!
> Your brother was the ruler's attendant, entering the great court of Chitral,
> The ruler awarded you presents: seven layers of silken gowns,
> Adorned in those [robes] you came out, and the 'white butterfly army' was surprised!
> Crossing over into Bashgal [in Nuristan], you danced the hero's dance at Kamdesh,
> At Gangalwat Pass [from Bashgal] you danced with shields, in that far-off high valley,
> [The god] Sajigor protected you, and it woke up [with rejoicing] your 'gateway and mulberry arbour' [family]!

In this simple praise song, the singer typically addresses a living elder through a shifting set of patrilineal identities: referring initially to the elder's deceased father's brother, who was an official 'headman' (*asakāl*) of Rumbur valley in the early decades of this century, and who successfully pleaded at the court of the prince of Chitral to settle Kalasha land disputes with neighbouring Chitrali peoples (lines 1–4); he then refers to the elder's own father, who is renowned for reclaiming a herd of goats stolen by Nuristani peoples, several of whom he killed in his warrior raid, thus earning the rank of 'hero' (*šura muč*) in a subsequent commemorative feast held at the altar of the god Sajigor (lines 5–7). Informants further indicated that the singer evidently alluded to the similar achievements of the elder's son, a dominant factional leader of Rumbur, who had recently replicated the ancestral renown of his grandfathers in both successfully winning court cases in Chitral and also attacking Nuristani rustlers in the mountain pastures of Rumbur. Conflating several generations of patrilineal identities, a singer may thus obliquely eulogise collateral descent groups or specific personalities beyond the immediate address of his song. Several formulaic phrases of this song also intentionally echo or 'quote' a well-known reflective song earlier composed by the elder being praised here (see Parkes 1993: Song C), which itself alluded to the same lineage ancestors and events. Given an audience's interpretative sensitivity to such intertextual allusions, within an intimate cognitive context of shared mutual knowledge about both ancestral and contemporary personalities, formulaic language may thus be used to communicate nuanced personal messages and relationships despite its apparent verbal guise of traditional honorific epithets.

The formulaic conventions of Kalasha praise songs do, however, provide a protective veil of potentially ambiguous expressions for the effective disguise or distancing of personal opinions, which may only be inferred with the aid of tacit contextual knowledge. Yet indexically impoverished praise lyrics, which manifest few inferential clues about a singer's personal intentions of communication or specific evaluations of other elders, will be deprecated for their lack of 'significance' (*mahanā*), itself implying ignorance or indifference towards the specific achievements of the elders and ancestors addressed. Some of the most memorable and valued praise lyrics are indeed openly critical complaints addressed to other elders, as in the following song (Appendix: Song 2):

> Bravo to you my in-law, the officer of Rumbur!
> Crossing into Bomboret, they hatched a plot – the assembled Bomboret people
> My [god] Sajigor protected [him], averting their arrowheads and bullets
> Our grandfathers' offshoots blossomed, in the upper valley
> I myself gave [a daughter] into your beehive, for my son-in-law is a bee
> [But] your father entered a wasp's nest, and he stirred up the wasps
> My good-faith [to you] was sweet food, from beginning to end
> My hope indeed is now ended, [I feel] no happiness from human-beings

The singer here is one of the most senior elders of Rumbur, already over sixty years old when this song was composed in the early 1970s. He addresses a fellow in-law (*khaltabār*), his son's father-in-law as well as an elder of his daughter's husband's lineage, effectively blaming this affine for instigating an attack on his son at a funeral celebration in the neighbouring Bomboret valley. As one knowledgeable commentator explained:

> His son was beaten with stones by the people of Bomboret for 'standing with' one of their women, but it was known that people of the Dremese-nawau lineage [that of the addressed elder] had falsely suggested this out of wickedness: that is the meaning of the first lines. Then he mentions that he had given his own daughter to that lineage and he addresses his son-in-law [line 5], explaining how his 'father' [the lineage elder] had stirred up the people of Bomboret, making them 'sting' his son like a swarm of wasps. His lineage had earlier given many female agnates (*jamīli*) to them in marriage: so he refers to them as 'offshoots of our grandfathers' like blossoming vines stemming from his own lineage women [line 4]. But they had repaid his loyalty with evil, and so he notes his unhappiness and complaint (*gilā*): that is the meaning of his song (*īsa gřūas mahanā*).

Such reflective songs, expressing complaints as often as praise, tend to be a prerogative of only the most senior elders in any community: its *gāḍa baṣāra* 'ceremonial elders' whose advanced age and accumulated achievements entitle them to represent personal opinions and critical observations of other people in the form of ancestral homilies of advice (*wasiāt*). Active elders (*gaḍērak*) and political leaders, however, can rarely afford to take such risks of personal allusion, which would be more likely to be interpreted with reference to their divisive factional allegiances. Active elders, usually aged between thirty and forty-five, indeed rarely compose and perform memorable praise songs, although they may be required to recite brief 'name-naming' eulogies in reciprocal honour of senior elders whose songs have addressed their own lineage ancestors. The pragmatic ability to compose referentially dense praise lyrics is therefore almost necessarily acquired after retirement from active political leadership.

The Poetics of Personality and Sexuality

Although the praise songs of senior elders are the predominant subject of *dražaīlak* recitation at major festivals and feasts, panegyric is not the only form of lyric appropriate to this prestigious genre. There is also a vast repertoire of traditional as well as newly composed 'love songs' (*aṣekī gřū*), expressing sentiments of yearning affection, admiration or complaint between lovers. As noted in the introduction to this essay, sexuality and adultery play a prominent role in Kalasha social life, where extra-marital affairs also have important political implications for lineage elders through the prevalent elopement of married women. Adultery and elopement are thus intrinsic issues of inter-lineage as well as interpersonal rivalries; so it is scarcely surprising that erotic song lyrics should be a subject of equivalent aesthetic elaboration as panegyric. Focusing upon the preoccupations of youths (j́uān) rather than elders, however, the recitation of love songs mainly occurs during informal periods of seasonal festivals such as Joshi and Uchao, when senior elders are not present at the dancing-ground, as well as during the summer 'night dances' (rat-naṭ) of young people.

In contrast to panegyric, love songs are overtly self-expressive and ideally focus upon the individual mannerisms of both lover and beloved as well as the peculiar circumstances of their affective relationship. Many of the idioms and formulaic epithets of such songs are evidently borrowed from the love poetry of surrounding Khowar speakers in Chitral, itself largely derivative of classical Persian and Urdu *ghazāl* topoi of rose and nightingale (cf. Morgenstierne and Wazir Ali Shah 1959: 31; Buddruss 1982: 12–13). But Kalasha love songs place less introspective emphasis upon the romanticised agonies of unrequited passion and alternatively allude to particular problematic events in a relationship that again need to be inferred by an audience with background knowledge of the persons concerned. One brief example may serve as an illustration (Appendix: Song 3):

> You go little bird, look and observe this wandering world!
> At night, resting in the mountains, sleep will not come:
> 'She is at Sendik' I think
> Rising at dawn I am despondent at my white goat-pen
> I look here and there: from afar the monal pheasant chirps on the mountain peak
> Searching for your likeness, I wander through the three Kalasha valleys
> You yourself will not chirp: a golden oriole on a copper-green tree
> Moon and sun confront one another, seated in the sky for their contest
> I was enamoured of your beauty, but I grieved for two of your deeds

> If you have no true intentions, make clear the talk of your tongue
> Even if it should not happen [our elopement], life passes while the world remains

The opening line conventionally addresses an imaginary 'little bird' or sympathetic messenger between the lovers, and the song also ends with a typical trope of contemplative resignation, as also used in some reflective songs of senior elders. The first part of the song evokes a vision of the young singer isolated in his mountain pastures, alerting an audience to the possible identity of his beloved with a toponymic reference to her father's fields. He refers to himself as a splendid 'monal pheasant' (*loïṣṭ*) of the mountains, while the girl is typically portrayed as a bright-yellow 'golden oriole' (*ṭiṭayũŋ*) in the valleys. Sun and moon are conventional poetic metaphors for women and men, and the singer further alludes to a whimsical myth of the sibling luminaries endlessly chasing each other over the sky to represent his pursuit of the young woman's fickle affections. He finally mentions his grief over her inconstancy – her 'two deeds' of suspected compliance with rival lovers – ultimately demanding a clear statement of her intentions.

Similar love songs in the *draźaïlak* form are composed by women, again alluding to their clandestine affairs with extramarital lovers which an audience may more or less plausibly infer from current gossip. Many women's love songs are indeed more highly valued than those of men, and this genre seems peculiarly expressive of Kalasha women's particular interests in the politico-erotic intrigues of interpersonal affections that become publicly expressed in adultery and elopement feuds. Women, however, do not publicly perform such songs at festivals, but usually arrange for kinsmen to sing on their behalf. Yet there is one type of song in the *draźaïlak* genre, stylistically related to love songs, which *is* predominantly sung by women in public festival performances: these are 'dream songs' (*isprāpasa gř̃ũ*) received in sleep from the spirits of recently deceased kin. Although disguised in peculiarly oblique verse, spirit songs communicated through women are often overtly critical of disputes and factional antagonisms between related male elders, as in the following dream song recited by an elder woman at the Rumbur Joshi festival in 1976 (Appendix: Song 4):

You go little bird, make a greeting to the world-above-earth!
My heirs and descendants fight and quarrel, son with grandson
Not knowing your [kinship], he coveted your rights and property
You think like this: I am hidden from your eyes, I am not seeing [your dispute]
But I look as if through a telescope at the world-above-earth
Do not despair my little daughter, in dark purgatory light comes from the child
I am a petitioner [at God's court]: a leaf-bud will be shown to the world-above-earth

The singer explained that this song had been revealed in her sleep by a recently deceased lineage sister, who had also been married into the same affinal lineage as herself. Speaking from the underworld (*parilōi*), she upbraids the rival factional leaders of these two lineages, whose disputes over property had been a major issue of factional polarisation in Rumbur throughout the 1970s. She further accuses her still living husband of concealing his ill motives, which she clearly perceives from the underworld. The final two lines are addressed to another lineage sister married into her husband's lineage, whose infant child had recently died – a misfortune that had been divined as caused by ancestral spirit 'anger' (*křũ*) over the same interlineage dispute (cf. Parkes 1983: 459–68) – promising her the birth of a new child (leaf-bud).

A similarly critical perspective on social events and interpersonal relations betraying kinship is also commonly expressed in women's lullabies or 'kissing songs' (*iṣpaḍēk gřũ*) addressed to their infant children. Mothers may thus indirectly berate their husbands or fathers-in-law for demanding that sons rather than daughters should be born, or swear that they will not allow their infant daughters to be betrothed by male elders outside their valley communities; and lullabies are also commonly employed by women to convey grievances with their own male relatives. Yet women's lullabies are equally used to convey praise lyrics about their male relatives, often comparable in narrative elaboration to the *draẓaīlak* panegyrics of senior elders although far more direct in their allusions to the personal achievements of close kin. But these songs are not, of course, publicly recited at seasonal festivals (although their lyrics are similar in style to traditional čā refrains chanted by young women while dancing). Such women's songs are indeed musically distinctive from the predominantly two-tonal recitative chants of public festival performance: they are sung to a range of colourful melodies, employing a full heptatonic scale, which appear to be largely borrowed from the song repertoires of neighbouring Chitrali and Nuristani peoples (cf. Morgenstierne 1967; Pressl 1976).

Many of these melodies are also employed as unison chants, accompanied by a regular clapping, in the obscene 'shaming song' (lač gřū) contests of the midwinter Chaomos festival. Chanted by rival dancing parties of opposed men and women, these 'shaming songs' consist of vulgar taunts and ripostes that often specify real or imagined acts of adultery between named individuals (cf. Loude & Lièvre 1984: 214–16). Mainly instigated and improvised by women, these obscene songs also typically portray women's potential independence from men during the sacred festival period of sexual seclusion, when women take over Kalasha villages as their exclusive domain. Epitomising Bloch's (1992) ritual scheme of 'rebounding violence' – entailing a chaotic reversal of normal sexual hierarchy contrastively to reinforce the symbolic authority of senior elders – the Chaomos festival also comprises an exaggerated ritual dramatisation of the tripartite structure of segmentary identities that we have already noted in the musical and choreographic orchestration of other seasonal festivals: moving from personal to group-antagonistic to collective representations of selfhood. It is therefore thematically consistent that an otherwise exclusively female genre of melodic unison singing, itself typically expressive of personalised and socially critical sentiments, should be musically employed in this festival alone to express intersexual antagonisms – in strong contrast to the restrained two-tonal recitative songs and heterophonous choruses of other festivals.

Song Performance and the Aesthetic Construction of Collective Identity

I have suggested in this essay that Kalasha song performance is implicitly structured in its musical, choreographic and lyrical expression to manifest and successively integrate personal, group and collective identities according to a progressive segmentary schema of self-representations. Acknowledging and presupposing the personal idiosyncrasies and erotic passions of young men and women, this performative schema ultimately privileges representative lineage elders and senior ceremonial elders as vocal embodiments of community solidarity, whose solo recitations are communally echoed in heterophonous choral acclamation. Asserting a musically manifest sense of social solidarity, song performance thus realises a relatively harmonious integration of normally competing personalities during festival celebrations, at least temporarily overcoming the interlineage and factional animosities characteristic of quotidian social life within the egalitarian enclave.

The socially integrative effects of group singing and dancing have of course been supposed by many Durkheimian anthropologists and ethnomusicologists since Radcliffe-Browne (1922: 247–54), while the affective inter-relationship of personal and collective identities or 'fellow-feeling' in music-making have been especially elaborated by Blacking (1976; 1983; cf. Baumann 1987: 173–83). Beyond the aesthetically satisfying mutual experience of singing together in Kalasha song performance, however, I have suggested that it is also implicitly organised by a series of congruent thematic contrasts in its three successive genres of song-and-dance, making aesthetically manifest an otherwise latent scheme of dialectically related segmentary representations. Rather than overtly 'reflecting' social structural principles, the organisation of festival music is itself necessarily informed by the same 'generative schemes' (Bourdieu 1977) or 'cultural scenarios' (Schieffelin 1976) that inform other collective social performances. Yet this sequential and antithetical framing of personal and group identities is almost uniquely experienced in Kalasha vocal music and dance as a subjectively sensible as well as objectively audible and visible aesthetic product, its culminatory collective synthesis being resoundingly manifest in the echoing heterophony of *dražaīlak* choral chant.

A comparable structuring of personal and group identities is also evident in the style of delivery of songs in each of the three genres of festival performance, as well as in the thematic organisation of their lyrics. In indicating how personal meanings and intentions may be communicated through the formulaic language of panegyric, I have further suggested that the seemingly constrictive semantic medium of song may be well suited to implicate private opinions within an oral context of extensively shared mutual knowledge, while at the same time conforming to a traditional repertoire of conventional imagery in public performance. Rather than being empty vessels of a depersonalised collective identity (Bloch 1974: 79), the praise songs of senior elders are precisely those expected to convey the most personalised and critical evaluations of other people, albeit to be inferred by indirect allusion that entails the provision of supplementary knowledge by an audience (cf. Barber 1991: 28–9). A similarly allusive expression of personal identities and private sentiments is conveyed in the *dražaīlak* love songs of young men and women; while the direct expression of personal and critical sentiments appears to be peculiar to women's lullabies and the ludic 'shaming songs' of the Chaomos festival – which are significantly differentiated from normal festival performance by their employment of a contrastive musical style of unison melodies.

Rather than being immediately expressive of everyday social conditions and values in Kalasha society (as are women's songs), I suggest that festival song performance, informally orchestrated by male elders, presents an idealised *ceremonial* enactment of recurrent social processes: one that implicitly recognises the disruptive passions of young people, the keenly competitive interests of lineage elders, as well as the more serious factional rivalries of major political leaders; yet which renders these practical antagonisms subordinate to, and symbolically supportive of, the performative authority of senior ceremonial elders – the *gaḍa baṣāra*. To this extent, the public organisation of song and dance plausibly legitimates the traditional authority of senior elders, as Bourdieu and Bloch suggest; but this is a specifically 'ceremonial' ideology that appears to have little persuasive power outside of festival performance. Furthermore, collective identity is here constructed by a musically framed recognition and accentuation of personal idiosyncracies rather than by their ritual eclipse through formalisation. Kalasha song performance thus manages to reconcile many of the inherent contradictions of personal and collective identity in the egalitarian enclave (cf. Stewart 1989), also answering that central problematic of all affective culture outlined by Blacking (1983: 54): 'how to relate the individuality of music and musical experience to its social use as a sign of ethnic identity'.

References

Barber, K., *I Could Speak until Tomorrow: Oriki, Women and the Past in a*

Yoruba Town, Edinburgh, Edinburgh University Press, 1991.

Baumann, G., *National Integration and Local Integrity: The Miri of Nuba Mountains in the Sudan*, Oxford, Oxford University Press, 1987.

Blacking, J., *How Musical is Man?*, London, Faber and Faber, 1976.

——, 'The Conception of Identity and Folk Concepts of Self: A Venda Case Study', in A. Jacobson-Wilding (ed.), *Identity, Personal and Socio-Cultural*, Uppsala, Studies in Cultural Anthropology 5, 1983, pp. 47–65.

Bloch, M., *Prey into Hunter: The Politics of Religious Experience*, Cambridge, Cambridge University Press, 1992.

——, 'Symbols, Songs, Dance and Features of Articulation: Is Religion an Extreme Form of Traditional Authority?', *Archives Européennes Sociologiques*, vol. 15, 1974, pp. 55–181.

Bourdieu, P., *Outline of a Theory of Practice*, Cambridge, Cambridge University Press, 1977.

Brandl, R.M., 'Zum Gesang der Kafiren', in R.M. Brandl and K. Reinhard (eds), *Neue Ethnomusicologische Forschungen: Festschrift Felix Hoerburger*, Berlin, Laaber Verlag, 1977, pp. 191–207.

Buddruss, G., *Khowar-Texte in arabischer Schrift*, Wiesbaden, Steiner (Mainz Akadamie der Wissenschaften und Literatur), 1982.

Castile, G.P. & G. Kushner (eds), *Persistent Peoples: Cultural Enclaves in Perspective*, Tucson, University of Arizona Press, 1981.

Douglas, M., *In the Wilderness: The Doctrine of Defilement in the Book of Numbers*, Sheffield Academic Press, 1993.

Feld, S., 'Sound Structure as Social Structure', *Ethnomusicology*, vol. 28, no. 3, 1984, pp. 383–409.

Finnegan, R., *Oral Poetry: Its Nature, Significance and Social Context*, Cambridge, Cambridge University Press, 1977.

Galaty, J.G., 'Models and Metaphors, On the Semiotic Explanation of Segmentary Systems', in L. Holy and M. Stuchlik (eds), *The Structure of Folk Models*, New York, Academic Press, 1981, pp. 83–121.

Herzfeld, M., *The Poetics of Manhood: Contest and Identity in a Cretan Mountain Village*, Princeton, Princeton University Press, 1985.

Kojima, R., 'Spring Festival of the Kalasha, Joshi and its Music [in Japanese]', in Tomoaki Fujii (ed.), *Girei to ongaku [Ritual and Music] II*, Tokyo, Tokyo Soseki, 1991.

——, 'The Structure and Social Context of the Dajahilak of the Kalasha: Musical Performance of the Uchao Summer Festival [in Japanese]', *Ongakugaku* (Journal of the Musicological Society of Japan), vol. 32, no. 2, 1986, pp.97–115.

Lord, A.B., *The Singer of Tales*, Cambridge, Harvard University Press, 1960.

Loude, J.-Y. and V. Lièvre, *Solstice Päien: Fêtes d'Hiver chez les Kalash du Nord Pakistan*, Paris, Presse de la Renaissance, 1984.

Morgenstierne, G., *The Kalasha Language*, Oslo, Institutet for Sammenlignende Kulturforskning, Universitetsforlaget, 1973.

———, 'Some folksongs from Nuristan', in *To Honour Roman Jakobson: Essays on the Occasion of his 70th Birthday*, The Hague, Mouton, 1967.
———, and Wazir Ali Shah, 'Some Khowar Songs', *Acta Orientalia*, vol. 24, 1959, pp. 29–58.
Opland, J., *Xhosa Oral Poetry: Aspects of Black South African Tradition*, Cambridge, Cambridge University Press, 1983.
Parkes, P., 'Alliance and Elopement: Economy, Social Order and Sexual Antagonism among the Kalasha (Kalash Kafirs) of Chitral', D.Phil. thesis, Oxford University, 1983.
———, 'Clan Temples and Descent Group Structure among the Kalasha (Kalash Kafirs) of Chitral', in K. Au, H. Nelson & H. Leung (eds), *Proceedings of the 6th International Symposium on Asian Studies*, vol.4, Hong Kong, Asian Research Services, 1984, pp. 1164–76.
———, 'Kalasha Domestic Society, Practice, Ceremony and Domain', in H. Donnan & F. Selier (eds) *Family and Gender in Pakistan*, Delhi & Leiden, Hindustan Publications & Brill, n.d.
———, 'Kalasha Oral Literature and Praise Songs', in E. Bashir (ed.) *Proceedings of the 2nd International Hindu Kush Cultural Conference*, Karachi, Oxford University Press, 1994.
———, 'Kalasha Rites of Spring: Backstage of a Disappearing World Film', *Anthropology Today*, vol. 6, no. 5, 1990, pp. 11–13.
———, *Kalasha Society: Practice and Ceremony in the Hindu Kush*, Oxford, Oxford University Press, in press.
———, 'Livestock Symbolism and Pastoral Ideology among the Kafirs of the Hindu Kush', *Man* (n.s.), vol. 22, no. 4, 1987, pp. 637–70.
———, 'Reciprocity and Redistribution in Kalasha prestige feasts', *Anthropozoologica* (L'Homme et L'Animal), vol. 16, 1992, pp. 35–44.
———, 'The Social Role of Historical Tradition among the Kalash Kafirs of Chitral', B.Litt Thesis, Oxford University, 1975
———, 'Temple of Imra, Temple of Mahandeu: A Kafir Sanctuary in Kalasha Cosmology', *Bulletin of the School of Oriental and African Studies*, vol. 54, no. 1, 1991, pp.75–103.
———, and J. Stock, 'Kalasha Praise Songs', MS (with musical transcription), n.d.
Pressl, H.M., *Musik aus Afghanistan*, Nuristan (recording), Graz, Adevaphon, Akademische Druck-u. Verlagsanstalt, 1976.
Radcliffe-Brown, A.R., *The Andaman Islanders*, Cambridge, Cambridge University Press, 1922.
Robertson, G.S., *The Káfirs of the Hind-Kush*, London, Lawrence & Bullen, 1896.
Saifullah Jan, 'History and Development of the Kalasha', in E. Bashir (ed.) *Proceedings of the 2nd International Hindu Kush Cultural Conference*, Karachi, Oxford University Press, 1994.

Schieffelin, E.L., *The Sorrow of the Lonely and the Burning of the Dancers*, New York, St Martins Press, 1976.

Shepherd, J., 'The Kalasha Rites of Spring', Granada Television Film, 'Disappearing World' Series (Anthropologist, P. Parkes), 1990.

Stewart, M., '"True Speech" Song and the Moral Order of a Hungarian Vlach Gypsy Community', *Man* (n.s.), vol. 24, no. 1, 1989, pp.79–102.

Woodburn, J., 'Egalitarian Societies', *Man* (n.s.) vol. 17, no. 3, 1982, pp. 431–50.

Appendix: Kalasha Song Transcriptions

Transcriptions follow the phonetic orthography of Morgenstierne (1973), with an apostrophe preceding stressed syllables (elsewhere indicated with a macron over the stressed and lengthened vowel). Songs 1 and 2 are marked with the caesura (/) or breath pause of sung *dražaīlak* recitation. Song 1: praise song of Gumara (Begalye-nawau lineage) for elders of the Mutimire-nawau lineage (addressing ancestors Fauch and Sakdar), recorded at Rumbur Joshi festival, 14 May 1976. Song 2: praise song of Buda (Mutimire-nawau lineage) for elders of the Dremeses-nawau lineage, recorded in Rumbur 1974 and 1989. Song 3: love song of Tajamul (Lataruk-nawau lineage) recorded in Birir valley, October 1976. Song 4: dream song of Panjarash (Dremese-nawau lineage), recorded at Rumbur Joshi festival, 15 May 1976.

Song 1:
ṣab'aṣ o tai h'atia / o Kal'aṣa ša, Mutim'ir naw'au
b'ayo khan'ẽas ṣ'adar / ath'una pai, Chetr'au gh'ona šar'an
khan'ẽ baṣ'es tai k'ada / sat p'uruna, khimkh'ap dragal'äi
šat'o sambh'i b'ien ni'ae / hair'an h'ula, g'ora pač'āřik b'au
Ç'atruma-deš bih'oṭi / gh'ona gr'omuna d'ita, š'ura lail'o
Gřāŋgřāwat son křẽ'ayak / n'aṭan 'ala wh'eno prh'āŋgai aw'at
tai Sajig'or s'araŋe / abh'ujis tai dur'uṣṭ že mraṭ-nəř'ik

Song 2:
ṣab'aṣ ta tai h'atiae / mai khaltab'ar, Rukm'ulä hawald'ar
pai Mumur'et pil'io / dro ab'inan M'omala sari'ai
mai Sajig'or s'araŋe / ne gre'ala, ša že břū thi
w'awai niš'er ta sanjal-/'ila h'ula, n'osani wh'ẽa dai
a-m'i ta tai mačh'erik / mř'ūai pr'ae, mačh'erik mai jam'ou
d'adalao pai trum'užak / mř'ūai at'i, trum'užak uguẓ'al
mai ta um'et ačh'ise / ne kia khoš'an tai band'aas pi

Song 3:
tu p'ario pach'iak, lūṛi de paı̄ tai k'asta duny'a
rat ta basth'onyuna ispr'ap mai ne hiu, Send'ikai 'asau gr̃õi
l'uṣuna uṣṭi, n'e as'alak hiu mai gori bas'ir san'eš
and'ä al'ai jag'eme, d'ešä b'ašau p'airan s'onao loh'iṣ
tai perug'ai kh'oji, ak'asis mai tre Kal'aṣa deš
tu ta tu-m'i ne baš'es, har'ilak muth'ikai ṭiṭay'uŋ
mastr'uk ze sw'iṛak dubad'u nis'una, di th'arä tamaš'a
a tai sur'atani aš'ek ne 'asis, du kr'omani abs'us
tai-o khi'al pe ne h'au, nasi čhal'ai de tai j'ipani mun
ne pe hau ne h'ulae, 'umbur ta par'iu duny'ao th'au

Song 4:
tu p'ario pach'iak, sal'am kari chom-th'ara duny'a
war'ista mai war'ise in'at ṣat'ai, putr že naw'ala sum
tai ta ne jh'onik h'au, kab'u 'arau tai hak že mulak'at
tu ta šeh'ẽ ačh'ti, ghečos'ar pačh'an mai gh'eči ta ne
s'ūr̃a par'eči kai durb'in jag'ese chom-th'arai duny'a
mo čh'iti mai čhul'iko, ch'ui kiam'at mas'umas pi rošt'i
a arzid'oyu 'asam, pr̃ā'iu paš'al, chom-th'arai duny'a

10

Music, Literature and Etiquette: Musical Instruments and Social Identity from Castiglione to Austen

Hélène La Rue

There are a number of ways in which a musical instrument can be a marker of social status. The mere ownership of an instrument may be limited to those of high social status and these instruments may in turn become insignia of that status. In the case of a person of high rank, their rank may be demonstrated by the instruments used in their presence as well as those that they might themselves play. The design or decoration of the instrument itself also indicates the status of the musician or listener. Musical instruments can be markers of culture, as well as status; they can also imply the status of gender. They can confer status on the high-ranking person with whom they are associated, the professional musician who plays or indeed even the amateur. The relationship between instrument symbolism and social identity is clearly a complex matter, but I hope to illustrate these points through this chapter with a series of examples from different areas. I then propose to examine the subject more closely with reference to musical instruments as markers of social status in England from the late sixteenth century until the early nineteenth.

I will begin by giving a number of examples of these from several different cultural traditions. Perhaps one of the most familiar instruments denoting national identity is the Irish harp. It is not associated with the country because many of its inhabitants play it. In fact, the small harp used today, the *clarsach*, is only played by a very small number of musicians. Moreover the modern tradition of this particular instrument can be traced back no more than one hundred years to the foundation of the *clarsach* society. The link of the small harp and Ireland is however far older than this, growing from the use of this type of harp as an important cultural unifier and tool before the earlier political divisions in the middle ages. Though long obsolete the instrument has a substantial history as a symbol of Ireland, together with the clover leaf. It has been exploited by various state agencies as a symbol of legitimacy and integrity, for example being used on Irish coins in Eire, and as the emblem of the Royal Ulster Constabulary in the North. Commerce is never far behind: the harp can be seen today on cans of Harp lager and Guinness stout.

Trumpets have an equally long tradition of association with high status groups, in their case with royalty. Until the sixteenth century in England, possession, or use of certain types of trumpet was limited to the king and his immediate family. Pairs of silver trumpets, such as those presented by Henry VIII to Louis of France on the Field of The Cloth of Gold in 1520, were the ultimate in royal gifts. A trumpet of precious metal, or possession of one, became a symbol of royal power or presence. The magnificence of a town or borough could only be shown by the possession of the carved ivory oliphants, intricately carved horns of ivory, still to be seen in various towns in England today. It is interesting to note that Queen's College, Oxford, by virtue of being a Royal foundation still makes use of its dispensation to have a trumpeter in office, and the pair of fine silver trumpets used for the most important occasions were in fact a replacement set from the king's own band at the time of the Restoration.

Among the Miao people of Guichew Province in the South West of China a bronze drum was, until at least the late eighteenth century, the supreme status symbol. These were kept in the head man's house and no Miao army marched without their drums, together with the bronze cooking pots, as the sound of the drums formed the essential communication network between different groups. For this reason the Han Chinese confiscated the drums when they tried to subdue the Miao in various battles from the sixteenth to the eighteenth centuries. The Meo, in Burma, used similar drums and one would be buried with the head man. This gradually became too expensive an operation and pieces were broken off the handles or rim instead (Kempers 1988).

In some traditions an ability to play a certain instrument might confer status on the musician, as was the case with the *mbira*. A skilled musician who played the *mbira* could advance in social status, but a boy already of noble birth would give up musicianship for the more important duties of his birth status. As John Blacking points out:

> The Venda may suggest that exceptional musical ability is biologically inherited, but in practice they recognise that social factors play the most important part in realising or suppressing it. For instance, a boy of noble birth might show great talent, but as he grows up he will be expected to abandon musical performance for the more serious (for him) business of government (Blacking 1976: 46).

In the greater part of my paper I would like to concentrate on these same themes as seen in English society and music making. Study of the English tradition shows that not only the type of instrument played, but also the amount of time spent in learning how to play could both be markers of social identity. Ethnomusicologists have studied this type of material within other cultures, but, as yet, studying our own is fairly new territory. Richard Leppert, in his book *Music and Image* (1988), deals with portraiture of the eighteenth century as sociological evidence of the interrelationships between music, gender and power. He states that his aim is to analyse 'less the music itself that amateurs played, or how they played it, than why they played in the first place and what the playing meant' (Leppert 1988: 2). My survey will also be an historical one, although covering a wider time scale, from the early sixteenth century to 1816. My main source of evidence is contemporary literature, including books on education and etiquette.

We have many sources which enable us to learn about musical instruments and their symbolism and use in English society. For the earliest period we have iconographical material, inventories, wills, court cases and much written evidence from theoretical treatises to literature. We also have some early texts which deal with the problems of the education of children. One such example is *The Romance of Horn*, a French poem written by Thomas in England in the third quarter of the twelfth century, in which the teachers of the king's son are advised to 'Teche him to harpe with his nayles sharpe' as well teaching him to serve at table (Pope 1955–64: 12–13).

The period which will form the main part of this chapter is that of the sixteenth to the early nineteenth centuries. During this period there are three musical skills which are discussed or mentioned in the texts I have read; singing which is normally held to be a good activity as it can strengthen the lungs and improve the diction (with the added advantage that the texts sung can also be of an improving nature); dancing, which can be beneficial for posture; and Music. The term 'Music' has been generally used in most Western European languages to mean the playing of instruments as opposed to singing. It has been used interchangeably for the word 'band' or 'orchestra'. Throughout this paper I shall use a capital letter for the word when using it in this sense.

For my first example I wish to quote from the book often considered to be the most influential to be published in England on the subject of etiquette. This was *Il Cortegione* by Castiglione, which was translated as *The Booke of the Courtyer* by Thomas Hoby, and published in 1561. It then had a remarkable number of re-editions in the sixteenth and seventeenth centuries. This book takes the form of a conversation between a count and his courtiers. Here we find the typical and traditional tensions between having a knowledge of music, together with a good education in the theory of music, and being able to play an instrument or sing. This becomes a focus for one of the debates between the count and the courtier, Gaspar. Gaspar voices one of the typical criticisms of musical practice at that time early in the dialogue, describing Music as an effeminate pursuit: 'I beleve musicke together with many other vanities is mete for women and paradventure for some also that have the lykenes of men, but not for them that be men in dede: who ought not with suche delicacies to womanische their mindes, and brynge themselves in that sort to dreade death' (Hoby 1561: 89).

The count contradicts this and has much to say about good examples of precedence – giving as examples earlier teachers and statesmen who practised music, one of these being the example of Chiron, who taught Achilles. 'And the wise maister would have those hands that should shed so muche Troyan bloude, to be oftentimes occupyed in playing upon the harpe? What souldyer is there (therefore) that will think it a shame to follow Achilles . . .' (Hoby 1561: 91). The count then strengthens his argument by listing those accomplishments that he considers to be necessary of a courtier and a 'Watyng Gentylwoman'. He says that the courtier must show a modest reluctance when called upon to play an instrument:

Therefore let oure Courtier come to shew his musicke as a thing to passe the time withall, and as he wer enforced to doe it, and not in the presence of noble menne, nor of any great multitude. And for all he be skillful and doth well understand it, yet wil I have hime to dissemble the study and penes that a man must needes take in all thinges that are well done (Hoby 1561: 118).

The total accomplishments of Castiglione's courtier are:

> To daunse well without over nimble footinges or to busie trickes
> To sing well upon the booke
> To play upon the lute, and singe to it with the ditty
> To play upon the vyole, and all other instrumentes with freates
> (Hoby 1561: 370).

The woman's attainments are more circumscribed:

> I would not see her use ... those and often divisions that declare more coonninge then sweetnesse. Likewise the instruments of musicke which she useth ought to be fitt for this pourpoise. Imagine yourselfe what an unsightly matter it were to see a woman play upon a tabour or a drumm, or blowe in a flute, or trumpet, or anye like instrumente: and this because the boisterousness of them doeth both cover and take away that sweete mildeness which setteth so furth everies deede that a woman doeth (Hoby 1561: 220).

He makes a short list of her possible attainments:

> Not to come on loft nor use to swift measures in her daunsing
> Not to use in singinge or playinge upon instrumentes to much division and busy pointes, that declare more conning then sweetenesse
> To come to daunce, or to show either musicke with suffringe herself to be first prayed somewhat and drawen to it
> (Hoby 1561: 375).

From these passages we see the existence of two points of view held about playing musical instruments. Also we discover that certain instruments are preferred for the use of the courtier and others which are forbidden to the gentlewoman. These instruments are not only listed but their merits and disadvantages discussed. In the case of the courtier the preferred instruments are all bowed and plucked strings. In the case of his female equivalent the list is not of those instruments most suitable but of those most incongruous, an incongruity based on the fact that it makes the player look 'unsightly'. This seems to be of more concern for a woman. There is also the requirement of a difference in style. A man must hide the effort that he had to make to acquire the skill of playing, and must always be asked to play. Also, interestingly enough, it is considered inappropriate for him to play in front of company more noble than himself or in front of a large number of people. These last two points are not included in the description of a woman's Music making, but she must not, in either her singing or playing, perform too cleverly, declaring more 'conning then sweetenesse'. Also she must be persuaded to play rather than pushing herself forward. Reticence, modesty and passivity are required of a woman in musical as well as all other aspects of social performance.

So we have here a statement of the instruments considered proper, or improper, a statement of preferred style, and it might be said, performance practice. The courtier, when asked, is to perform as if 'he wer enforced to doe it'; the woman 'to come to daunce, or to show either musicke with suffringe herselfe to be first prayed somewhat and drawen to it'. We will see that these conventions are repeated over and over again in the writings which follow.

This is, of course an Italian text translated into English, even though it was a very well-known one in England, as demonstrated by the large number of editions it went through from its publication in 1561. It could be argued that it still could represent different points of view from those held by most of the people of England. I would also like to add that, in contrast to some other popular publications, a large number of copies of the *Booke of the Courtyer* survive in libraries in Britain in almost pristine condition. This might imply that it was more a book to be displayed than one of frequent study. Ten years later an Englishman, Roger Ascham wrote his book *Toxophilus*. Ascham was most famed as the tutor of the three children of Henry VIII. In his book he deals exclusively with a boy's education and opens his passage on music thus.

> Muche Musicke Marreth Mannes Maners, sayth Galen, although some men wil say that it doth not so, but rather recreateth and maketh quycke

a mannes mynde, yet me thinke by reason it doth as hony doth to a mannes stomacke, which at first receyveth it well, but afterwarde it maketh it unfit to abyde any good stronge norishynge meate, or do any holsome sharpe, and quicke drinke. And even so in a maner these instrumentes make a Mannes wit so softe and smoothe so tender and quaisie, that they be laise able to brooke strong and tough studie (Ascham 1573: 39).

Of playing a musical instrument he says 'fine minnikin fingering' being 'farre more fitte for the womannishnesse of it to dwell in the courte amonge ladies, than for any great thing in it, which shoulde helpe good and sad studie' (ibid.). He too appeals to examples from the Classical world, but to show how musical learning could be used to put men at a disadvantage, he cites Croesus's subjugation of a rebellion in which he made 'them weare long kyrtils to the foot lyke women, and that everyone of them shoulde have a harpe or a lute, and learne to play and sing ... you ... see them quickly of men, made women' (Ascham 1573: 39). But he does add, with some sarcasm, 'perhaps you knowe some great goodnesse of such musicke and suche instrumentes, whereunto Plato and Aristotle his brayne coulde never attayne, and therefore I will say no more agaynst it' (Ascham 1573: 39).

It might be interesting at this point to remember the descriptions of the musical attainments of Henry VIII and his children. In 1531 the Venetian Ambassador painted an unbelievable picture of the young Henry.

> He is so gifted and adorned with mental accomplishments of every sort, that we believe him to have few equals in the world. He speaks English, French, and Latin; understands Italian well; plays on almost every instrument, and composes fairly; is prudent and sage, and free from every vice' (*Calendar of State Papers Venetian* 1527–83: 293).

And looking at what was said to be a typical day, which included the composition of two complete masses, it is difficult to believe the veracity of the reports of his accomplishments and perhaps tempting to think that in these he was being flattered in his role of the true Renaissance prince. It is true that he had a rich collection of musical instruments at each of his establishments[1] but this is not in itself evidence that he himself played them. They would have been there

---

1. These lists are transcribed in Galpin's *Old English Instruments of Music*, 1910, pp. 292–300.

as a collection or for the use of the musicians in his employ.

His daughter Elizabeth played both the lute and the virginals. She is seen in a miniature by Holbein playing the former and there is an interesting description of her playing the latter in the Memoirs of Sir James Melville, the Scottish Ambassador. He writes,

> The same day, after dinner, my lord of Huntsdean drew me up into a quiet gallery that I might hear some music . . . where I might hear the Queen play upon the Virginals . . . Seeing her back was towards the door, I entered . . . and stood a pretty space, hearing her play excellently well; but she left off immediately so soon as she turned her about, and came forward, seeming to strike me with her hand alleging, she was not used to play before men, but when she was solitary to shun melancholy' (Melville 1752: 50).

These early texts were followed by an ever increasing number of books on the subject. These were of two sorts, either concerning the education of noble children or describing the rules of etiquette. Although other Continental books were translated into English there seems to be a definite development of an English style which is influenced by the puritanical view. This first surfaces in a fairly virulent form in *Anatomie of Abuses* written by Stubbes and published in 1583. Most of these texts not only deal with Music as an abstract concept, but carefully consider the suitable differences between the amount of performance allowed to men or to women. Many of the texts say specifically that they are concerned with the behaviour, or education of, the children of gentlemen. It may well have been that those from the growing middle classes who had pretensions to being 'gentlefolk' would have also used these books as a clue to correct behaviour. It becomes necessary to examine the differences in convention between the sexes as well as the amount of music making allowed to those of high or low status. Stubbes describes the effect of Music on the morals of children of both sexes:

> Of a Sonne If you would have him, as it weare, trans natured into a woman, or worse, and inclyned to all kind of whoredom and abomination, set him to dauncing school, and to learn musicke, and than shall you not faile of your purpose. And if you would have your daughter whoorish, bawdie and uncleane, and a filthie speaker, and such like, bring her up in musick and dauncing, and, my life for yours, you have wun the goal (Stubbes 1583: 76).

Here Music is associated with effeminate behaviour for boys, whereas for the girls it endangers their morals. This, in more moderate form, is the same view expressed in *The Necessary, Fit and Convenient Education of a Yong Gentlewoman* of 1598 which recommends 'leaving musicke to people that are riotous and idle'. Some of the more moderate texts, such as Cleland's *Hypometa or The Instruction of a Young Nobleman* point out that playing is not appropriate, for it 'doth disgrace more a Nobleman than it can grace and honour him in good companie, as manie thinke. For he should rather take his pastyme of others, then make pastyme unto them' (Cleland 1607). This text also disagrees with Castiglione that a nobleman should play the lute, arguing that holding the lute has 'made manie crooked bodies'.

The theme of the amount of time taken to become a good player being a waste for a gentleman is the most common excuse given for not playing. Seventy years later Obadiah Walker dismisses playing an instrument in the following terms: 'Musick I think not worth a Gentleman's labour, requiring too much industry and time to learn, and little to lose it. It is used chiefly to please others, who may receive the same gusto from a mercenary ... at a very easy rate' (Walker 1673: 110). The same comment was being made a hundred years later in *Education of Children and Young Students* (Education 1752). Increasingly it seems that for a man to play on any musical instrument at all is for him to put himself in the place of the servant, and that even if he is skilled he should not play to any except his social equals. The position does seem to have been different for women. Although there are early tracts which do state the same position as Stubbs, it seems to have been a much more common point of view to think that playing a musical instrument was a suitable feminine accomplishment, one through which she could attract attention before her marriage but one which was then most suitably practised, privately and at home. As a late seventeenth century text points out:

> To dance or play on any suitable instrument of Musick is commendable; but in the first place Remember that the end of your Learning of it was, That you might the better know to move more gracefully, for it is only an Advantage so far, and when it goeth beyond it, one may call it excelling in Musick, which is no great Commendation. As for the latter, it is to Delight the Sadness of the Mind, and Tune over Melancholy Hours: but be careful not to do these often because you do them well; the easiest and safest method is to do it in Private Company amongst Particular Friends, and then carelessly, like a Diversion, and not with study and

Solemnity, as if it was a Business, or yourself overmuch affected with it' (*The Whole duty of a Woman* 1696).

Other records of musical practice show that although there were such books recommending practical musical skill, such as Morley's *Plaine and Easie Introduction to Practicall Musick* (1597), the more common approach was that which held music to be an entertainment that was bought with money, rather than with one's own time.[2] Within the accounts there is a very clear idea of the status and social value of different instruments. The bowed string family was usually slightly more socially acceptable than wind instruments, and most of these more acceptable than the bagpipe. In 1608 Robert Armin describes Christmas festivities in the following way: 'Amongst all the pleasures provided, a noyse of minstrells,[3] and a Lincolnshire bagpipe was prepared: the minstrels for the great chamber, the bagpipe for the Hall: the minstrels to serve up the knights meate and the Bagpipe for the common dancing' (Armin 1608: B).

However, the violin could be given many names and these could be used to imply the social status of the musician. Throughout the period I have so far been describing, professional musicians themselves had a hierarchy, with the common fiddlers described as equal to beggars and the Gentlemen of the Chapel Royal of equal status to the keeper of the King's menagerie. Queen Elizabeth was responsible for the first piece of legislation which was to punish itinerant musicians with branding for the first offence and execution for the third. These musicians were those described by John Earle:

> A Poore Fidler is a man and a fiddle out of case and he in worse case than his fiddle ... He is just so many strings above a beggar, though he have but two ... A country wedding, and Whitsun ale are the two main places he dominiers in, where he goes for a musician and overlooks the bag-pipe (Earle 1629: E10)

The use of different names for the violin could enliven a text and spice up the irony. The term 'fiddler' was often a term of abuse although, in 1594, the Bishop's court in Wells that dismissed a fiddler named John Hewishe seem to have treated him leniently because he was such an established musician. In spite of this, it is clear from

---

2. It is also interesting to note from the account books of noble English families it is generally the daughters that are favoured with instrumental instruction, as their brothers will only learn dancing and possibly singing.
3. We later discover that 'the noyse of mistrells' is that of violins.

the records that Hewishe, described somewhat dismissively as 'such a one as goeth from parishe to parishe, to playe on his fiddle uppon revill daies and Churchales' was 'a very poore man, and not worth ... xls ...' (Bishop's Court, Wells, leaf 90 v., 1594–5.)

One treatise, *The Way to Health*, written by Thomas Tryon in 1683, listed all the different types of musical instruments, and the type of music played upon them to show their social position, their character and their proper astronomical sign and character. According to Tryon, for example, the bagpipes, half a century earlier described as 'an ill wind that begins to blow upon Christmasse eve, and so continues very loud and blustring all the twelve days' (*Whimsies* 1631: 27), are described in the following way: 'The sounds and harmonies thereof are more effaeminate and Venerial, than Martial, fitter for Peace than War, and for the Shades of Venus than the Fields of Mars, Being an excellent sort of Harmony for Shepherds, to entertain their innocent flock with, which sheep much delight in' (Tryon 1683: 654).

Other instruments are given a much more predictable turn. Flutes and recorders, described by Pepys as used in the theatre to accompany the arrival of the *Dea ex machina*, have 'sounds and harmonious Tones ... grave and full of Majesty, attractive and delightful'. Of the wind instruments, the flageolet is described as having 'sounds and Harmonies ... more youthful than Grave, being a good field Musick, more proper for shepherds and Herds-men, or Carters, and drivers of horses, and the like, than for Consorts in Houses', (Tryon 1683: 655) and the oboe 'For such as look after Cattel' (ibid.).

Time and time again in poetry on pastoral themes the shepherd or swineherd is described as playing a pipe. In an anonymous seventeenth century description of the epitome of the lazy swineherd, the poet writes

> This sluggish Swinhard met me ...
> He can nor pipe nor sing,
> Nor knowes he how to digge a well,
> Nor neatly dress a spring:
> Nor knowes a trappe nor snare to fill,
> He sits as in a dreame,
> Nor scarce hath so much whistling skill
> Will hearten-on a team
> (The Shepheards Pipe, the second Eclogue 1614: D).

In Tryon's book the string family rank high in the list, but with the useful caveat 'Grave, noble, great and delightful, pleasant and alluring; but the Musitian must have skill and hand, or else Mars will spoil the harmony by his rough jarring sounds' (Tryon 1683: 655). So far then we have a picture in which some musical education could be considered a good thing for a man of good family (outside of the extreme Puritan circles) but only possibly so far as it taught him to appreciate the music he heard produced by professional musicians. Professional musicians also had their own levels of status. By the late sixteenth early seventeenth century, the bagpipe was the instrument of the lowest order, and the fiddle (when played well) at the top. It was suggested by several contemporary writers that the early training in Music given to the sons of gentlemen would develop the critical facilities in those who would themselves be responsible for being the patrons of musicians in later life. However, apart from the case of the royal family, this does not seem to be an accurate conclusion as stately homes which employed musicians, such as Hengrave Hall in Suffolk where the composer Wilbye was employed for more than fifteen years, and which also had a large collection of musical instruments, were very few in number. Even if a man could play he had to be sure not to play in any company which would undermine his social position and put him by implication, at the level of a servant.

The position for a woman does seem to have been different. This use of musical instrument playing, as well as singing and dancing, is celebrated in popular verse such as the following, entitled *A Lady and her Musig*:

> Upon an Instrument of pleasing sound
> a lady played, most pleasing to the sight
> I being askt in which of these I found
> greatest content my sense to deliyght
> Ravisht in both at once as much as may be
> said sweet was musig sweeter is the layde
> (Queens Coll. Ms. 414. no 16)

This position is confirmed by the advice given in the various etiquette books and books on education produced for women. That these conventions continued from the seventeenth century through to end of the nineteenth can be seen from contemporary literature. In Goldsmith's *The Vicar of Wakefield* (1766) the vicar's daughters play the guitar to the socially desirable Mr Thornhill. He then takes the instrument and plays, for them, although not very well:

> They gave us a favourite song of Dryden's. Mr Thornhill seemed highly delighted with their performance and choice, and then took up the guitar himself. He played but very indifferently; however, my eldest daughter repaid his former applause with interest and assured him that his tones were louder than even those of her master (Goldsmith 1766: 30).

I would like to finish by showing how much the points that I have raised so far were an integral part of English social life by looking closely at two particular texts. These are not books on education or behaviour but novels: *Pride and Prejudice* and *Mansfield Park* by Jane Austen. In most of Austen's novels, music and discussions of what accomplishments are necessary to a lady form a useful way of delineating character. Interestingly enough most of these scenes happen at the beginning of the books and set the scenes for the later action. It is interesting too that these texts mention the women as being practitioners and the men observers. Also that the women with the better social standing, or pretensions, are those with the skill. The men on the other hand are skilled in discriminating the quality of music performed. The instruments considered proper to young ladies are, at this period, (1813–14), the piano and the harp. In *Pride and Prejudice* an accomplished woman 'must have a thorough knowledge of music, singing, drawing, dancing, and the modern languages' (Austen 1894: 51). In *Mansfield Park*, we find the following conversation:

> 'How many Miss Owens are there?'
> 'Three grown up.'
> 'Are they musical?'
> 'I do not at all know. I never heard.'
> 'That is the first question, you know,' said Miss Crawford, trying to appear gay and unconcerned, 'which every woman who plays herself is sure to ask another. But it is very foolish to ask questions about any young ladies – about any three sisters just grown up; for one knows, without being told, exactly what they are – all very accomplished and pleasing, and one very pretty. There is a beauty in every family, – it is a regular thing. Two play on the pianoforte, and one on the harp – and all sing – or would

sing if they were taught – or sing all the better for not being taught – or something like it' (Austen 1897: 261).

Fanny Price on the other hand had no education in the necessary accomplishments, being unable to play an instrument. As her aunt pointed out it should be kept that way so that there was no doubting the difference in her position from that of her cousins:

> 'all things considered, I do not know whether it is not as well that it should be so, for, though you know (owing to me) your papa and mamma are so good as to bring her up with you, it is not at all necessary that she should be as accomplished as you are; on the contrary, it is much more desirable that there should be a difference' (Austen 1897: 15–16).

At no point in either of these books do any of the (male) heroes play musical instruments. They might discuss the virtues of a woman's accomplishments as well as gamble, run up debts, and elope with younger sisters, but play a musical instrument – never! The only mention of a man playing is of the violin playing servant who most conveniently comes to work in the servants' hall of Mansfield Park in time to provide music for a ball.

As in the literature of social improvement it was important that a woman should not perform in the wrong company. As Darcy says in *Pride and Prejudice* when Lizzie explains that she has not wanted to waste over much time in learning to play, 'You are perfectly right. You have employed your time much better. No one admitted to the privilege of hearing you can think anything wanting. We neither of us perform to strangers' (Austen 1894: 220). The sensible heroines all have to be persuaded to play and appealed to in just such a manner that would have pleased the sixteenth century writers. Early in the novel, an interesting elaboration of the social etiquette of female musical performance in this period emerges. Mary requests a performance from Elizabeth, but first of all Elizabeth is most unwilling to play: 'You are a very strange creature by way of a friend! – always wanting me to play and sing before anybody and everybody! If your vanity had taken a musical turn, you would have been invaluable; but as it is, I would really rather not sit down before those who must be in the habit of hearing the best performers' (Austen 1894: 32).

On Miss Lucas's persevering, however, she plays after saying a dismissive 'Very well; if it must be so, it must.' Austen goes on to describe her short performance and then its appropriation by her sister Mary.

> 'Her performance was pleasing, though by no means capital. After a song or two, and before she could reply to the entreaties of several that she would sing again, she was eagerly succeeded at the instrument by her sister Mary, who having, in consequence of being the only plain one in the family, worked hard for knowledge and accomplishments, and was always impatient for display . . . Mary had neither genius nor taste; and though vanity had given her application, it had given her likewise a pedantic air and conceited manner, which would have injured a higher degree of excellence than she had reached. Elizabeth, easy and unaffected, had been listened to with much more pleasure, though not playing half so well; and Mary, at the end of a long concerto, was glad to purchase praise and gratitude by Scotch and Irish airs, at the request of her younger sisters, who . . . joined eagerly in dancing at one end of the room (Austen 1894: 32).

So in fact Mary ruins her otherwise accomplished performance by her lack of etiquette. Her punishment for using the moment to attract attention to herself is to be left accompanying those who want to dance – not at all the result that she must have hoped for.

The effect she had no doubt so earnestly desired was acquired however by Miss Crawford in *Mansfield Park*, who having upset the whole district by her unreasonable requests for a farm cart to fetch her harp at the middle of harvest time, invites Edmund to listen.

> The harp arrived, and rather added to her beauty, wit, and good humour; for she played with the greatest obligingness, with an expression and taste which were peculiarly becoming, and there was something clever to be said at the close of every air. Edmund was at the Parsonage every day, to be indulged with his favourite instrument: one morning secured an invitation for the next; for the lady could not be unwilling to have a listener and everything was soon in a fair train.
>
> A young woman, pretty, lively, with a harp as elegant as herself; and both placed near a window cut down to the ground, and opening on a little lawn, surrounded by shrubs in the rich foliage of summer, was enough to catch any man's heart. The season, the scene, the air, were all favourable to tenderness and sentiment. Mrs Grant and her tambour frame were not without their use: it was all in harmony; and as everything will turn to account when love is once set going, even the sandwich tray, and Dr Grant doing the honours of it, were worth looking at (Austen 1897: 57–8).

The strong line taken in these writings, which considered Music not worth wasting a gentleman's time, might seem to be contradicted by the many portraits showing men playing, or posing with, musical instruments. An analysis of them shows, however, that many of these are either of professional musicians or young gentlemen. It has been shown that to learn to play an instrument was suitable for a boy; the use of instruments in caricature imply that the men shown are acting childishly. Here we may return to Leppert' s question of what this inclusion of the musical instrument is trying to say. He concludes that 'as a visual experience music is paid homage for what it said about one's position' (Leppert 1988: 146). For the eighteenth century gentleman, ambitious for worldly knowledge, the most pointed representations are of music as vanitas. 'Music was a reminder of the fact, in its inherent immateriality that fades into the silent void and thereby ironically renders the void more absolute. Music for men was a reminder of the necessary failure of all they typically held dear' (Leppert 1988: 146).

For a woman a musical instrument was learnt as a necessary accomplishment before marriage; after this they only played within the domestic environment, as is shown in many of the portraits of the period. Status was measured by the wealth gained to provide the leisure to play and develop skill without this being used as public entertainment. As Leppert notes, 'the implications of the privatisation of women's performances are very great for the music history of England, for among the leisured élite theirs was the gender that had the time and cultural "permission" to study music seriously, yet by and large the talents they developed could not be heard beyond their own drawing rooms'. (Leppert 1988: 149). So the playing of musical instruments has a certain set of purposes which continues unchanged throughout a long period of English tradition, defining and shaping values of gentility and nobility, reflecting and in turn contributing to the formulation of distinct gender ideologies. One could extend this to show how this position was maintained throughout the whole of the nineteenth century. Even then, with the opening of colleges for music, when a musical career was becoming more allowable to those with a higher social status there was still great debate in popular literature (for example such magazine stories as found in *The Girl's Own*) as to whether a musical career was suitable for a well brought up young lady, and if so whether she should be admitted to play before all audiences. Whether such a career were suitable for a man is never even discussed. Such musicians with a wish to be part of the social élite, such as Edward Elgar, even with such a skill as his, never found that the honour given to them as composers was matched with a true rise in social status. To the end of his life he suffered from the social stigma of having worked in a shop.

References

Anon, *The Necessary, Fit and Convenient Education of a Yong Gentlewoman*, London, 1598.
——, *The Shepheards Pipe, the second Eclogue*, London, 1614.
——, *Whimsies: Or A New Cast of Characters*, London, 1631.
——, *The Whole duty of a Woman: or a guide to the female sex from the age of sixteen to sixty. Being directions, How women of all qualities and Conditions ought to Behave themselves in the Various Circumstances of this life, for their Obtaining not onlyPresent, but future Happiness. Written by a Lady*, London, 1696.
Armin, R., *A Nest of Ninnies*, London, 1608.
Ascham, R., *Toxophilus, or the Scholemaster*, London, 1573.
Austen, J., *Pride and Prejudice*, London, (1813), 1894.
——, *Mansfield Park*, London, (1814), 1897.
Blacking, J., *How Musical is Man?*, London, Faber, 1976.
Calendar of State Papers Venetian, 1527–83.
Cleland, *Hypometa, or The instruction of a Young Nobleman*, London,1607.
Earle, J., *Microcosmographie, or a peece of the world discovered. In essayes and characters*, 5th ed., 1629.
Education of Children and Young Students, London, 1752.
Goldsmith, O., *The Vicar of Wakefield*, London, 1766.
Hoby, T., *The Booke of the Courtyer done into English*, London, 1561.
Kempers, A.A. Bernet, *A Bronze Age World and its Aftermaths. Modern Quarternary Research in South East Asia*, no. 10., Rotterdam, A.A. Balhema, 1988.
Leppert, R., *Music and Image*, Cambridge, Cambridge University Press, 1988.
Melville, J., *Memoirs*, London, 1752.
Morley, T., *Plain and Easie Introduction to Practicall Musick*, London, 1597.
Pope, M.K. (ed.),*The Romance of Horn*, 2 vols., Oxford, Anglo-Norman Text Society, ix–x, 1955–64.
Stubbes, P., *The Anatomie of Abuses*, London, 1583.
Tryon, T., *The Way to Health*, London, 1683.
Walker, O., *Of Education. Especially of Young Gentlemen*, Oxford, 1673.

Index

advertising, 4
aesthetics, 5, 152, 180
Afghan Turkestan, 50–1
Afghanistan, 45–60 *passim*, 11, 158 *see also* Pashtun identity, Pashtun regional music, Pashtun poets
Hindustani music in, 52–3, 58
Andrade, M. de, 14, 71, 76, 79–91 *passim* 93
Macunaíma – The Hero with No Character, 71–94 *passim*
Essay on Brazilian Music, 72–4, 80–1, 89
Ardener, E.W., vii, 7, 20, 32, 33
Attali, J., 24
Austen, Jane, 201–3
Australia, 21, 135–56 *passim*
Aboriginal identity, 147, 135–7, 153 *see also* Yolngu, Yothu-Yindi, yothu-yindi idealogy
and land rights, 21, 148–9, 151, 152, 153
authenticity, 20, 21, 42, 103, 126, 133
and discourse, 6–7, 117
and music press, 118

balladry, 3
bağlama, 101, 106–8, 110–12
bagpipes, F., 37–8, 42, 198–200
Barth, F., 6, 48
Basque identity, 20 n.8, 43 n.6
Baumann, G., 12, 17, 181

Beatles, 123, 120
Blacking, J., 12, 46, 99–100, 181, 182, 191
Bloch, M., 180, 182
boundaries, 4, 6, 13, 23–4, 120, 130, 133
categories, 36
gender, 22
maintenance, 48
Bourdieu, P., 4, 8, 181, 182
Boze Cos Polske, 67
Brazil, 14, 71–96, *passim*
'Brazilian psyche', 81, 73, 74, 83, 85, 86, 88
Creole identity in, 72
Mestiço identity in, 80, 81–3, 93
Música Viva movement in, 93
tri-racial ethnicity in, 72, 80, 94
Brazilian modernist movement, 71, 74, 75, 78
and intelligentsia, 76, 91, 93
Britain, 20–1, 40–1, 43, 117–134 *passim*
Black Music in, 16, 123
Bristol, 121
Brittany, 30–1, 34 n.1, 37

Celtic ethnicities, 32, 34–6 *see also* Basque identity, Brittany, Ireland, Northern Ireland, Scotland
and excess, 38–40
an otherness, 36–7

207

and romanticism, 40–2
  as 'folk', 42–3
  in relation to mainstream
    European culture, 37–8
Celtic languages, 30, 33–5
Celtic music, 6, 29–44 *passim*
Celts, 29–31, 32–6
Cercles folkloriques, 30–1
ceremonial, 137, 139, 160–2,
  182 *see also* ritual
Certeau, M. de, 4
Chambers, I., 16, 132
China Crisis, 126, 127
Chopin, F., 13–14, 61–9 *passim*
class, 4, 10, 18–21, 47, 77–8,
  129, 196
Clifford, J., 98
Cohen, A., 4, 132 n.14
colonialism, 7, 14–15, 76–7,
  79, 136, 145
  and world exhibitions, 98
Comhaltas Ceoltori Eireann,
  109
Congress of Arab Music 1932,
  15
conjunto, 18–19
  and Chicano identity, 19
'Country and Irish', 3
Country and Western, 18, 146
  in Ireland, 18
commodification, 99, 146 *see
  also* media, tourism
creole identities, 14 *see also*
  Brazil, *mestiço* identity

Dabrowski Mazurka, 62, 67
dance, 10, 18, 192, 193, 197
  and gender, 22–3, 201
  and possession cults, 82
  candomblé, 85
  ceremonial dance, 157–8,
    160, 164–9, 172, 180
  and 'traditional authority',
    181–2
  clubs in Turkey, 101
  music, *see* House music
descent groups, *see* lineage
  identity, segmentary identity
D'Erlanger, R., 15
dernek, 100–2
diaspora, 103, 105
difference, 3, 15–18, 19, 119,
  129–30, 132–3, 153
domination, 8, 10, 19–20, 159
  and gender, 22
  ritual, 142, 147
Douglas, M., 159–60
Dreamtime, 136, 137
drums, 190–1

ethnic cleansing, 7
ethnic festivals, 34, 35, 99–100,
  102–3
ethnic jokes, 112
ethnic violence, 7
ethnicity, 6–10, 48, 117, 129,
  132, 136, 182
  and inter-ethnic contact, 46
  belonging, 35–6
  'musical ethnicity', 42
  pluralism, 16
  tri-racial ethnicity in Brazil,
    72, 80, 94
etiquette, 192–8, 200, 203
Eurovision Song Contest, 15,
  100, 102
enclave cultures, 158–60
England, 191–205 *passim*
ethnomusicology, 1, 73, 46–8,
  191
  and locality, 97–8
  and multiculturalism, 98

and tourism, 98–9
  in Brazil, 81, 91, 94
exchange, 146, 99–100, 110
exoticism, 32–3, 119

fado, 83
fiddle, 110, 198–99, 200, 202
  see also violin
'folk music', 42–3
folklore, 6, 7, 15, 20 n.8, 30, 90
folklorismus, 99
formulaic structure, 173–6, 177
  and 'traditional authority', 181–2
Foucault, M., 13
functionalism, 47

Gaelic choirs, 34
gender, 21–3, 117, 120, 204
  and dance, 22–3
  and love songs, 178–180
  and musical performance, 22, 192–8, 200–4
  and music education, 196–7
  and political order, 22, 180
  and power, 191
  and ritual rights, 139
Germany, 24, 78–9
  Turks in, 104, 114
ghazal, 53–4
Giddens, A., 3
globalisation, 21, 133, 153–4
Greece, 22–3

Hall, S., 13
harp, 41–2, 201, 203
  and Irish identity, 43, 189–90
Hebdige, R., 19–20, 132
Herder, 78–9
heterophony, 158, 170–1, 181

and political order, 158
hierarchy, 4, 106–8, 160–2 *see also* rank, status
  sexual, 180
hip-hop, 21, 132
Hobsbawm, E., and T. Ranger, 61, 99
House music, 132

iconography, 191
ideology, 61–2, 99, 107, 130, 137 *see also yothu-yindi* ideology
  and authenticity, 130
  and performance, 162
  and sound structure, 160
identity, 24, 113–14, 135
  and art, 152
  and instrument symbolism, 189–91
  and modernity, 114
  categories, 23, 132
  clan, 140, 135–6, 143–4, 147–50, 153 *see also* lineage identity, segmentary identity
  enclave, *see* enclave culture
  'local', 31, 129, 133 *see also* Bristol, Liverpool, locality, Manchester
  moiety, 2, 143
  national, 10–15, 20, 45–59 *passim*
    in Afghanistan, 61–69
    in Brazil, 76–81
    in Turkey and Ireland, 89, 113–14
  regional, 105, 113–14
  relation of personal and group, 158, 169, 171, 172, 180–1
  rural, 18

tribal, 14
urban, 120–1
Il Cortegione, 192–4, 197
International Council for Traditional Music, 98–9
Ireland, 8–10, 15–16, 43, 100, 105–14, 126
Irish harp, 38, 189–90
Irish music session, 16, 20, 109–110
Islam and music, 59

Japan, 14 n.7, 63

Kabul, 52, 54–5, 57, 59
Kabul radio, 57–8
Kerman, J., 1, 18
kemençe, 106–8, 110–12
kiliwâli, 55
kinship, 129, 120, 179 *see also* lineage identity, segmentary identity and ritual, 138
  Yolngu system, 138 n.10

land, *see* topography
land rights, 21, 148–9, 151, 152, 153
Lévi-Strauss, C., 1
Leppert, R., 191–204
literature, 200–4, 67
lineage identity, 160, 162–4, 172–3, 176–7, 181–2
Liverpool, 21, 117–34 *passim*
  Black music in, 123
  Kirkby, 125, 127
  North and South End, 124–5, 128
locality, 21, 30–1, 98, 117–21, 125, 130, 133
  and anthropological theory, 98

'local scenes', 118
Lomax, A., 47–8

Manchester, 117, 121, 122, 123–4
Marxism, 59, 75
  historical materialism, 80
  Marxian cultural theory, 19
mbira, 191
meaning, 105, 140, 145, 172
  and formulae, 181–2
Mediterranean, 16, 23, 126
memory, 114, 121, 169, 172
  and lineage history, 172
  and post-modernity, 131
mestiço identity, 80, 81–3, 93
Mexico, 18
media, 10, 11, 20–1, 38, 123, 136
  and definition of folk, 42–3
  and indigenous music, 145–6, 147–54
  and locality, 118
  and radio broadcasting, 11–12, 57–8 *see also* Kabul Radio, Turkish Radio and Television
  imagery, 119
  multinational corporations, 130
  and post-modernity, 131
Merriam, A., 2, 17, 47
metronome sense, 85 *see also* rhythm
Middle East, 15
migration, 3, 4, 18, 103–4, 105, 114
minorities, 31, 129 n.8, 159
mode, 38–9, 110 *see also* pentatonicism
modernity, 3, 114, 130

modernism, 130–1
Morphy, H., 138 n. 11,143 n. 16, 145
music education, 194–5, 196–8
Musicultura, 98

nation-state, 10–15
 and intelligentsia, 13, 14
 in Brazil, 76, 91, 93
 in Poland, 63
 and modernisation, 11, 12
 and media systems, 11–12
 regionalism in, 12
national anthems, 61, 62, 66, 67
national flags, 61–2
Nettl, B., 18, 43
New York, 47
Northern Ireland, 8, 16
 British identities in, 8, 10
 Irish identities in, 8, 9–10
 lambeg drumming, 9
 12 July parades, 8, 9

Orientalism, 15, 16

Paderewski, I., 65
Pakistan, 8, 157–188 *passim*
Pashtun identity, 49, 50, 52
Pashtun poets, 56–7
Pashtun regional music, 53
periphery, 36, 37–8, 41, 113–14
Peña, M., 4, 18
pentatonicism, 38–9 *see also* mode
performance, 97, 108, 111–13, 119, 162, 164–72 *passim*
 aesthetic quality of, 5, 153
 and gender, 22, 192–8, 200–4
 and ritual, 138, 139, 141–4
 and place, 135

theory in ethnomusicology and anthropology, 91–97
 relations between musical and social, 181
pianoforte, 201
place, 3, 98, 114, 117–8, 132–3, 135
placelessness, 131, 132–3
pleasure, 13
poetics, 176–80 *passim*
Poland, 61–70
Polish intelligentsia, 63
 'national prophets', 64
popular literature, 204
portraiture, 204
post-colonialism 68
post-modernity, 16, 21, 130–1

qaum, 49

race, 79–80, 81, 120
racism, 120
rank, 22, 189 *see also* hierarchy, status
reinvented traditions, 14, 99 *see also* Hobsbawm E. and T. Ranger
religion, 117, 120, 127–9
refugees, 18, 59
resistance, 13, 136, 140, 146–8, 159
'remoteness', 33, 110, 113–4
rock music, 130
romanticism, 37, 40–2, 122
royalty, 190, 195–6
rubâb, 53, 54
rhythm, 80–1, 82, 84, 85–6, 110
 'beat', 125–6
ritual, 5, 139, 146, 149 *see also* ceremonial

and tribal identity, 141–5
language, 152
'magical-ritual' musics, 83–6, 87
rights, 138, 19, 145
song texts, 136

Said, E., 15
Saussure, F. de, 40
Scotland, 32, 33–4, 42, 121
Seeger, A., 2
segmentary identity, 158, 160–4, 172
sexuality, 176–180
Slobin, M., 46, 48, 50–51
Smith, A.D., 65
Soft Sands, 135 n.1, 146, 147
South Africa, 12
Soviet Union, 68
space, 133, 153
and post-modernity, 131
urban, 121, 124, 128, 129
status, 22, 189, 200 *see also* hierarchy, rank of musicians, 198–200, 204–5
subcultures, 19
Sudan, 17
Suyá Indians, 2, 17–18
syncretism, 82

tribal identities, 14
tourism, 98–9
topography, 113, 139–41
transnationalism, 130 *see also* globalisation

travel, 98, 112–13
Turkey, 4, 10, 11, 15–16, 50, 97–116 *passim*
Black Sea region, 103–5, 113–14
Black Sea musicians, 15–16, 103–8, 110–14
Turkish music conservatories, 100
Turkish Radio and Television, 100, 101, 104–5, 107, 108, 111
Tunisia, 15

United States of America, 17, 18, 19, 114
USSR *see* Soviet Union

Vargas, G., 87, 90, 91, 92, 93
Villa-Lobos, H., 73, 92
violence, 8–10
violin, 198–99, 200, 202 *see also* fiddle

Waterman, C., 5, 23
Waterman, R., 85
World Music, 98, 100, 105, 131, 153

Yolngu, 136–9, 140–54 *passim*
kinship, 138 n.10
Yothu-Yindi, 147–153
yothu-yindi ideology, 136, 137–9, 145, 146, 147, 149, 154